D1559483

Promoting *creativity* across the Life Span

Edited by
Martin Bloom and
Thomas P. Gullotta

CWLA Press
Washington, DC

CWLA Press is an imprint of the Child Welfare League of America. The Child Welfare League of America is the nation's oldest and largest membership-based child welfare organization. We are committed to engaging people everywhere in promoting the well-being of children, youth, and their families, and protecting every child from harm.

CHILD WELFARE LEAGUE OF AMERICA, INC.
HEADQUARTERS
440 First Street, NW, Third Floor, Washington, DC 20001-2085
E-mail: books@cwla.org

CURRENT PRINTING (last digit)
10 9 8 7 6 5 4 3 2 1

Cover design by Jennifer Geanakos
Text design by Peggy Porter Tierney

Printed in the United States of America

Library of Congress Cataloging-in-Publication Data
Promoting creativity across the life span/edited by Martin Bloom, Thomas P. Gullotta
   p. cm.
   Includes bibliographical references.
   ISBN 0-87868-811-0
    1. Creative ability--Congresses. 2. Creative thinking--Congresses.
   3. Medicine, Preventive--Congresses. I. Bloom, Martin, 1934- II. Gullotta, Thomas, 1948-

BF408 .P76 2001
153.3'5--dc21

                                              2001025530

Issues in Children's and Families' Lives
An Annual Book Series

Senior Series Editor
Thomas P. Gullotta, *Child and Family Agency of Southeastern Connecticut*

Editors, The University of Illinois at Chicago Series on Children and Youth
Arthur J. Reynolds, *University of Wisconsin-Madison*
Herbert J. Walberg, *University of Illinois at Chicago*
Roger P. Weissberg, *University of Illinois at Chicago*

Drawing upon the resources of the Child and Family Agency of Southeastern Connecticut, one of the nation's leading family service agencies, **Issues in Children's and Families' Lives** is designed to focus attention on the pressing social problems facing children and their families today. Each volume in this series will analyze, integrate, and critique the clinical and research literature on children and their families as it relates to a particular theme. Believing that integrated multidisciplinary approaches offer greater opportunities for program success, volume contributors will reflect the research and clinical knowledge base of the many different disciplines that are committed to enhancing the physical, social, and emotional health of children and their families. Intended for graduate and professional audiences, chapters will be written by scholars and practitioners who will encourage readers to apply their practice skills and intellect to reducing the suffering of children and their families in the society in which they live and work.

Thomas P. Gullotta
Chief Executive Officer
Child and Family Agency of
Southeastern Connecticut

Contents

Tables

Figures

Acknowledgments

I wish to acknowledge my sources of creativity—my grandson Paul and my granddaughter Beth, and their remarkable parents, Sara and Laird Bloom; Vicki and Bard Bloom, creative gamesters as well as scientists; and Lynn, my life partner and spouse of 43 years whose creativity never ceases to delight, amaze, and inspire me.

-Martin Bloom

I wish to acknowledge Mrs. A. P. Grint, who had the vision to create the New London Day Nursery in 1906, and Miss May Taylor and Miss Mary Nahas, whose kindness and love of all children set an example emulated to this day by Pat King, Leslie Lohr, and the other caring child care professionals at Child and Family Agency.

-Thomas Gullotta

Chapter 1

Creativity and Primary Prevention: Terms of Engagement

Martin Bloom and Thomas P. Gullotta

To put the matter bluntly, we are trying to unite in a productive union two lovely if shy and demure bodies—creativity and primary prevention. As the matchmakers, we had better define the terms of this engagement, while describing what each party brings to the table in the exchange. Then, in what we candidly admit are marketing terms, we propose to sell the idea of the union to the parties of the first part, so we can all get on with producing bundles of joyous products for relevant audiences. Ah, gardens of earthly delights, heaven only knows.

This anthology is based on a set of papers presented at the Hartman National Conference on Children and Their Families, the fifth biennial meeting, held at Mystic, Connecticut, on a beautiful and historic maritime coast, in May 2001. This conference was organized under the auspices of the Child and Family Agency of southeastern Connecticut. The theme of the conference was "Promoting Creativity Across the Life Course," thus joining two pursuits that have been, at best, distant cousins. Why join together creativity and primary prevention?

Our answer is contained in this introductory chapter. It involves our assumption that each can contribute significant insights and suggested courses of action for the other. To reach this conclusion, we have to travel across several territories. Initially, we prepared for the trip by reviewing our own thinking and experiences with primary prevention. Then we reviewed the literature on creativity, both to understand this new territory (relatively new to us) as well as to find good guides in our travels. The authors of this anthology are those guides, each expert in his or her own domain.

Interestingly, we invited each author of these chapters with the exciting proposition of connecting primary prevention with their own work in creativity, and they all said, in words to this effect, that they knew their own domain but were not as prepared for a journey in primary prevention. To this we said, in our exuberance, that this is exactly what we expected, because now we could bring together experts in diverse areas, all of whom would be exploring with us how to bridge these different domains. It is a tribute to our authors that they tolerated our exuberance and produced a variety of road maps for new thinking about promoting creativity across the life course. This is what we offer readers. However, we want to introduce this travel adventure with some of the basic tools of the trip. First, we will review our approach to primary prevention. Then, based on the literature, which now includes these fine chapters from our colleagues, we will offer a definition of creativity that is oriented toward primary prevention. This term, and related others, will be developed and expanded in other chapters, but here we provide some terms for engagement with the two sets of basic ideas. Thirdly, with our last burst of enthusiasm, we will attempt to link these two topics, at least into kissing cousins, if not closer. Ah, garden of earthly delights, heaven only knows.

Definitions of Primary Prevention

There has always been a folk understanding of primary prevention, whose origins are hidden in the mists of time, such as, "An ounce of prevention..." and "A stitch in time..." These express more the wish than the actual reality of how the world works, as ordinarily we are largely occupied with putting out fires rather than preventing them. (About 95% of government funding for health goes to treatment and rehabilitation efforts.) Yet, wishes and dreams are the first step toward actions and solutions. In our very recent times, there have been some basic steps taken toward these dreams of primary prevention, and while there is much more to be done, we have begun (Albee & Gullotta, 1997; Bloom, 1996; Price et al., 1988). It will be useful for this anthology to reflect on the paths taken, as well as those not taken, in order to look ahead with greater assurance.

The word *prevention* had evolved from a core western European definition by at least the 15th century (Oxford English Dictionary, 1971), meaning to anticipate, to take precautions against (a danger or evil), and hence to evade that danger. Its Latin root—to come before—is still central: to take actions *before* some untoward set of events occurs, in order to preclude, delay, reduce, or stop completely its occurrence in some population at risk. However, there was also a positive meaning of the term—to come before another, to excel—which has reappeared in some contemporary definitions as well.

There have been at least four main scientific paths to current definitions of primary prevention. The first began with public health and medical writers, such as Leavell & Clark (1953), who distinguished the following elements:

- *Health promotion.* The furthering of health and well-being through general measures such as education, nutrition, and the like, aimed at a host population.

- *Specific protections.* Measures taken toward particular diseases to intercept the pathogenic agent before it affects the host population.

- *Early recognition and prompt treatment.* The use of screening and disease control through standard medical practices.

- *Disease limitation.* The delaying of the consequences of clinically advanced cases.

- *Rehabilitation.* Bringing the affected person back to a useful place in society, as far as possible.

This definition opened up ways of thinking about the idea of acting or intervening before a problem occurred, and employed a number of basic public health strategies to do so. However, this definition lacks a term for palliative care, which, in the meaning provided by the contemporary hospice movement, allows for a death that minimizes pain for the patient, and increases as much as possible comfort-giving social reconciliation for the patient and survivors.

A second approach involved an epidemiological perspective as interpreted by psychiatric theorists, such as Caplan (1964), who defined the set of terms: *primary prevention, secondary prevention,* and *tertiary prevention.*

Primary prevention involved the lowering of the incidence (the rate of new cases) of mental disorders in a population. Secondary prevention concerned reducing the disability rate due to a disorder by lowering the prevalence of the disorder in the community, by lowering the number of new cases and shortening the duration of old cases. This connects primary prevention with the first (lowering new cases), while secondary prevention focuses on the second (shortening the duration of old cases), so that secondary prevention, by Caplan's definition, includes primary prevention. *Tertiary prevention* involves reducing the rate of defective functioning in a community, or the lowered capacity remaining as a residue after the disorder has terminated. (Tertiary prevention focuses on the latter [lowered capacity], while primary and secondary prevention address the former [rate of defective functioning]. Thus, by Caplan's definition, tertiary prevention includes the other two.) These terms are widely used, but they are also commonly misused or confused, possibly because of the complex interrelationships of their meanings.

The third approach began in the United States Congress, which mandated the National Institute of Mental Health (NIMH), and other agencies within the Department of Health and Human Services, to provide a long-term agenda for prevention research.

This task was given to the Institute of Medicine, and ultimately, a group of scholars (Mrazek & Haggerty, 1994) proposed a variation on the prior two models. Prevention was to be limited to those interventions designed to prevent the onset of disease, divided into *universal preventive interventions* (aimed at the general public or to those who have not been identified by their increased risk of some problem) and *selected interventions* (aimed at those whose risks have been identified). *Indicated prevention intervention* involved persons with minimal symptoms. This was something like Caplan's concept of secondary prevention, while Caplan's concept of tertiary prevention was to be discarded entirely. Much has been written about this revision of thinking about prevention of mental illness or disorder and its emphasis on *risk* and *protective* factors (Munoz et al. 1996), but we chose not to use this as the guiding definition of terms because it intentionally omits having health and well-being be constructively *promoted*. Rather, it takes a more limited disease-oriented approach that appears to put primary prevention into the hands of medical personnel, rather than involving the persons and groups whose lives are at stake, as well as a wide range of other possible helping professions whose services in and out of medical settings can be activated. Mental health is but one small piece of a larger continent of social and cultural health.

The fourth approach may be characterized as embodying a psychosocial or systemic perspective, which attempts to give all of the components a place at the table of well-being. In its simplest form, it has been described as the distinction among prevention, treatment, and rehabilitation (Klein & Goldston, 1977). Albee (1983) gave this approach substantial form in the equation: The incidence of mental disorder is a function of organic factors plus social stresses plus social exploitation, reduced by personal competence, self-esteem, and social supports. Several others suggested modifications of Albee's formulation. We will use a definition of primary prevention that goes beyond personal physical or mental health, to include social, economic, and physical environmental health.

FIGURE **1.1** *Primary Prevention Equation*

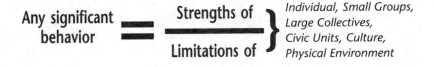

This equation is to be read as follows:

Any significant personal or collective behavior is equal to some function of the pushes to increase

- individual strengths,

- small group and large collective supports,

- constructive civic laws,

- helpful cultural mores, and

- resources from the physical environment,

as against the pulls regarding

- individual limitations,

- small group and large collective stresses,

- destructive civic laws,

- social/environmental pollution, and

- restraints from the physical environment, all viewed over certain time periods. (There are impacts of human actions on the physical environment, but we are focusing on individual and collective behaviors in this discussion.)

Thus, our working definition, derived from this theoretical tradition, is as follows: Primary prevention involves the simultaneous (a) prevention of predictable problems, (b) the protection of existing states of health and healthy functioning, and (c) the promotion of desired states of affairs for populations of affected persons. This definition uses the strengths perspective as an intrinsic perspective, and also involves the possibility that a strength in one area may compensate to some degree for a limitation in another.

This is a very complicated structure, and lest it fail because of its complexity rather than its utility, we propose a shorthand approach. Think of a cube, with three sides facing us, and three sides hidden. The three facing sides would be represented by the strengths of (1) the individual involved, (2) all of the sociocultural and civic units, and (3) the physical environment. The three hidden sides would be represented by the limitations of (4) the individual involved, (5) all of the sociocultural and civic units, and (6) the physical environment (Bloom, 1996). What is important about the choice of the symbol, the cube, is that if any one side does not receive due consideration in primary prevention planning, the entire cube (project) stands in danger of collapse for neglect of a potentially vital aspect.

The definition of primary prevention with regard to any particular topic directs us to ask six basic questions, represented by faces of the cube: how to optimize the strengths and neutralize the limitations of involved persons, social units, and physical environments, recognizing that the limitations of one may, to some degree, be compensated for by the strengths of others.

A Definition of Creativity Oriented to Primary Prevention

Why be coy? Our primary prevention-oriented definition of creativity may be stated as *involving the ecstatic resolution of a challenge involving unknowns, whose solution has social value.* We hasten to explain the component terms and phrases.

Resolution of a Challenge

A creative activity is about something, and that something represents a challenge, either in the form of a predictable harm, risk, or danger facing us, or in the form of a potentially valued experience, desired objective, or goal not yet present in our lives. The creative activity moves us toward a resolution—either reducing the risk, or increasing the desired potential. The creative product may attain either all or some of the resolution; we may reduce or eliminate the risk, or we may achieve all or some of the desired objectives. The challenge may involve fine arts or the sciences, but it may also involve the practical arts of everyday living, if not everyday survival. We cast the widest net on the objects and products of creative efforts.

Involving Unknowns

If we knew all about a situation, it would be easy just to step in and make the changes we wanted to achieve the ends we desired. But every situation contains unpredictable elements, some beyond our control. A creative solution is new; it has never been known in exactly this form. Therefore, achieving this uniquely new outcome necessarily involves unknowns. Once achieved, the unknowns become known (at least to those sophisticated enough to engage in the technical process).

Ecstatic

With this term, we refer to the personal involvement in the creative act, the engrossment, the pleasure and delight, the intensity of the experience—all of which seem to pull the creator toward an attempted solution. Just because the creator is ecstatic with his or her effort (the process and the product) does not guarantee that the public will judge the outcome successful or creative.

This term also brings into focus a wide array of personal attributes that lead to this personal thought-feeling-action state we call ecstasy. We will hear much more about these personal attributes in many of the following chapters. Ecstasy is something like a mystic experience—we know when we're in it, but it is hard to explicate afterward. The feelings, thoughts, and actions are...wonderful. (Words fail us.)

However, just because creativity is wonderful doesn't mean it is not a lot of hard work often involving some pain—as Edison said: 2% inspiration, 98% perspiration. It may be very difficult. There is no free ecstasy lunch.

Solution has Social Value

This is the contextual aspect of the definition. It refers to the fact that any creative effort is judged and eventually approved—or else it never reaches the level of being "creative." The social value is wide open, as one group's meat is another group's poison; so audiences will vary as will their responses. But some significant portion of a society must value the product for it to be creative. Truly creative solutions come to be recognized by wider groups, and over longer periods of time. But almost no creation will necessarily be popular forever. The awesome pyramids were at several times in their three thousand year history totally neglected and covered by the sands of perceived irrelevancy as well as by the real stuff.

Thus, this primary prevention-oriented definition of creativity has a distinct problem-solving, or potential-enhancing, quality that involves both a creator and an audience, where the wonderfully engaging but often hard-work process leads to novelty that is accepted as socially useful to some significant sector of the public.

We are not limiting this definition to a fine arts or hard science arena, but include the practical arena of everyday life, which requires creative solutions to novel and persistent challenges. This means that every problem solver, young and old alike, may be involved in the creative process, although their products will differ in sophistication. One must be absolutely relativistic in this creativity business.

We find it interesting that creative activities emerge in the process of living. No one has to explain the underlying process, although "students" have to learn the language, the tools, and the methods that permit creative expressions. The creative (adult) person keeps working at it because of the rewards of the chase itself (of course, these are not the only rewards—even the creative have to eat and live within a society) and because the unknowns in the situation are of continual interest to the creator. Once the creator connects with the challenge, then a self-generated dynamic system ensues which also keeps the creator working toward an acceptable solution. The aesthetic effect comes into play when the resolution is proposed, whether or not it fits (an aesthetic judgment), works (a demonstrable pragmatic effect), and is accepted by its audience (a social judgment).

Eventually, the product of this creative endeavor is displayed before some public in an appropriate fashion, and the public makes its reaction known. The public may not always be right, especially with regard to aesthetic efforts for which there is as yet no context or language by which the public can understand the novelty. Twelve tonal patterns were difficult for an audience to listen to, for whom eight tones were normative. The impressionists' fragments were difficult for audiences to accept at a time when realism was normative. But audiences can learn, and if the decision is favorable, then the creative effort has a stronger chance of remaining in force for a period of time—until displaced by the next creative activities on similar topics.

To put this entire conceptual exploration in a different light, let us offer the notion of a creativity cube. In parallel with the primary prevention cube discussed above, we suggest that there is a side involving individual strengths—the enormous array of factors and characteristics that have been assigned to creative people. Yet, as authors of this anthology clearly document, there are strengths of small groups and larger collectives that clearly support the creative efforts of individuals, and without whose presence those individual efforts might never have come to pass. Some authors are aware of the effect of resources from the physical environment, from the intentional isolation of the painter Georgia O'Keeffe to the intentional gathering of the impressionists in beautiful Provence.

On the other hand, the authors in this anthology also recognize how individual limitations, and especially small group and large collective stresses, can impede the creative process and completely negate it for some. Also, some of the demands from the physical environment may interfere with creative activity as well. Thus, we see creativity as involving the pushes and pulls of the strengths and limitations of individuals, groups, and environments. Just how these six facets interact in particular segments of the life course is the subject of this book. Let us briefly introduce our authors.

Mark Runco emphasizes individual strengths. Individuals must (1) construct original interpretations of their own experience, (2) exercise discretion to know when and when not to rely on and defend these interpretations, and (3) have the ego-strength to defend the interpretations when appropriate. Strongly implicated in this definition of optimal functioning is the socio-cultural context in which originality and conventionality achieve some delicate balance—not too original (or it won't be accepted as creative) and not too conventional (or it won't be considered as creative). The resultant is a state of individual health (healthy functioning), but implied is a contribution to the health of society to some degree.

Charlotte Doyle emphasizes the creative paradox in the very young child and necessarily in the sociocultural context of that child. The paradox turns on the fact that sometimes creativity involves freedom and spontaneity, but at other times it demands its opposite, the tight rigor of following well-honed technologies. Sometimes creativity can be emotional, other times rigorously intellectual. Sometimes creativity is pure joy, other times long, hard work. Her resolution: These are parts of the phases in a creative process. She discovers this up-and-down-and-sideways process in her studies of young children and their social world, and offers many insights as to the nature and flow of this process. Creativity in children involves a true interaction between individual and environment; parents and other adults can offer opportunities and facilitate particular activities, but they cannot force creativity as such. They can be a receptive and encouraging audience, but being a good audience is a difficult task, a paradox, a careful balancing between saying too little and saying too much, either of which may discourage a budding talent.

Alice Sterling Honig offers a panoply of instances in which creativity, giftedness, and talents may be promoted in young children at preschool and in the early grades. In the socioemotional domain, she emphasizes teacher creativity in helping children toward more mature solutions to the emotional tasks of early childhood, which will enable them to take steps toward creativity. Children have to trust their caregivers as they move toward generating new hypotheses about the world and also to feel comfortable with its ambiguities. She discusses the use of small peer groups in creating a climate favoring creativity, through word games, shared tasks, and mutual encouragement (including those wonderfully awful puns of early youth). Various social devices may also be employed to encourage creativity, from musical instruments to art supplies and drama, always within the social context of an encouraging audience. Teachers can encourage creativity in young children, but they may also unintentionally inhibit creativity, a fact that requires continual reaffirmation of what encouragement involves. Interestingly, Honig also discusses the physical environment as a stimulus to creativity in young children, such as the creation of special places for different activities that may attract a curious mind. Some of these may be individual spaces, while others may involve group activities such as the reading circle or "show and tell." By encouraging the collection of things, the teacher enlarges the physical world wherein these things lie. Perhaps most important, it is necessary to connect the educational world with the home world, which requires teachers to make alliances with families in order to help parents find and recognize their child's special gifts. In any case, Honig touches on all six facets of the cube of creativity.

Joseph Renzulli and *Sally Reis* report on a rich vein of theory, research, and demonstrations, stemming over the past quarter of a century, on promoting creativity in school-age children through the Enrichment Triad Model. They introduce a number of important distinctions, including those between "schoolhouse giftedness," which is the type of giftedness that emerges in lesson-learning or test-taking abilities, and thus is most valued in conventional school settings; and "creative-productive giftedness," which involves the production of original ideas and products, and thus uses nontraditional means to attain unexpected ends—these may not always be appreciated in a conventional school setting. Renzulli and Reis emphasize individual strengths in their discussion of giftedness in young people— above average ability, high levels of task commitment, and high levels of creativity. Fundamentally, they advocate a change in the way giftedness is to be viewed. Rather than labeling the educational services received by students, they propose to emphasize a concern with the development of gifted and creative behaviors in youth who have a high potential for benefiting from special educational opportunities outlined in the Enrichment Triad Model. Indeed, all students can benefit from social actions to make schools more creative places for talents to develop in young people. Various research programs are reviewed that offer support for this model. Thus, their approach to creativity involves both the strengths and limitations of individuals and social groupings.

Peter Wyman and *Emma Forbes-Jones* reflect on their past and current research with youth and families who are exposed to chronic adversity such as poverty, family problems, and violence in the community. These circumstances can make it difficult for young people to be creative in the conventional senses of the arts and sciences. Rather, their creativity may be expressed in the creative adaptation to and eventual surmounting of their adversity. These researchers and their colleagues have long been involved in studies of resilience, in which a sizable proportion of such young persons coming from great disadvantage become effective adults against all odds. This basic fact has led many to study the causal factors so that perhaps yet other disadvantaged youth might be aided to attain successful adulthood. This chapter focuses on two new sets of data: (1) The first study considers how parents attributed positive meaning to their own negative childhood parenting experiences in order to construct useful models for parenting their own children. Understanding how certain of these parents are successful in doing this may be helpful in supporting other parents to do likewise. (2) The second study involves how youth's future expectations appear to influence their current school functioning, social adjustment, and problem behaviors. Positive expectations for the future are correlated with current functioning, and thus present another point of entry into how we may promote creative adaptations in these disadvantaged youth. Thus, these authors consider both individual and sociocultural levels in their studies.

Lita Linzer Schwartz takes us on another path toward understanding creativity, this time in the processes involved in becoming a female artist—oftentimes against the social norms that have emphasized women's conventional activities, towards independence and mastery of new, nonconventional activities. Through an historical review and a contemporary research study, she recognizes the forces that inhibit women from becoming creative artists, as well as those factors that contribute to their success. Her formula for achievement of artistic success includes two individual factors, personal talent and personal commitment to the creative process, along with one social factor, the opportunity situation in which talent and commitment are expressed. Thus, Schwartz enables us to see as much of the negative factors that can influence creative efforts in women—the negative individual and sociocultural factors inhibiting the expression of creative talents—as much as she offers insights into the positive factors. Her current research, reported in this chapter, supports both strengths of women and the limitations or barriers of the environment. She raises another interesting point, the importance of mentors in the development of women artists. This notion reverberates in the Reis and the Wyman and Forbes-Jones chapters as well. No creative woman—or creative man—is an island unto herself or himself alone.

Sally Reis offers a wide-ranging theory on creativity in women, based on her long-term research studies among culturally diverse women. Theories on creativity have been, heretofore, theories on male creativity. This chapter presents some sharp contrasts to the single-minded, often abstract contributions of males, by recognizing the important sociocultural contexts in which women have largely inhabited. Reis, like Schwartz, discusses many of the

individual and sociocultural barriers to creativity in women—
that is, creativity in the male template. Reis goes on to recognize
the diversity of women's creativity into multiple areas of their
lives. So, women's creativity may be expressed in human relationships, in family contexts, in personal interests, and in aesthetic sensitivities—as well as in more traditionally creative
contexts of the sciences and the arts. It is not that women are less
creative than men are, so much as it is that women are differently
and diversely creative, with the need for new perspectives to
evaluate their creative efforts apart from those present in the
traditional (male) domains. This insightful perspective provides
many opportunities to promote a wide-range approach to creativity in young girls and women of all ages.

Robert Kastenbaum addresses creativity in the later adult
years—perhaps this may surprise readers more used to discus-
sions of creativity in the young and the very young. He presents
some challenging answers about older persons, and, in effect,
invites us to make up the appropriate questions. We'll accept that
challenge: the answers Kastenbaum proposes involve mostly the
strengths of individuals, but importantly, these individual characteristics often reach out to others and the world, and thus
become sociocultural in nature as well. Creative acts in the old are
as unpredictable as they are in the young, making use of accessible resources within available energy limits. Creative acts express the truth of the person in the situation, and transform the
limited human condition to an optimal or mastery level. Creative
acts are both gifts to others and expressions of self, now and
beyond death where we transcend the particular to the symbolic.
Kastenbaum moves the discussion of creativity into spiritual or
mystic realms because creativity is not necessarily nice nor is it
safe. It is playing with fire, the spark of untamed creative spirit.
Fire burns, and so may creativity, and in burning, destroy. We
destroy the conventional in order to build the unconventional,
the new way of looking at the world. This may be disturbing, but
it is also the generative spirit of the universe. Creativity and
destruction are opposite sides of the same coin that the great

students of the human condition find in us all, in both the creating and the destroying, the risk taking and the security seeking. And the funny thing is that as we get older, these are exactly what we become aware of in ourselves, and hence the great potential—that we may promote creativity across the entire life course, albeit in expressions so very different at each step along the way. So, it is not the answer we seek, but to understand the question.

References

Albee, G. W. (1983). Psychopathology, prevention, and the just society. *Journal of Primary Prevention, 4*(1), 5–40.

Albee, G. W., & Gullotta, T. P. (Eds.) (1997). *Primary prevention works.* Thousand Oaks, CA: Sage.

Bloom, M. (1996). *Primary prevention practices.* Thousand Oaks, CA: Sage.

Caplan, G. (1964). *Principles of preventive psychiatry.* New York: Basic Books.

Klein, D., & Goldston, S. (1977). *Primary prevention: An idea whose time has come.* (DHEW Publication No. ADM 77-447). Washington, DC: Government Printing Office.

Leavell, H. R., & Clark, E. G. (Eds.) (1953). *Textbook of preventive medicine.* New York: McGraw-Hill.

Mrazek, P. J. & Haggerty, R. J. (Eds.) (1994). *Reducing risks for mental disorder: Frontiers for preventive intervention research.* Washington, DC: National Academy Press.

Munoz, R. F., Mrazek, P. J., & Haggerty, R. J. (1996). Institute of Medicine Report on Prevention of Mental Disorders: Summary and commentary. *American Psychologist, 51,* 1116-1122.

Oxford English Dictionary (Compact edition) (1971). Glasgow, Scotland: University of Oxford Press.

Price, R. H., Cowen, E. L., Lorion, R. P., & Ramos-McKay, J. (Eds.)(1988). *14 ounces of prevention: A casebook for practitioners.* Washington, DC: American Psychological Association.

Chapter 2

Creativity as Optimal Human Functioning

Mark A. Runco

Optima are by definition desirable. This is what differentiates optima from simple balances and compromises. A balance may indicate that two things are involved, such as nature and nurture or cognition and affect. Optima usually involve a balance of some sort, but it is a special kind of balance: It is an effective balance. The balance is optimal in that it leads to effective behavior, and this in turn leads to unquestionably desirable conditions, including physical and psychological health.

Not surprisingly, optimal functioning results from optimal experiences. To understand the former, it is useful to explore the latter. The present chapter does just that by (1) reviewing influences on optimal functioning, and (2) constructing a theory and definition of optimal behavior itself. Runco and Gaynor (1993) and Runco and Sakamoto (1996) have already presented an extensive list of optimal influences. They have not, however, defined optimal functioning. Their focus was on optimal experiences—on the influences rather than the outcome. They did tie optimal influences to creativity. And indeed, the definition of optional human functioning presented here involves creativity, and, in particular, mature, tactical, and postconventional creativity. Each of these terms—maturity, tactics, postconventionality, and creativity—is defined and the connection to optimal functioning defended in this chapter.

After addressing the two objectives mentioned above—(1) and (2)—we will have enough information to consider the proposition that creativity is indicative of optimal functioning.

As a matter of fact, a brief review of the influences on optimal functioning will give us a very good start at defining creativity and tying it to optimal functioning. That relationship will be further defended after a review of the influences. In addition to setting the context for a definition of creativity as optimal functioning, the specific influences are meaningful in the practical sense. If creativity is indicative of optimal functioning, these influences should be carefully considered when promoting creativity or optimal functioning. The final section of this chapter will summarize the practical implications of the definition of creativity as optimal functioning.

Influences on Creativity

Recall here the definition of "optimal functioning" as an efficient balance. For influences, this means that a certain amount of an influence facilitates creative behavior, but beyond that amount the same influence will inhibit creativity. Thus, for each of the following, this position has been supported: X can take different forms and contribute to creative work in various ways. In some instances, however, too much is inhibitive. For X, any of the following potential influences could be substituted.

Experience and Education

Experience can supply information, and both declarative (factual) and procedural (strategic) information may contribute to creative success. On a simple divergent thinking task, like what is used on tests of creative potential (Guilford, 1968; Runco, 1991), the information supplied by experience can supply the individual with options and perspective. Experience is also necessary for expertise, which can contribute to creative work—but can also inhibit it (Martinsen, 1993, 1995). Expertise often allows the individual to make assumptions, and thus the individual is not mindful and spontaneous (Minsky, 1998).

Interestingly, education is a kind of experience, and there are optima specifically in educational levels. Simonton (1984) demonstrated that different careers and domains have different optimal levels of education. This research demonstrated that work in the sciences benefits from a fairly high level of education—but not a PhD! The other domains examined by Simonton had even lower optimal levels of education. One explanation for optimal rather than maximal education involves the student's convergent thinking and susceptibility to dogma.

One way of describing experience is as investment. At the very least, experience requires an investment of time. More often than not, the individual actively selects his or her own experiences (Scarr & McCartney, 1985). When there is a large investment, any loss is very costly. If you invest $100,000 in a new invention, for example, and it turns out to be worthless, you have lost more than if you had invested only $100 in that same invention. With the $100,000 you have more at stake—and you are more likely to defend the investment. If an expert has invested 10,000 hours into an invention, he or she will have more at stake and be more resistant to criticisms and the like. Thus, investing in particular experiences can make us resistant to alternatives and inflexible (Rubenson & Runco, 1995). Creativity often requires flexibility, so it may be undermined by any sizable investment.

General Intelligence and the IQ

The threshold theory has been demonstrated several times (e.g., Guilford, 1968; Runco & Albert, 1985). This indicates that creative ideation and creative problem solving may require a moderate amount of general intelligence. Beyond that moderate amount, the individual may or may not be creative, but below it the individual ostensibly cannot be creative. This would suggest that there is a lower limit of general intelligence. The upper limit, which must be present if we are to conclude that there is an optimal level of intelligence, is suggested by findings that children can have IQs that are too high for creative thinking (Hollingworth, 1942). These children put all of their resources into convergent thinking (i.e., finding the correct or conventional answer) and value convergent thinking and correctness to the exclusion of divergent thinking and originality.

Even in the early years it may be easiest to fit in if one has an optimal level of ability. Sadly, some persons may not invest in their intelligence or creativity if they feel like they will not fit in with their peers if they continue to perform at higher than average levels. Hollingworth (1942), and Hollingsworth (1998) both noted problems frequently encountered by gifted children which may result specifically from their having too high of an IQ.

An interest in fitting in may explain why in adolescence some girls stop doing well in mathematics. We do not want the same thing to happen to creative skills, which means that ego strength and the confidence it affords may be among the most important things we can encourage and reinforce. Children can think originally and express themselves, and with ego strength they resist pressures and expectations and will have the confidence to use and build on their creative talents.

The individual does not merely stop expressing him- or herself when there is pressure to conform. He or she also loses out in that talents are not maximized and developed. This is again analogous to investment, but here the issue is accrued interest. When talents are not reinforced, they are not exercised, so they do not grow. There is thus both a loss of opportunity in the present but also a loss of opportunity for growth. No wonder, then, educationally and professionally, "the rich get richer and the poor get poorer" (Walberg, et al., in press).

There are other costs of very high levels of traditional intelligence. Simonton (1994), for instance, reported that effective interpersonal communication often requires an optimal level of traditional intelligence. It may not surprise anyone that U.S. Presidents tend to have only moderate IQs. This may allow them to communicate to unselect populations. The optimum is suggested by the fact that U.S. Presidents not only need to communicate to a wide audience but also need to minimize the possibility that intelligent persons will criticize their ideas.

There are problems with high levels of traditional intelligence, especially if they preclude originality. So, too, are there problems with high levels of divergence and originality.

Divergence and Originality

Tests of divergent thinking (DT) are probably the most common paper-and-pencil assessment of the potential for creative problem solving. DT is not synonymous with creative thinking but instead indicative of one aspect or component of creative thinking. Runco and Chand (1993) suggested that creative thinking also requires problem finding, the evaluation of solutions, motivation, and information (see Fig. 1).

The easiest way to see the optimum of DT is to consider a wildly divergent idea. One of the simplest DT tasks used with school children involves an examinee being asked to "name all of the square things you can think of." "Box" is a common response; "my dad's music" is quite unusual and therefore original. It is also appropriate and fitting to the task, at least metaphorically. "Basketball," on the other hand, is widely divergent and original, but difficult to justify as an appropriate answer for "square things," even with metaphorical logic. The point is that neither divergence nor originality is alone sufficient for creativity. Moreover, you can be too original and too divergent. Entirely unrealistic ideas, including at the extreme, psychotic ideas, will tend to be extremely original—but useless. Just as creativity is not synonymous with DT, so too is it not synonymous with originality. Originality is probably the most commonly recognized facet of creativity, and it may be necessary, but it is not sufficient. Creativity probably requires an optimal level of originality such that it is not too extreme and such that it leads to appropriate ideas. Originality will probably be the most creative when it works with convergent thinking.

This idea of a balance between divergence and convergence is contrary to much applied work. Some individuals still rely on the brainstorming model for problem solving, for example, the

FIGURE 2-1 *The Two-Tiered Model of the Creative Process.*

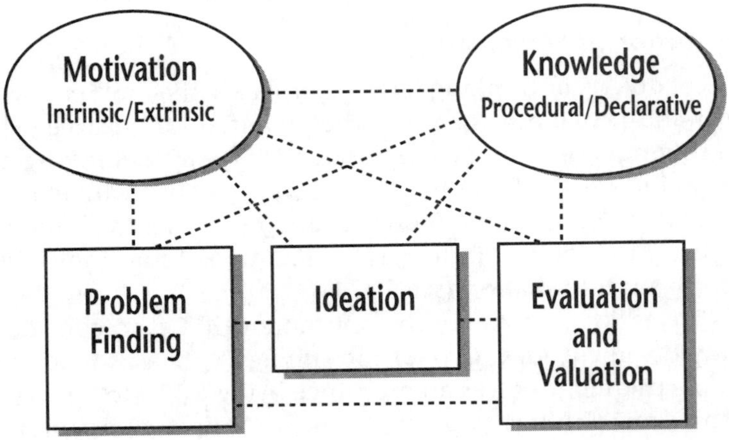

assumption being that judgment and evaluation of solutions be postponed. In other words, early in problem solving, divergence is all-important. Elsewhere I suggested that it simply is not possible to avoid judgment, and indeed judgment and discretion are vital throughout the creative process, not just at the end (Runco, 1994). I suggested that instead of avoiding judgment, it should be practiced and utilized.

The same problematic assumption of brainstorming is implied by Wallas's (1926) classic problem solving model, with preparation, incubation, illumination, and verification as discrete stages. What I am suggesting may be applied here as recursion and interaction among stages, including divergence and convergence. Basadur (1994) suggested that such a balance as I am recommending can be defined in terms of *optimal ratios* of ideation and evaluation.

In many ways, the DT model is compatible with associative theories of creative thinking (Mednick, 1962). In contemporary associative models, truly creative insights (as distinct from bizarre ideation) are uncovered when the person is open to loose associations—but not too open. As Martindale (1999) put it, the individual "must cut down on the associative horizon—to a reasonable level." Otherwise, the individual will be too original. His or her ideation will be more psychotic than creative.

Problem Finding

Problem finding and its various expressions (e.g., problem identification, problem definition; Runco, 1994) are very important for creative work. They may require optimization, for

> creative individuals may have a penchant for finding and solving problems that are neither too easy nor too difficult. It may seem like eminent creators would solve only very difficult problems, but in fact they avoid problems which have no solutions....There are several personal benefits to the finding of optimally difficult problems, in addition to the maintenance of some likelihood of success. One is the staying in a position for a flow state, with subsequent benefits for self-esteem, avoidance of boredom, and heightened attention... Another is the social benefit, alluded to above, where if you work on problems which others think are important, you are most likely to earn a high reputation. If you solve problems that are so difficult that few see the relevance, your reputation will probably not change much at all. (Runco & Sakamoto, 1996 p.125)

Simonton's (1984) data cited previously, showing that communication tends to be optimal when the individual has a moderate intelligence, is relevant to this last point about reputations.

Runco and Sakamoto (1996) noted that a problem depends on one's interpretation of the situation (an observation supported again and again in the stress research), and a challenge is simply a problem that captures one's interest. If the problem is too easy, the person is bored. If the problem is too difficult, the person quits. This is precisely why IQ tests begin with an estimate of the examinee's mental age and the examiner terminates that particular test when the examinee answers several sequential problems incorrectly. If a problem is optimal, the individual is intrigued and challenged. Moreover, if a problem is intriguing, it is probably optimal (for the individual); if it is not intriguing, it is probably not optimal. Clearly, optimization is individualistic. This may be why Skinner, Piaget, and many other notables who looked to education agreed that the best instruction is individualized.

Not surprisingly, creators often report a "disappearance of the problem" because they are intrigued and challenged. The problem is not a disturbance, then, but instead a joy. When a problem is suboptimal, there is no interest. William James put it this way: "we feel neither curiosity nor wonder concerning things so far beyond us that we have no concepts to refer to them or standards by which to measure them" (quoted by Henle, 1974, p. 33).

This view of challenges and problems assumes wide individual differences. Just as in the stress research, what is a problem (or stressor) for one person may be an intriguing challenge to another.

Strategic and Tactical Behavior

Creative persons are often strategic (Root-Bernstein, 1988; Runco, 1999b). A tactic that has recently received a great deal of attention is that of the contrarian (Sternberg & Lubart, 1991; Rubenson, 1991; Runco, 1991b, 1991c). Being a contrarian can insure that one's behavior is original. The individual is, after all, doing what others are not; at least metaphorically, he or she is "buying low and selling high." The metaphor of buying and selling may sound entirely economic, but to the extent that creative persons invest their time and resources into a style, theory, or line of work, the metaphor applies well. The problem arises when persons take the contrarian strategy to the extreme—beyond an optimal level. If they do this, they may never be able to ground their thinking in the work that others are doing or share their work enough to earn a reputation. Moreover, the contrarian may value something (an idea, theory, procedure, or product) just because it is unconventional and original, but some things may be commonly viewed as valueless because they are in fact worthless. The contrarian strategy can easily be taken too far. No wonder that Perkins and

Weber (1992) described the use of strategy for invention as a "balancing act" (p. 327).

Consider the case of the Wright brothers, who adopted various strategies, including *visualization* (of the wing), the *breaking down of the general problem of flight into small and workable problems* (e.g., power, control), *the use of analogies* (birds), and *the obtaining of good information* (by writing letters to others studying flight and by collecting a great deal of their own data—even making their own wind tunnel). They also argued, which was tactical in the sense that Orville would fight for one side of the technical problem and Wilbur on the other; after exhausting those perspectives, they switched sides of the argument. Runco (1998) recently explored the value of argument as tactic.

The numerous letters written by the Wright brothers are most relevant here. They wrote to the National Aeronautics Commission, to journal editors who had published relevant articles, and to many other individuals studying flight. The Wrights were not all that contrarian; instead, they wanted to be in as close a contact as possible with others studying flight. They may have done things differently from others, but not just for the sake of being different. If others found something that worked, the Wrights would follow. If anything, this eclectic approach is an optimizing strategy, sometimes contrarian and sometimes not.

A second example may help, even though it is hypothetical. In his discussion of the contrarian strategy, Rubenson (1991) used baseball as a metaphor. Surely it is most effective in a baseball game for a base runner to steal only when it is unexpected. That is a kind of contrarian behavior; but consider other, wilder, and contrarian yet ineffective base-running strategies. The runner could steal second base when the person at second base had the ball, for example, which would be very uncommon—but the runner would surely be tagged out. The strategy would be unexpected but ineffective. The same is true of pitch selection: The best pitches are unexpected. Even very slow "offspeed" pitches can be very effective. Hitters in the major leagues can hit pitches thrown 90 mph, but sometimes miss balls thrown half that speed, because the offspeed pitch is unexpected. But again, the pitcher can throw an offspeed pitch when it is contrarian (to baseball strategy) and unexpected, and this can be entirely ineffective. The offspeed pitch is never thrown as the first pitch to a batter, unless that batter is expecting "the heat." Most often a batter first needs to see some speed on a pitch, so the fastball is used before an offspeed pitch. As the first pitch, the slow offspeed pitch may come as a pleasant surprise to the batter, and he or she may promptly hit it out of the park.

Cognitive Style

Martinsen (1993) demonstrated that there is a "joint effect" between cognitive styles and problem-solving experience, and, more importantly for the present purposes, a curvilinear relationship between experience and problem-solving success. As he explained it, "A-E (assimilator-explorer) styles describe different strategy dispositions that are associated with competence in utilizing experience and in coping with novelty. *Good performance occurs when there is an optimal match between strategic disposition and the task condition.*" (Martinsen, 1993, italics added). This optimal match between the person and the task parallels what was said earlier about good problems. The optimal match can also be viewed as evidence of why it is so important for an individual to find the career that matches his or her own interest and talents (Albert, 1993).

Other Influences

A large number of other influences have been identified by Runco and Gaynor (1993) and Runco and Sakamoto (1996). They suggest that *mood and affect*, for example, can be optimal for creativity. Even the mood swings that characterize bipolar disorders (Andreasen, 1997; Schuldburg, 1997) may contribute to creative thinking and creative work if they are not extreme (Richards & Kinney, 1997). Depression is one side of the mood swing, but in milder forms depression may allow the creative individual to take a critical look back at his or her own efforts and act as an editor or personal critic. *Time* can be optimal for creative work. Karau and Kelly (1992) found that originality of essays was the highest when those writing the essays were given a moderate amount of time. *Independence* given or allowed by parents may be optimal for creative work (Albert & Runco, 1985). Parents should be explicit about their support for a child, while correspondingly not being too obtrusive. A child needs to know that the parents care, but that they will respect autonomy and individual efforts. *Mentors* might be optimal in the sense of being not too similar but not too different from the student (Simonton, 1994). If they are too different they may disagree on the value of a particular line of thought. If they are too similar, the student may not be comfortable or capable of breaking away and doing his or her own (creative) work. *Age* may be optimal. High-impact mathematics, for example, is typically produced fairly early in one's career, while high-level physics may occur later. Even *procrastination* may sometimes be optimal (Subotnik, et al. 1992). Some procrastination may allow incubation. Too much, however, and details are forgotten and nothing gets done. Perhaps procrastination is for some an optimal use of time or a consistent style of work.

The list of influences is extensive. Presumably we have covered enough ground to conclude that the influences on creativity most often need to be optimal. We can therefore propose that creativity is itself in many ways a result of optimization. One of the best rationales for viewing creativity as a form of optimal functioning is provided by the research on the relationships between creativity and health.

Creativity and Health

As a starting point, consider a definition of creative behavior presented by Runco (1996):

> Creativity reflects the intentional transformation of experience into original and useful interpretations that result from self-expressive intentions and depend on the

discretion to know when to be original and when to be conventional.

The inclusion of self-expression in this definition may imply a revamped theory of self-actualization. Rogers (1961) and Maslow (1971) each had difficulty separating creativity from self-actualization. At one point Maslow (1971) concluded that creativity and self-actualization "may turn out to be the same thing" (p. 57). Similarly, Rogers (1961, pp. 351-352) suggested that "the mainspring of creativity appears to be the same tendency which we discover so clearly as the creative force in psychotherapy—man's tendency to actualize himself, to become his potentialities...the individual creates primarily because it is satisfying...because this behavior is felt to be self-actualization." Mathes (1978), Murphy, Dauw, Harton, and Fredian (1976), and Runco, Ebersole, and Mraz (1991) each presented data supporting the relationship between creativity and self-actualization.

Note that creativity is not just self-expression. This is important in distinguishing creativity from self-actualization (and the theory presented here from those of Rogers and Maslow). There is some overlap with earlier theories but important differences exist (e.g., the possibility that certain aspects of creativity can be found in unhealthy persons). This will be emphasized throughout this chapter.

For Rogers (1961) and Maslow (1971), psychological health involves self-actualization. Self-actualization occurs when there is a fulfillment of potential and authentic self-expression (Jones & Crandall, 1991; Runco et al., 1991). Self-actualized persons are spontaneous rather than inhibited, have a tendency toward lifelong development, and are very self-aware—accepting themselves for what they truly are. The self-actualized individual will recognize his or her strengths *and* weaknesses but see both as part of him- or herself. To the extent that (1) psychological health is valuable, and (2) self-actualization is tied to creativity, a point made by Rogers (1961), Maslow (1971), and various investigators (Crandall, 1999; Runco et al., 1991), creativity is indicative of optimal functioning.

The inclusion of creative self-expression as a part of optimal functioning might be questioned. Evidence can, however, be marshalled that creative self-expression is a vital part of psychological well-being. To the extent that psychological and physical health interact (Pennebaker, 1996), creative self-expression may also be important for physical well-being. And interestingly, this may be one point on which the full range of psychological theorists agree. Humanists such as Rogers (1961) and Maslow (1971) felt that self-actualization was the epitome of health and involved self-expression; Freudian theorists often define ill health in terms of a reliance on defense mechanisms and a failure to admit what one is truly thinking or feeling. In other words, ill health from a Freudian perspective can be construed as a lack of self-awareness. There is, then, agreement from various quarters about the benefits of self-awareness and about an openness about one's self.

Some of what is being suggested here may seem contrary to the corpus of work on the disturbances of creative persons. Some unambiguously creative persons seem to be schizophrenic (Schuldburg, 1997), bipolar (Andreason, 1998; Jamison, 1998; Richards, 1994), and suicidal (Mraz & Runco, 1994; Runco, 1998), and there is evidence that some have the potential for psychosis (Eysenck, 1993). Earlier, I included longevity in my list of examples of signs of physical health; and here again are data that could be interpreted as contrary to my proposal of creativity as indicative of psychological well-being. I am referring to Kaun's (1990) data showing that "writers die young." Yet these data were based on unambiguously creative persons—the eminent, the famous, the dead. This is a critical point because what is found in that population may not generalize to persons with more ambiguous forms of creativity. Findings from studies of unambiguously creative persons may not generalize to those of us with *everyday* creativity (Runco & Richards, 1997) or with creative *potential* (as distinct from manifest and mature creative skills; Runco, 1995). There are other problems with research focusing on unambiguously creative persons, including the reliance on biographical, autobiographical, and archival data and generational (historical) differences.

Still, the eminent are often studied, probably because their creativity is unambiguous. This allows for the highest level of objectivity in that research, at least about the labeling of the "subjects" as creative, and this is especially important in studies of creativity because of the long-standing *criterion problem* (Vernon, 1970). Unfortunately, the implication is that creativity is not widely distributed in the population. Martindale (1999, p. 137), for example, recently claimed that "creativity is a rare trait." The related assumption is that creativity is always manifested in products—publications, works of art, whatever the tangible and quantifiable results are within each particular field. This in turn implies, first, that children are not creative, for they do not produce things that change the way others think or things that are original in comparison to normative data. It also implies that we should focus on persons who are already behaving in a creative fashion and ignore persons who have the potential and who will eventually be creative but are not quite doing it yet.

The alternative view is that the cognitive potential for creative performance is very widely distributed, and perhaps even universal. Indeed, it is a function of a process that each of us probably uses each day. I am referring to the assimilatory process, or, in other words, the process by which individuals construct original interpretations of their personal experiences. This process has also been conceived as transformational because objective experience is transformed into personally meaningful interpretations (Runco, 1996). Keep in mind, however, that creativity involves discretion and ego strength as well as interpretive power.

Creativity is thus not just a matter of special or extraordinary skills. It is instead a part of the universal human capacity to construct personal interpretations of experience. Surely there are individual differences in creative behavior, but more often than not these reflect variations in discretion (the judgments about when to be original and creative and when to conform) and ego strength (the confidence to stand up for one's own judgments).

The definition of creativity given earlier in this chapter emphasizes that the interpretive power each of us commands requires appropriate intentions as well as discretion for actual creativity. The role of intentions was apparent in the discussion of the radical contrarian tactic and how the likely intention here is just to be different. It is *contrarianism for contrarianism's sake.* The intentions of the radical contrarian are likely to be directed towards others' attention or simply as confirmation of one's own uniqueness. For true creativity, one's intentions are likely to be directed at creativity itself, or the solution to a problem (including the challenges of self-expression with which artists are often faced). Creativity may therefore involve contrarianism, but it will not be contrarianism for contrarianism's sake, and instead will be directed at unconventionally for the sake of creativity.

As I stated earlier, the Wright brothers were "sometimes contrarian and sometimes not." They were capable of being unconventional, but their intentions were directed at solving the problem of flight and not at uniqueness. They were capable of being original and finding new options which might be used to solve the problems of flight. The Wright brothers had the potential for originality and unconventional behavior, but they were interested in solving a problem (rather than in contrarianism for contrarianism's sake), and capable of knowing when to be conventional and when to be unconventional. To simplify, they were capable of creative insights precisely because they found optimal originality and conventionality, autonomy and conformity, divergence and convergence.

Implications

In many ways, development involves increased conventionality and conformity. This general trend is apparent, to varying degrees, throughout the life span. There is, for example, a common trend towards rigidity and a loss of flexibility (Chown, 1961; Mumford, 1984; Rubenson & Runco, 1995; Schultz et al., 1980; Treutt, 1993). As we age we develop effective routines that often require that we make assumptions and force new experiences into existing structures (Bruner, 1957; Runco, 1999a). As Bruner (1957, p. 52) put it, "to understand means to fit something into a structure."

Perhaps formal and informal education should attempt to stop that developmental trend when it reaches the optimal level. Perhaps it is a matter of optimizing the three components presented earlier (interpretive power, intentions, and discretion). Then again, given that the first of these is widely distributed in the general population, it would seem that the intentionality and discretionary components of creative behavior would be best targeted in formal and informal education. After all, students already have interpretive capacity. And given the connection between intentions and values, and the fact that values often reflect family background (Albert, 2001), it might be best to focus formal educational efforts on discretion—and ego strength.

Discretion may seem like a difficult educational objective. There is, however, a great deal that can be done. Consider a simple example of crossing the street. We want creative children who are capable of being original and unconventional—but when faced with a red light at a crosswalk, we want them to do what others do and stop, even though this is conventional behavior. There are many advantages of conventional behavior that are more important than originality. But it is the individual who should mindfully decide when to be original and when to be conventional. The stoplight example indicates that many people already work to exercise children's discretion. There is also a large body of research on decisionmaking that suggests various methods for exercising discretion (see Runco, Johnson, & Gaynor, 1999).

None of this implies that the environment must be balanced for creativity. First, the individual may not really balance originality and conventionality; it is more a shunting between the two. Second, there is already too much pressure toward conventionality in our society and our schools; what is really needed is an appreciation for the maintenance of originality throughout the life span. If there is any question about the overemphasis on conventionality, consider what occurs in most schools: Children spend much more time thinking convergently (about the one correct answer) than they do divergently (about original options).

Rubenson and Runco (1995) suggested that the overemphasis on conventionality may result from the unpredictable results of original thinking. They contrasted educational attainment with creativity, using an economic model, and suggested that if someone has educational attainment, we know pretty well what we are going to get. The latter, on the other hand, is by definition unpredictable. If someone is a highly original person, what exactly can be expected? Only that he or she will do the unexpected. If the behaviors of the person were not unexpected, he or she probably would not be considered original. Economic logic applies—if people are going to invest time, money, or the like, they tend to invest in a predictable commodity. Originality and creativity are not very predictable.

March (1987) seemed to be thinking about emphasizing creativity when he outlined a *technology of foolishness*. In his terms this involves play and reason, which can be balanced by treating (1) goals as hypotheses, (2) intuition as real, (3) hypocrisy as a transition, (4) memory as an enemy, and (5) experience as a theory. March suggested that these five methods be used alternatively, with a temporary suspension of "reasoned intelligence." As he put it:

> Play and reason are functional complement…They are alternative styles and alternative orientations to the same situation…Our design problem is either to specify the best mix of styles or, failing that, to assure that most people and most organizations most of the time use an alternation of strategies rather than perseverate in either one. (p. 77)

Children and adults share the capacity to construct personally meaningful interpretations, but they are creative in different ways. Children may be spontaneously original. They hold fewer assumptions, have fewer cognitive structures into which their experiences neatly fit. They are uninhibited. Kohlberg (1987) and Rosenblatt and Winner (1988) labeled children *preconventional*.

Adults, on the other hand, must be tactfully, strategically, mindfully, and intentionally original. Adults must fight routine, at least when it inhibits appropriate originality. Unlike the spontaneous originality of children, ours must be *tactical creativity*. We must use tactics (or what are more frequently called strategies) to maintain or regain our originality and to find our balance. For this reason, it may be most helpful to view adult creativity as *postconventional creativity*. Postconventional behavior involves the individual knowing what the conventions are but choosing not to abide by them (Kohlberg, 1987). This again is indicative of optimal functioning: there is a recognition of norms and conventions but an openness to individual decisionmaking.

Practically speaking, then, while children may need to learn discretion, adults may benefit the most when they practice tactics and strategies (see Runco, 1999b). Given that we have the potential for original interpretations, some of the best tactics and strategies help adults to recognize the blocks that inhibit our spontaneous use of our interpretive capacity. Adults may benefit most by not focusing on what to do but instead on what to avoid (e.g., routine, conventions, blind conformity).

Conventional tendencies arise early on in moral, artistic, and linguistic domains (e.g., Gardner, 1982; Kohlberg, 1987; Rosenblatt & Winner, 1988). They may cause the widely-recognized 4th grade slump in originality (Raina, 1980; Torrance, 1968). Many persons grow beyond the conventional state and become postconventional. That is one way of describing what children need for optimal functioning: practice at evaluating conventions and ego strength to violate them, if appropriate. Adults, in contrast, probably need tactics to avoid assumptions and similar blocks.

Creativity Can be Maladaptive

At this point a tactic should be applied to the present chapter to ensure that it is original and yet appropriate, or fitting. Originality can be addressed by stating explicitly how this theory of "postconventional creativity as optimal functioning" differs from parallel views.

The view presented in this chapter may seem to suggest that creativity is merely a kind of adaptability. The connection between creativity and adaptability was explored by Cohen (1989) and Flach (1996). Evolutionary theory has also been used to explain creativity (Campbell, 1960; Simonton, 1997) and this of course assumes adaptations are made. The view presented in the present chapter can be distinguished from these theories in that it does not equate creativity and adaptability. Creative skills may provide the individual with the means for adapting—but do not guarantee that the person will use them. In fact, adaptations often require a kind of conformity, which is antithetical to creativity. What would an adaptable person do when it is best to conform?

Even more convincing may be the seemingly maladaptive nature of some creative actions. Kaun (1990) found that "writers die young," for example, and inferred that the profession of writing may pull an individual into an unhealthful lifestyle. *That lifestyle is, however, chosen by the individual—consciously and intentionally.* In this sense, the difference between the theory presented in the present chapter and theories of creativity as adaptability hinges on what I have called discretion. Adaptations are not always discretionary and can sometimes lead to conformity. Optimal functioning is discretionary and rarely leads to conformity. Creativity, one kind of optimal functioning, never leads to conformity. It may lead to maladaptive behaviors but not to conformity.

We should also keep in mind that the emphasis here is on the creative process rather than the end result or creative product. There are different ways to construct a creative product or find a creative solution. One way involves optimal functioning, as defined in this chapter. But some creative products may be found from other processes, including analogical thinking (where the result is not truly original but adapted from or somehow suggested by an existing product or idea), serendipity, experimentation, or simply accidentally. Just as creative potential does not guarantee creative performances, so too must we be careful in assuming that the same creative process is used for all creative products.

Admittedly, the seemingly maladaptive nature of some creative behaviors assumes that the individual is all important. Creativity may be maladaptive for the individual if it is associated with short life expectancy. From the social or cultural perspective, creativity may be highly adaptive, even if certain individuals suffer from their originality. There is a clear parallel in Darwinian theory in the sense that creative persons may increase the variation within which fit behavior patterns (and personalities) are selected. Those persons who are outliers and in a sense deviants because of their creativity and originality may not be selected, but they do increase the range of possibilities. For the individual, creativity merely provides the potential for adaptability. The individual may or may not use his or her talents to that end when behaving creatively.

The separation of creativity and adaptability is further suggested by the fact that the former can be proactive (Heinzen, 1994; Richards, 1996; Gruber, 1993). Adaptability is typically reactive. Such proactive creative work also shows again the role of discretion. Proaction occurs by choice. This does not mean that creative thinking is always conscious, mindful, effortful. Discretion is one of those judgmental processes that may involve both mindful and preconscious processes. This is even truer of creativity, which is often preconscious, as in case of incubation, and may have a logic of its own (Runco, 1996).

It may seem that a theory of creativity that emphasizes postconventional thinking and interpretations is also close to parts of Freudian theory. Much of what is suggested by the optimization of convention and originality, for example, boils down to the individual's perspective as it conflicts with social pressures. Freud said much the same in *Civilization and its Discontents*. That title helps separate the present theory from Freudian theory, for discontent only plays a role in creativity some of the time (Runco, 1994a, 1998). Separation is also suggested by the emphasis on decisionmaking in the interpretive theory and on the mindfulness necessary for tactical behavior. As the term "postconventional" creativity implies, the individual is aware of conventions but chooses not to abide by them, at least while being creative. As the term "proactive creativity" implies, the creative individual is often thinking ahead, again, in a mindful fashion. Creative work is not sublimation nor catharsis, or at least it need not be. It can also be quite conscious and tactical.

A third and final difference between the interpretive theory and Freudian theory involves testable hypotheses and operational aspects of the theory. Freudian theory is often criticized for lacking testable hypotheses. What about the interpretive theory of creativity? To the extent that discretion is related to decisionmaking, it can be easily tested (Halpern, in press; Runco et al., in press). Runco et al. suggested that interpretive tendencies can be examined using technologies from studies of heuristics (Nisbett & Ross, 1980). Intentions may be slightly more difficult to test, though some expressions of them can be found in the empirical research on intrinsic motivation (e.g., Amabile, in press; Hennessey, 1989; Runco, 1993) and on goal structures (Mehr & Shaver, 1996; Shalley, 1991).

Testable predictions are particularly feasible because there is a direct connection between the concept of optima and objective statistical procedures. Optima can be easily tested in regression analyses with exponential terms (e.g., Runco & Albert, 1986). These identify curvilinear trends, each of which will have a peak, zenith, or optimal level of the predictor or predictors.

A final attraction is the generality of optima. "Moderation in all things" is a useful reminder because "all things" is not much of an exaggeration. Of course, optima may not be completely sufficient for a realistic picture of behavior, though they certainly help in this regard. Again using statistical thinking, interactions (product terms) are likely to increase the realism and accuracy of predictions. This has been demonstrated in research on judgment, where simple models are the most replicable and complex models (containing curvilinear and interaction terms) are the most accurate and realistic (Meehl, 1980). As a matter of fact, interactions may be as important for models of creativity because creativity itself is typically defined as a *complex* or *syndrome*.

(MacKinnon, 1960; Mumford & Gustafsson, 1988; Runco & Albert, 1985) The model used in the present chapter involves at least three components: interpretive (and assimilatory) capacity, intentions, and discretion. Interactions have been suggested by the recursion and joint effects that were mentioned earlier in this chapter.

The present theory of optimal functioning is, then, not too similar to theories of adaptation nor to the Freudian view of creativity. The testing and further exploration of this theory will be worthwhile, given that creativity is very frequently a key part of optimal human functioning.

References

Albert, R. S. (in press). Identity, experiences, and career choice among the exceptionally gifted and eminent. In M. A. Runco, & R. S. Albert (Eds.), *Theories of creativity* (Rev. ed.). Cresskill, NJ: Hampton Press.

Albert, R. J., & Runco, M. A. (1989). Independence and cognitive ability in gifted and exceptionally gifted boys. *Journal of Youth and Adolescence, 18,* 221–230.

Amabile, T. (in press). Within you, without you: The social psychology of creativity, and beyond. In M. A. Runco & R. S. Albert (Eds.), *Theories of creativity* (Rev. ed.). Cresskill, NJ: Hampton Press.

Andreasen, N. C. (1997). Creativity and mental illness: Prevalence rates in writers and their first-degree relatives. In M. A. Runco & R. Richards (Eds.), *Eminent creativity, everyday creativity, and health* (pp. 7–18). Norwood, NJ: Albex.

Basadur, M. (1994). Managing the creative process in organizations. In M. A. Runco (Ed.), *Problem finding, problem solving, and creativity* (pp. 237–268). Norwood, NJ: Albex.

Bruner, J. S. (1957). What social scientists say about having an idea. *Printer's Ink, 260,* 52.

Campbell, D. N. (1960). Blind variation and selective retention in creative thought as in other knowledge processes. *Psychological Bulletin, 67,* 380–400.

Chown, S. M. (1961). Age and the rigidities. *Journal of Gerontology, 16,* 353–362.

Cohen, L. M. (1989). A continuum of adaptive creative behaviors. *Creativity Research Journal, 2,* 169–183.

Eysenck, H. (1993). Creativity and personality: Suggestions for a theory. *Psychological Inquiry, 4,* 147–148.

Flach, F. (1990). Disorders of the pathways involved in the creative process. *Creativity Research Journal, 3,* 158–165.

Gardner, H. (1982). *Art, mind, and brain.* New York: Basic Books.

Gruber, H. E. (1993). Creativity in the moral domain: Ought implies can implies create. *Creativity Research Journal, 6,* 3–15.

Guilford, J. P. (1968). *Creativity, intelligence, and their educational implications.* San Diego, CA: EDITS.

Halpern, D. (in press). Thinking critically about creative thinking. In M. A. Runco (Ed.), *Critical creative processes.* Cresskill, NJ: Hampton Press.

Heinzen, T. (1994). *Frustration and creativity in government.* Norwood, NJ: Ablex.

Henle, M. (1974). The snail beneath the shell. In S. Rossman & L. E. Abt (Eds.), *Essays in creativity* (pp. 23-44). Malabar, FL: Robert Krieger.

Hennessey, B. A. (1989). The consensual assessment technique: An examination of the relationship between ratings of product and process creativity. *Creativity Research Journal, 6,* 151–168.

Hollingworth, L. S. (1942). *Children above 180 IQ Stanford-Binet: Origin and development.* Yonkers, NY: World Book.

Hollingsworth, P. L. (1998). The world of the young gifted child viewed through systems concepts. In J. Smutny (Ed.), *The young gifted child: Potential and promise* (pp. 432–444). Cresskill, NJ: Hampton Press.

Hunt, J. McV., & Paraskevopoulos, J. (1980). Children's psychological development as a function of the inaccuracy of their mothers' knowledge of their abilities. *Journal of Genetic Psychology, 136,* 285-298.

Jamison, K. R. (1997). Mood disorders and patterns of creativity in British writers and artists. In M. A. Runco & R. Richards (Eds.), *Eminent creativity, everyday creativity, and health* (pp. 19–31). Norwood, NJ: Ablex.

Jones, A., & Crandall, R. (Eds.). *Handbook of self-actualization.* Corte Madera, CA: Select Press.

Karau, S. J., & Kelly, J. R. (1992). The effects of time scarcity and time abundance on group performance quality and interaction process. *Journal of Experimental Social Psychology, 28*, 542–571.

Kaun, D. E. (1991). Writers die young: The impact of work and leisure on longevity. *Journal of Economic Psychology, 12*, 381–399.

Kohlberg, L. (1987). The development of moral judgment and moral action. In L. Kohlberg (Ed.), *Child psychology and childhood education: A cognitive developmental view* (pp. 259–324). New York: Longman.

Mackinnon, D. W. (1960). The highly effective individual. *Teachers College Record, 61*, 276–278.

March, J. G. (1987). The technology of foolishness. In J. G. March, & J. P. Olsen (Eds.), *Ambiguity and choice in organizations* (pp. 69–81). Bergen, Norway: Universitets-Forlaget.

Martindale, C. (1999). Biological bases of creativity. In R. J. Sternberg (Ed.), *Handbook of creativity* (pp. 137–152). New York: Cambridge University Press.

Martinsen, O. (1995). Cognitive styles and experience in solving insight problems: A replication and extension. *Creativity Research Journal, 8, 291-298.*

Martinsen, O. (1993). Insight problems revisited: The influence of cognitive styles and experience on creative problem solving. *Creativity Research Journal, 6*, 435–447.

Maslow, A. H. (1971). *The farther reaches of human nature.* New York: Viking Press.

Mathes, E. W. (1978). Self-actualization, metavalues, and creativity. *Psychological Reports, 43*, 215–222.

Mednick, S. A. (1962). The associative basis for the creative process. *Psychological Review, 69*, 200–232.

Meehl, P. (1954). *Clinical versus statistical prediction.* Minneapolis: University of Minnesota Press.

Mehr, D., & Shaver, P. R. (1996). Goal structures and creative motivation. *Journal of Creative Behavior, 30*, 77–104.

Minsky, M. (1997). Negative expertise. In P. J. Feltovich, K. M. Ford, & R. Hoffman (Eds.), *Expertise in context* (pp. 515–521). Cambridge, MA: MIT Press.

Mraz, W., & Runco, M. A. (1994). Suicide ideation and creative problem solving. *Suicide and Life-Threatening Behavior, 24,* 38–47.

Mumford, M. D. (1984). Age and outstanding occupational achievement: Lehman revisited. *Journal of Vocational Behavior, 25,* 225–244.

Mumford, M. D., & Gustafson, S. G. (1988). Creativity syndrome: Integration, application, and innovation. *Psychological Bulletin, 103,* 27–43.

Murphy, J. P., Dauw, D. C., Harton, R. E., & Fredian, A. J. (1976). Self-actualization and creativity. *Journal of Creative Behavior, 10,* 39–44.

Nisbett, R., & Ross, L. (1980). *Human inference: Strategies and shortcomings.* Englewood Cliffs, NJ: Prentice Hall.

Pennebaker, J. W., Kiecolt-Glaser, J. K., & Glaser, R. (1997). Disclosure of traumas and immune function: Health implications for psychotherapy. In M. A. Runco & R. Richards (Eds.), *Eminent creativity, everyday creativity, and health* (pp. 287–302). Norwood, NJ: Ablex.

Richards, R. (1996, Summer). Beyond Piaget: Accepting divergent, chaotic, and creative thought. *New Directions for Child Development, 72,* 67–86.

Richards, R., & Kinney, D. (1997). Mood swings and creativity. In M. A. Runco & R. Richards (Eds.), *Eminent creativity, everyday creativity, and health* (pp. 137–156). Norwood, NJ: Ablex.

Rogers, C. R. (1961). *On becoming a person.* Boston, MA: Houghton Mifflin.

Root-Bernstein, R. (1988). *Discovering.* Cambridge, MA: Harvard University Press.

Rosenblatt, E., & Winner, E. (1988). The art of children's drawings. *Journal of Aesthetic Education, 22,* 3–15.

Rubenson, D. L. (1991). On creativity, economics, and baseball. *Creativity Research Journal, 3,* 205–209.

Runco, M. A. (Ed.) (1991a). *Divergent thinking.* Norwood, NJ: Albex Publishing Corporation.

Runco, M. A. (1991b). On economic theories of creativity [Comment]. *Creativity Research Journal, 4,* 198–200.

Runco, M. A. (1991c). On investment and creativity: A response to Sternberg and Lubart [Comment]. *Creativity Research Journal, 4,* 202–205.

Runco, M. A. (1993). Operant theories of insight, originality, and creativity. *American Behavioral Scientist, 37,* 59–74.

Runco, M. A. (1994a). Creativity and its discontents. In M. P. Shaw & M. A. Runco (Eds.), *Creativity and affect* (pp. 102–123). Norwood, NJ: Albex.

Runco, M. A. (Ed.). (1994b). *Problem finding, problem solving, and creativity.* Norwood, NJ: Ablex.

Runco, M. A. (1995). Insight for creativity, expression for impact. *Creativity Research Journal, 8,* 377–390.

Runco, M. A. (1996, Summer). Personal creativity: Definition and developmental issues. *New Directions for Child Development, 72,* 3–30.

Runco, M. A. (1998). Tension, adaptability, and creativity. In S. Russ (Ed.), *Affect, creative experience, and psychological adjustment* (pp. 165–194). Philadelphia, PA: Taylor & Francis.

Runco, M. A. (1999a). Development and creativity. In M. A. Runco & S. Pritzker (Eds.), *Encyclopedia of creativity.* San Diego, CA: Academic Press.

Runco, M. A. (1999b). Tactics and strategies for creativity. In M. A. Runco & S. Pritzker (Eds.), *Encyclopedia of creativity.* San Diego, CA: Academic Press.

Runco, M. A. (in press). Idea evaluation, divergent thinking, and creativity. In M. A. Runco (Ed.), *Creatical creative processes.* Cresskill, NJ: Hampton Press.

Runco, M. A., & Albert, R. S. (1985). The reliability and validity of ideational originality in the divergent thinking of academically gifted and nongifted children. *Educational and Psychological Measurement, 45,* 483–501.

Runco, M. A., & Albert, R. S. (1986). The threshold hypothesis regarding creativity and intelligence: An empirical test with gifted and nongifted children. *Creative Child and Adult Quarterly, 11,* 212–218.

Runco, M. A., & Chand, I. (1993). Cognition and creativity. *Educational Psychology Review, 7,* 243–267.

Runco, M. A., Ebersole, P., & Mraz, W. (1991). Creativity and self-actualization. *Journal of Social Behavior and Personality, 6,* 161–167.

Runco, M. A., & Gaynor J. L. R. (1993). Creativity as optimal development. In J. Brzezinski, S. DiNuovo, T. Marek, & T. Maruszewski (Eds.), *Creativity and consciousness: Philosophical and psychological dimensions* (pp. 395–412). Amsterdam/Atlanta: Rodopi.

Runco, M. A., & Johnson, D., & Gaynor, J. R. (1999). The judgmental bases of creativity and implications for the study of gifted youth. In A. Fishkin, B. Cramond, & P. Olszewski-Kubilius (Eds.), *Creativity in youth: Research and methods* (pp. 113–141). Cresskill, NJ: Hampton Press.

Runco, M. A., & Richards, R. (Eds.). (1997). *Eminent creativity, everyday creativity, and health.* Norwood, NJ: Ablex.

Runco, M. A., & Sakamoto, S. O. (1996). Optimization as a guiding principle in research on creative problem solving. In T. Helstrup, G. Kaufmann, & K. H. Teigen (Eds.), *Problem solving and cognitive processes: Essays in honor of Kjell Raaheim* (pp. 119–144). Bergen, Norway: Fagbokforlaget Vigmostad & Bjorke.

Scarr, S., & McCartney, K. (1983). How people make their environments: A theory of genotype-environment interactions. *Child Development, 54,* 424–435.

Schuldberg, D. (1997). Schizotypal and hypomanic traits, creativity, and psychological health. In M. A. Runco & R. Richards (Eds.), *Eminent creativity, everyday creativity, and health* (pp. 157–172). Norwood, NJ: Ablex.

Schultz, N. R., Jr., Kaye, D. B., & Hoyer, W. J. (1980). Intelligence and spontaneous flexibility in adulthood and old age. *Intelligence, 4,* 219–231.

Shalley, C. E. (1991). Effects of productivity goals, creativity goals, and personal discretion on individual creativity. *Journal of Applied Psychology, 76,* 179–185.

Simonton, D. K. (1984). *Genius, creativity, and leadership.* Cambridge, MA: Harvard University Press.

Simonton, D. K. (1997). Political pathology and societal creativity. In M. A. Runco & R. Richards (Eds.), *Eminent creativity, everyday creativity, and health* (pp. 359–378). Norwood, NJ: Ablex.

Sternberg, R., & Lubart, T. (1991). Short selling investment theories of creativity? A reply to Runco. *Creativity Research Journal, 4,* 200–202.

Subotnik, R., Steiner, C., & Chakraborty, B. (1992). Procrastination revisited: The constructive use of delayed response. *Creativity Research Journal, 12,* 151–160.

Torrance, E. P. (1968). A longitudinal examination of the fourth-grade slump in creativity. *Gifted Child Quarterly, 12,* 195–199.

Treutt, K. R. (1993). Age differences in conservatism. *Personality and Individual Differences, 14,* 405–411.

Vernon, P. E. (Ed.) (1970). *Creativity.* Middlesex, England: Penguin.

Walberg, H. J., Zhang, G., Cummings, C., et al. (in press). Childhood traits and experiences of eminent women. *Creativity Research Journal.*

Wallas, G. (1926). *The art of thought.* New York: Harcourt Brace Jovanovich.

Weber, R., & Perkins, D. (1992). *Inventive minds: Creativity in technology.* New York: Oxford University Press.

Chapter 3

I'm Too Busy: The Creative Paradox and the Young Child

Charlotte L. Doyle

Once upon a time when we all were children, we spent time in a creative activity called pretend play. Franklin (1983) tells of a continuing drama she played with her cousins from the time she was around five. The girls called themselves the Fancy Ladies of North Poo-Poo. They dressed in large floppy hats and evening gowns, and wherever they found themselves in the imaginary worlds of their own creation, they were contrary and did the opposite of what was expected. In an elegant restaurant, they ate mashed potatoes with their fingers. On the subway, they entered by leaping through windows instead of walking through doors. At the circus, instead of laughing at the antics of a clown, they cried.

In this chapter, I feel a little like a Fancy Lady of North Poo-Poo. Many observers from Freud (1908/1925) to Picasso (Penrose, 1981) look to the creations of children for insight into the adult creative process. I have followed a contrarian path. I have come to understand creativity in children and the ways in which it can be facilitated by first looking at the creative process in adults. Bear with my naughtiness. Just as some art teachers direct drawing students to turn common objects upside down to make the familiar strange, it may be revealing to look at creativity in children using concepts that capture the adult creative process.

The Experience of the Adult Creative Artist

My first attempt to articulate my understanding of creativity began some years ago when I was invited to be the keynote speaker for a conference on the creative process (Doyle, 1976). A funny thing happened on the way to writing that address. I began by trying to write what psychologists and creative people generally agree upon. But whatever I wrote down, the opposite also seemed to be true. I started out with: *The creative process involves freedom and spontaneity.* But then I recalled the words of Ezra Pound (1963, p. 42): "Any damn fool can be spontaneous." And even though as a psychologist I knew that was not totally true, I immediately straightened up in my chair and wrote: *The creative process requires intention, concentration, and a commitment to work.* I thought of Freud and wrote: *The creative process taps the primitive and the emotional.* And then I thought of Shakespeare and Rembrandt and wrote: *The creative process requires skill, insight, and maturity.* I thought of psychologists such as Guilford (1959) and Wallach and Kogan (1965) and wrote: *The creative process involves fantasy, inventiveness, the ability to diverge from what is.* But then I thought of my own interviews with artists and wrote: *The creative process demands honesty and a pull to truth.* Then statements began to crowd in on me: *The creative process is self-expression; the creative process cannot take place unless the creator forgets about self. The creative process is a joy; the creative process is fraught with anxiety and frustration. The creative process is its own reward; the creative process needs the support and encouragement of the social world.* This first phase of my inquiry led me to the title of my address: "The Creative Process: A Study in Paradox."

But this mystery of creativity, which seemed so full of contradictions when I tried to describe it as a list of attributes, became clearer when I looked at it as a *process.* From the beginning I had been convinced that creativity is not a trait, something a person is, but an activity, something a person does, an activity. And the activity does not happen in an instant; it is not a momentary flash of originality, a single clever idea, rather an episode that unfolds through time. I see the creative episode as the period in a person's life when he or she creates a work, the period from the impulse to create something, through the ups and downs of working on it, to the sense that the creation has been completed. My chief resources for illuminating creative

episodes came from firsthand accounts, both those in the literature and in interviews I and my students had done. So I sought
insight into the creative process by exploring its phenomenol-
ogy. (See Czikszentmihalyi, 1996 and Wallace & Gruber, 1989 for
similar approaches.)

The Creative Episode in Adult Artists

I began my probe of the experience of the creative episode with
a simple question: "How does the creative process begin?" The
answer was equally simple: It begins with some sense that the
creative process has begun. Something pulls at the mind and
engages the creative person. That very engagement points to
something else. The creator allows that something that pulled at
the mind to structure activity, makes a decision to allow that
something to take shape. A process sustained over time has to
become an intentional project, something the creator as an active
agent undertakes to do. This was true of Picasso in his painting of
his mural *Guernica,* William Faulkner in his writing of *The Sound
and the Fury,* and Albert Einstein in the creation of relativity
theory. The creator DECIDES to work on a particular kind of
thing. Now the kinds of things creators decide to work on depend
on the society in which they grow up (Feldman, 1980; Gardner,
1983). Before the modern era, there was no modern physics;
before the invention of printing, there were no novels. Every
known human society has developed linguistic, visual, musical,
and movement arts of some kind and every known human
society has developed systematic ways of understanding the
natural world. But the media, the forms, the ways people in a
particular society spend time on creative projects, vary from
culture to culture. Creative people see themselves and their work
as part of a cultural tradition, a culturally prescribed way of
working in a medium. Picasso knew and saw himself as part of the
tradition of painting; Faulkner saw himself as a novelist among
other novelists; Einstein was a physicist immersed in the work of
other physicists.

Yet part of the mystery of the creative process is that even
though it takes place in the context of a tradition, it involves an

intention to do something that does not yet exist, so there is no clear path ahead. There may be a germ of an idea at the beginning—Faulkner (1959) began *The Sound and the Fury* with an image of a little girl in a tree with muddy drawers. Picasso committed himself to painting a mural when he got a commission and, soon after the bombing of Guernica took place, he knew that would be his subject. Sometimes the germ is more inarticulate. Katherine Ann Porter's stories start with a cloud in her head (Porter 1963). How do these germs develop into completed works? One answer is that the creator thinks in a medium. The painter thinks color and form; the novelist thinks characters and situations and dialogue; the physicist thinks mathematical, kinesthetic, and spatial representations of masses and forces. The forms, the characters, the spatial representations constitute a whole domain of experience,

Recently, I have been thinking about thinking in medium in a new way using Heinz Werner's (1948) concept of spheres of experience and Schutz's (1962) parallel concept, provinces of meaning. Both speak of a practical everyday realm, but also of other realms of experience: the dream sphere, a theoretical sphere, in which we make models of the world—a sphere frequently inhabited by scientists, the play sphere inhabited by children. According to Schutz, in each sphere, the very nature of experience changes with respect to time, causality, self, and sociality. We can apply this to the creative process as well. For example, fiction writers inhabit a sphere I have called the *fictionworld,* in which they experience the characters and events of their imagination so vividly, that, for moments, the ordinary time, space, causality, and self of the everyday world disappear (Doyle, 1998).

Though the creator may be residing in a world of imagination, he or she, at the same time, is doing something active, making something—writing words, placing colored shapes on a canvas, writing a formula. Now there is an object in the world facing the creator. The thing made real, the object facing the creator may grow and develop and realize the original intention, but it may not. Adult creators go in and out of their imaginary worlds in the course of a creative episode. Sometimes what throws them out of their imaginary worlds is the sense that something is wrong—doesn't look right or sound right or that couldn't be what happened next. At that point, they emerge from their imaginary worlds and reflect on what their lived, unselfconscious thinking in the medium has produced.

Sometimes they reflect on craft, their use of the medium. Creative people are drawn to their medium, enjoy both playing with it and studying it. Skill in the medium and confidence in that skill can be essential to carrying out intentions. I remember a story told by Herbert Kohl (personal communication, 1999) about his work on writing with children. One little girl raised her hand and said, "I would like to write a story about my father, if there is a word for him. But if there is no word for him, I don't want to write about him." Part of skill is learning to use a symbol system (Gardner, 1993) in increasingly sophisticated ways. Skill also involves learning what psychologists call *heuristics*—tricks of the trade that guide you in moving forward. Faulkner (1959) described his first image for *The Sound and The Fury* as a little girl in a tree watching her grandmother's funeral and reporting what was going on to her brothers below. Then Faulkner asked himself to imagine who these children were and what they were doing and how the pants got muddy. These questions are a novelist's guides to thinking in the medium, for developing a germ over time—and writing workshop teachers often direct students to ask themselves such questions to develop a germ into a story.

So, creative people reflect on their developing work once they find themselves outside the imaginary world, and part of that reflection may be studying their medium or applying heuristics. But the reflections that come to mind as the creator finds himself or herself outside the imaginary world do not always center on the problems of the work. Many creative people tell of their thoughts taking a harsher turn. As they step back from the world of the medium, thoughts can turn judgmental. Almost all adult creators are ruthlessly severe critics of their own work. The words or the forms or the formulas or the sounds may be so far from the original intention that it is easy to become discouraged. Sometimes the reflections become an attack on self. "I'm not a writer. I've been fooling myself..." wrote author John Steinbeck (1989, p. 56) in his journal. Other activities also pull at the creator and anything but the work becomes increasingly attractive.

Sometimes the creator gives up before what are the most wonderful, most joyous periods of the creative process. In 1976, I called it a period of total centration, but it has acquired some other names as well. Czikszentmihalyi (1996) called it flow; sports psychologists call it "the zone." These are the times when, for sustained periods, the creative person inhabits the creative sphere, when, for the novelist, the characters completely take over, when, for the composer, melodies flow without forcing. The creator is totally absorbed in the world of the work. That world fills consciousness for a sustained period. All the awkward- ness of the pragmatic, self-reflexive sphere—watching self at work; explicit attention to form; fear that the work is no good; careful, logical selection—are no longer a part of the flow of thought and action. The creator's head, hands, lips are totally engaged by the world as it is unfolding. All intellectual and emotional resources, all skills and experiences become sources that can be drawn into the imaginary world of the developing work. These are wonderful times: they have been described as moments of full spontaneity and freedom. But the freedom and spontaneity do not mean that there is no structure or direction to the mental flow; rather the total inhabitation of the creative world means that its structure and its direction determine the flow of experience, and resources are directed toward it. The creator is freed of self-consciousness, the paralyzing awareness of personal fears and hopes, and fully lives in the imaginary world. That freedom allows the creator to give shape to all sorts of things: observations not fully assimilated, ideas and aspirations only partially worked out, deep concerns which may or may not be reflectively known, perhaps which may be even too frightening to consider, wishes unacknowledged by our respectable selves.

Poet Jane Cooper once said, "A poem uses everything we know, the surprising things we notice, whatever we can't solve and keeps on growing." (Doyle, 1976, p. 13)

These centration periods are recalled as periods of joy, even ecstasy. Thought and action, interaction with the work, become as smooth and flowing as a dance and the imaginary world takes shape seemingly out of nowhere. From everything the creator knows, feels, and has done, just the right elements emerge and interact and organize the imaginary world in a way that gives flesh to the original germ. The work seems to create itself because the worried, self-conscious self of the everyday world does not inhibit the flow that results in the making of the work. Still, though self was not part of the experience of the imaginary world as it was being created, afterward it feels as though, "I have never felt more fully myself."

Periods of centration can be nurtured but cannot be commanded. They require a compelling idea, access to a world of a medium where the idea can take root and grow, willingness to keep going even when the imagined world seems to have come to a standstill. Centration emerges from a focus so steady and strong, there is no space for self-consciousness to intrude. This depends on trust. It is a risk to let go of self-consciousness and enter fully into a world where deliberate, pragmatic control has been suspended, difficult for someone who is deeply frightened to trust oneself in that way. Jane Cooper spoke of "the vulnerability that is always part of making decent poems." (Doyle, 1976, p. 14).

These periods of full inhabitation in the creative world come and go. Those in-between times can be agonizing and frustrating. The pull to bring the intention to fruition has to be strong. What is the pull? Short story writer Grace Paley says it is "an absolute compulsion to tell the truth, to know the truth and tell it somehow" (Doyle, 1976, p. 14). Composer Joel Spiegelman, speaks of composing both as "a moment of truth" and as a way of looking in the mirror—"extending mind and body in a way that you can do in no other way if you are sincere about it" (Doyle, 1973, p. 47). Frequently creators speak of journeys into their imaginary worlds as leading to discoveries. "What do you discover?" I asked several writers. "How we are," said one writer. "How life is," said another. The creative process at its best brings the creator closer to truth. (Doyle, 1976, 1998).

My students and I asked in our interviews, "How do you know when a work is done?" "It's like a door clicking shut," Jane Cooper said, quoting Yeats (Doyle, 1976, p. 14). Somehow the work facing the creator is a good-enough realization of the initial intention. Now comes another important period in the life of the creator: sharing the work. Creators, even when a group creation is involved such as in making a play, isolate themselves from other people and the flow of everyday life and live in the imaginary world of their own making. Now the creator turns back to the social world, the world of other people, and shows what he or she has made.

Sharing the work is also full of contradiction, a time of special self-consciousness and vulnerability, given that one's work may be rejected. One writer gave a draft of her first novel to an agent who returned it, saying it was the most depressing thing she ever read. The writer did not go back to writing for a year (Doyle, 1998). But sharing also has the possibility of being a self-confirming occasion, a celebration of the creation, bringing a special joy that comes when others truly understand something important you have said and done.

Does the Creative Episode in Children Resemble That of Creative Adults?

This was my account of the adult creative episode as it weaves its way in and out of imaginary worlds through time. Now, the time has come to give up being a Fancy Lady of North Poo-Poo and to consider young children and the issue of how to facilitate their creativity. But what are we talking about when we speak of facilitating creativity in children? Does it make sense to see creativity in 3-, 4-, and 5-year-old children in terms of episodes—periods in children's lives when they first undertake, then work on, and finally complete a creation? To what extent are these episodes structured by intentions, to what extent by the cultural opportunities available to them? Does it make sense to think about these episodes as creating imaginary worlds? Do children become explicitly aware of a medium as a system of representation that requires study? What are the sources they draw into their imaginary worlds as they create? How do children deal with getting stuck? What can lead them back in? To what extent are they pulled to complete what they started? Do they make discoveries in the process of creating? Do children know when their works are finished? What are the effects of sharing their work? And what is the impact of creative episodes on the children themselves?

To approach these questions, I will draw on several sources. For many years, I have been doing field observations on young children in a progressive nursery school and kindergarten. This has allowed me to see the ways in which gifted teachers facilitate creativity in children. Second, in more formal research on storytelling in young children (Doyle, 1989, 1990), young authors taught me a great deal about what supports and sustains the creative episode in young children. These observations are complemented by the testimony of parents and a grandparent who witnessed the developmental course of children's creative episodes in their families over several years.

Creativity in Preschool

Let me begin this section by noting that, today, fostering creativity in preschool children is not usually mentioned as a major goal. Instead, emphasis is on training in academic skills. The current rhetoric speaks of high standards, behavioral goals, and the measurement of the extent to which children meet those standards and goals with objective tests. Many parents and teachers train children to meet these standards using materials such as flash cards and arithmetic cards or their more technological versions, computer phonics and arithmetic programs. Now, even though creativity may be far from the minds of those who plan such activities, we need to acknowledge that such activities support one aspect of the creative episode—introducing children to the cultural symbol systems which are also the media for creation. And I have no problem with a little time spent in those activities if—and there are two big ifs—if those activities are games the child really enjoys and if there are opportunities for the child to engage freely in more complete creative episodes.

Of course, there are other ways to introduce those symbol systems, ways that are less decontextualized and center instead on the power of symbolic systems to represent and reveal significant meaning. Take the case of learning to read. I received the following in a letter from the parents of an 18-month-old:

> My 18-month-old son is in love with *You Can't Catch Me*...He absolutely squeals with joy when he sees your book...You cannot stop him from getting your book down from the counter when he wants it. My husband and I believe if *You Can't Catch Me* were locked in a safe, R. would find a way to get it out with his bare hands. He loves the entire experience of the story—the chasing, the racing, the hiding, the catching. He is wild for the buildup at the story's end. R. has been developing speech during the months my husband and I have been reading your book to him. Now R. likes to fill in words when we pause in our reading.

This child has learned something more basic to literacy than phonics. He has learned that books hold stories, and that reading is a loving, enjoyable, meaningful activity. This child will not need flash cards. He will learn about the written code in the context of this and other deeply meaningful books. (Wells, 1986; Wilford, 1998). Sharing the words and pictures of books, playing music, taking children to dance performances and plays, giving children toys that embody mathematical and scientific principles are all ways to introduce children to our culture's ways of representing and understanding experience symbolically and—and this is the part that is often left out—those introductions can convey the excitement and the joy of using those symbol systems.

Some parents who value the creative arts pay for structured lessons in music or dance. Again, these are ways of introducing children to the media in which creative episodes take place, and they can be useful as long as the lessons do not sap children of self-confidence and joy in the activity, and as long as there are opportunities for other kinds of activities as well.

Introduction to the use of systems of representation is necessary to the creative process, but that alone will not lead to creative episodes. To see such episodes, let us leave the realm of structured lessons and visit Sarah Lawrence's Early Childhood Center, a school for children between the ages of 2 and 7, one that follows a progressive, developmental-interactionist approach (Nager & Shapiro, 2000). Preschools such as these are sometimes criticized because it seems to some unsympathetic outsiders that "all the children do in them is play" (and you can just hear the denigration in the way the word "play" is uttered). But let us take a closer look.

First, the children do not play all the time. Here, too, I saw structured activities that put children in touch with the many media in which creative work goes on. Teachers read stories and poems. They play music. They have conversations with children about scientific topics like where rain comes from and why popcorn pops. They introduce number concepts and mathematical notation in ways that have meaning to the children (one of my favorites was a kindergarten graph that showed the number of teeth each child had lost).

But what about those periods when children did "nothing but play?" Then, too, teachers provided opportunities for children to try out many media. Each classroom had areas that invited making: a pretend corner for creating a drama, a painting area for creating visual representations, a place for block building, occasional opportunities to shape modeling clay or try woodworking. There were chances to explore the "I wonder" world of science: by noting the growth of plants and the behavior of animals, by using mirrors and magnifying glasses and magnets. The creative process takes root in a cultural and social context, one in which various media are available and which gives children opportunities to try them out. These everyday setups and activities were providing the preconditions of the creative process.

But these play periods had another very important feature, one typical of creative episodes in adults but that we do not focus on as much in young children. The children *chose* their own activities. During the free play period each day, no one told the children what they should do. The teachers respected the children as active agents with intentions and invited the children to allow their own intentions to structure their activities. Very occasionally, a child found the freedom of free play daunting, and then the teachers gave the children support, suggestions, and encouragement, but even then the activities themselves were self-chosen. Listening to an inner voice is an essential feature of the creative process, and these children were encouraged to do so.

Soon after the free play periods began, I began to see creative episodes unfolding all over the classroom: children painting at easels or drawing with magic markers, miniature architects creating buildings, young scientists studying their own fingers under magnifying glasses, young improvisers creating characters and stories in a pretend corner. I saw children intently concentrated, deeply engaged in what they were doing, engrossed in worlds different from the pragmatic world of everyday life.

As with adults, these creative episodes involved developing and using the skills of observation and representation, drawing on the symbol systems of various media. Children learned the tricks of their media by watching and listening to teachers and to each other and by their own discoveries. I saw children discover how to mix paints, rhyme words, use a stick to serve as a vacuum cleaner, realize that a large block on top of a small block can be unsteady, and discover how to draw a particular kind of thing such as an ant (more about drawing ants later).

The teachers facilitated the creative episodes in several ways. First, they showed respect for the children's discoveries and inventions, sometimes helping them to extend the episode. One day a little girl found a worm under the sliding board and wanted to keep it. The teacher admired her discovery and asked her to tell where she found the worm and what it felt like to pick it up— helping her to find words to describe the worm and the conditions that help worms thrive. Then the teacher gave her a cup to fill with the moist dirt the worm had lived in so she could take her precious worm home.

Some of the invented projects involved using materials in unorthodox ways. Teachers accepted and supported the unusual. When a child painted a green flower with red leaves, the teacher didn't say, as one adult still remembers her kindergarten teacher saying, "It doesn't look like a tulip." Instead, she asked the child to tell her about his painting.

One day a child discovered that magic markers could be lined up end to end like a train. She built a long magic marker train. The markers, which were sometimes put on the table for use in art projects, on this day had been on a shelf, not intended for use that day. The teacher did not say, "We're not using markers today," or "Markers are for drawing," or "Markers are not toys." She was genuinely impressed with her inventive construction. And when the girl said, "I want to leave it up," the teacher allowed the child to dictate words for a sign which said, "Don't knock down my train."

When a child is engaged in a creative episode, being abruptly routed from the created world can be a difficult moment. One way teachers supported the creative process was by how they dealt with those transitions—with respect and understanding. Three children invented a jumping game as the group was moving from free play to meeting time. Instead of saying, "You can't," or "You shouldn't," the teacher said, "Three more jumps and then it will be meeting time." The project was acknowledged and respected even though the teacher needed for it to stop.

With respect for the children went an amazing amount of trust. This was brought home to me in an experience surrounding a story I told children. The children asked for it again and again— it somehow became their story—so the teacher suggested to her kindergartners that they could do it as a play. "Maybe we could use the blockroom," she said. The children went immediately into the blockroom and began building a set out of blocks. They used what they knew of the story and about block building. They were concentrated and engaged as they invented it. Then came the problem of picking a cast. Two children wished to play the lead. The teacher did not suggest a solution. She trusted the children to find a creative solution even to this difficult interpersonal dilemma. When no solution emerged, she allowed the process of coming to a solution to take time. She asked the children to think about it until the next day. The next day, one of the children who wanted be the leading character suggested that the play be divided into two acts and that each child could play the lead in one act. The other children immediately recognized this as a good solution.

There were times when children could not solve a problem that emerged in the course of the creative episode, when they became discouraged at not being able to carry out their own intentions. Here, the teachers found ways to help children do what they wanted to do with hints and helps. They sometimes framed the situation so that the child could learn a *heuristic*, a trick of craft that would enable a child to carry out his or her own intention. A boy started out to draw something very large. One piece of paper could not contain his monumental creation. "It's no good," the boy told the teacher, "there's no room for the legs." "What could you do to make more room?" the teacher asked. The boy thought and then brightened and said, "Get another piece of paper." He did, but the papers kept slipping in relation to one another. The teacher brought out some tape. The boy found and used it.

A little girl was building a building and was becoming increasingly frustrated at the inability of a block to stay vertical. She became so angry she was about to knock down the rest of the building, as she had done several times before. The teacher guided her in buttressing the vertical block with supporting blocks on each side.

Did children know when their projects were finished? Young children's creative endeavors do not always have a clear beginning, middle, and end. Dramatic play, typically co-constructed by several children drifting in and out of it, often trailed off into another activity. But frequently children had a clear sense of project and knew when they completed it. A 4-year-old boy drew some lines, then drew an ant. (This class had recently established an ant farm.) The boy clearly wasn't satisfied with his representation of the ant, so he tried out another version and another and another. Then he took a second sheet and drew an ant farm with all the ants drawn in the same way, combining the best features of his earlier ants. Now he knew he was finished and proudly showed his picture to the teacher, moving into the next phase of the creative process, sharing the work (Eben Schwartz, personal communication, 2000).

The classrooms I observed were full of occasions that allowed children to share their creations and feel that their work has a valued place in the social world. Teachers modeled respect and interest. Often, at meeting time, each child had an opportunity to do something individual such as imitate a favorite animal or pick a favorite color. When shown creative projects, teachers did not offer empty praise, did not say, "I like your painting," or "I think your block building is great." Instead, they gave recognition to interesting features of the children's creations. "Wow. You drew all the parts of the ants," or "I like the way the polar bear is walking on the high plank so he can talk to the giraffe." One teacher often asked the children who painted a painting, "Can I use your picture to make the room pretty?" and she meant it. Children also had opportunities to share with each other, not only during the classic show-and-tell, but when talking to the others about the buildings they built, the worms they found, the discoveries they made by playing with mirrors. One child, then another experienced that special pleasure that comes from sharing and then finding recognition for what he or she created.

To summarize what I saw in the preschool classroom: I saw children becoming acquainted with wonderful uses of various media and being guided as they acquired skills. I saw a safe context that provided opportunities for trying out various media.

I saw children experiencing a sense of agency as they intentionally undertook their own projects. I saw them becoming completely absorbed in the worlds of dramatic play, block building, drawing, and painting. I saw respect and trust as the teachers supported unusual uses of materials, provided a transition time so that children were not abruptly uprooted from their imaginary worlds, and allowed children to come to their own solutions to problems. But I also saw teachers sensitive to the children's intentions and ready to offer just the help needed should the attempts to realize tasks become overly frustrating. I saw children developing increasingly sophisticated standards for their own creative endeavors as they made discoveries in how to use a medium. I often saw the children indicate a clear sense of when their projects fulfilled their intentions. And I saw the children's own projects given a valued place in their social world. Each aspect of the creative episode as it unfolded over time was encouraged and supported.

Young Children as Visual Artists

Occasionally, one medium will be especially meaningful to a child, and, given support, will become an oft chosen way to explore, entertain, invent, and discover. I interviewed the mothers of two children for whom drawing had become such a favorite activity. Because the mothers saved many of the children's drawings and remembered some of the episodes as well, this allowed a glimpse into the development of creative episodes in young children over time. It also allowed entrance into the creative process in the context of home. Admittedly, these two children were unusual. Winner (1996) suggests that children talented in the visual arts have some unique characteristics: precocious achievement; needing only minimal help in mastering the domain; and obsessive, intense interest. I certainly heard descriptions that echoed these qualities. But another way of looking at these qualities is to see them as amplifications of features of the creative episodes I saw among so-called ordinary children in the preschool classroom. Winner agrees that the burgeoning of an artistic gift is not merely the unfolding of genetic certainties; rather, the propensity toward a medium requires a supportive, inviting environment. The parents of these children whose creative gifts blossomed during the preschool years provided the same kinds of opportunities and supports that I saw in the progressive classroom.

First, both mothers introduced their children to a variety of media—music, stories, picture books, science museums. Both also noticed that the children were attracted to the visual world early and so provided the opportunity for art projects at home. Interestingly, neither provided paints, a medium difficult for very young children to control.

One mother provided magic markers. She, who herself is very sensitive to the visual world, also provided good paper rather than scraps for him to draw on. From the beginning, David loved to draw. His mother found that by having art materials with her all the time, David amused himself at the kinds of times children often find themselves at loose ends: in doctors' offices, restaurants, during visits to the homes of parents' friends.

His early drawings were designs and already showed a strong, confident line, a relaxed but expansive use of space. By age 3, a representational intention took over. In one drawing, he tried something, the inner critic rejected it (and the outer child crossed it out). Then, with the courage required of the creative process, he tried again and again, and finally drew what he intended to his satisfaction. He brought the finished drawing to his mother and told her "flower." We see a complete creative episode here: intention, trying out in the medium, judgment, rejection, reimmersion in the world of drawing, a sense of completion, and sharing.

Interestingly, this child didn't draw much at school. His mother told me he tended to draw, not when he was upset, but when he felt especially calm and relaxed, and for David that was at home. From the beginning, he drew a variety of things: a mother and child, a tree with a bug in it, a picture that some people might title "windows" and others "a study in vertical and horizontal," a tree. His mother said he tended to draw a kind of thing for a period, and then, once he knew he could draw that kind of thing to his satisfaction, he went on to drawing another kind of thing. It was as if once he could do the kind of drawing he wished, it was no longer interesting, and he sought a new challenge.

One of the major sources of inspiration for what to draw came from picture books. We tend to think of art in terms of paintings in art museums, but in the lives of young children, the major visual sources other than their own perceptions of the world around them are books, comics, and the images on packages of various sorts. Books probably inspired the animal series. By the time David was 4 or 5, his pictures often integrated several sources. A drawing of train tracks combined his own toy tracks which he could arrange in all sorts of interesting configurations but which didn't have ties and straight tracks with ties he had seen on the subway and in his books.

"Did you make a big fuss about his drawings?" I asked his mother. "I didn't," she said, explaining that she had an older son who also liked to draw, but who was not as precocious, and she didn't want to emphasize the difference between them. On the other hand, she was genuinely impressed by David's drawings and talked with him about them in a substantive way, much as the teachers did at the school. The boy also knew that his mother valued his drawings; she dated and saved most of them. Clearly the boy loved to draw. His pleasure in the activity included the completion of his own intentions, the challenge of learning how to represent things, a sense of the aesthetic, a sense of competence, and the pleasure in sharing.

For David the motivation for drawing seemed intrinsic from the beginning. He was attracted to the activity of creating visual experience with magic markers, and he varied the content from the beginning.

Ross's entry into drawing started earlier and in a different way, reminding us that there is no single developmental path to creativity, even in talented children. The very beginning of Ross's experience sounds much like David's. Ross's mother noticed her son's sensitivity to the visual world very early; she, too, provided art materials. In fact, she discovered crayons that could be attached to little fingers and markers in the shapes of animals, just the right size and shape so that a little hand could be cupped around them. This child made his first scribbles when he was less than 15 months old.

According to Ross's mother, very soon after he picked up his first crayon, he had a representational intention. Between the ages of 1 and 2, this little boy's favorite objects were balls; he had huge collection of balls of all sorts. So when mother and son sat down together with the crayons, he began with circular scribbles (as many children do). But as he was doing this, he kept saying his favorite word, "ball." The mom, a Vygotskian psychologist, was careful not to crayon anything beyond his zone of proximal development—what he did not do yet but was capable of learning. So as he kept saying "ball" and drawing round scribbles, she drew a very simple ball. But she told me that her son was so intent on what he was creating, so absorbed in his own creative world, he paid little or no attention to her ball. He wanted her company but the example didn't mean much. He just drew scribble ball after scribble ball until he was able to do one that satisfied him. Creating a ball, she told me, seemed like a way of possessing it to him. He continued drawing balls for several months, and then stopped drawing for a period of several months.

Ross did not return to drawing until he had a new intention. His next consuming interests around the age of 2 were dinosaurs and Batman. The parents allowed the Batman interest but really supported the dinosaur interest with books, toys, and trips to a museum. The child ended up with a huge collection of dinosaur toys and books and by age 3 knew the names of all the dinosaurs and quite a bit about their differences from one another. He had many dinosaur toys but no Dunkleosteus. He wanted one. The mother provided modeling clay, and Ross made one, but it fell apart in play. Next they tried downloading the outline off the Internet, coloring it in, and pasting it on cardboard. That led to the Ross's drawing many of his own dinosaurs, cutting and pasting them and then playing with them alongside his other dinosaurs. He said after pasting one drawing on a cardboard backing, "Now it's a real toy."

After a while, books became the inspiration for drawing dinosaurs in various positions and interactions. That became such a consuming activity that art materials, scissors, and paste had to be kept in every room. But dinosaurs were not his only consuming interest as he drew. He became fascinated with the problems of representation. At one point, frustrated with the problem of how to attach the dinosaur's legs to the body, he kept drawing the same dinosaur over and over again, until he was able to render the relation of legs to body to his satisfaction.

His dinosaur drawings progressed, until one spring day at day care, a classmate asked him to stop drawing dinosaurs because they were too scary. Like the writer who received a devastating review from an agent, Ross dropped his artistic activity completely; he drew neither at day care nor at home. He did not touch art materials during the summer months when he was no longer in day care. Now he attends a preschool that encourages art activities of all sorts. Ross had never painted; now he has had his first experiences with paint, first creating designs and later seeing how paint can be used as a representational medium. And drawing has again become a consuming activity. At 4 1/2, he is doing less copying than he did earlier. In fact, his latest interest involves combining from several sources, among them books, films, videos, and CD covers. Inspector Gadget is a current favorite subject. He made an Inspector Gadget valentine and has drawn himself as Inspector Gadget. He has also combined Santa Claus and the Grinch, a chipmunk and Batman.

Now these may be two special children, but they show in amplified form what I saw in an ordinary classroom. They benefited from opportunities to learn about and practice a medium, received permission and support to follow their own intentions, and their intentions allowed them to enter imaginary worlds with deep concentration, moving in and out of them as they puzzled over problems of representation. These children experienced satisfaction as they made discoveries and completed their projects, and also felt the positive and negative impacts of social reactions to their work. With Ross, art seemed to provide an opportunity to portray images of awesome power that he could possess and control. In both children, their desires to draw a particular kind of thing combined with a cognitive purpose—determination to solve the problems of representation in the visual medium.

Young Children as Authors

Some creative activities require scaffolding by adults. An example is "book making" by young children who are capable of telling stories but not yet capable of writing them. So, I invited children between the ages of 3 and 6 to tell me stories. (Doyle, 1989, 1990) One of the features of the creative process as I conceptualize it is that it results in an object, something real, something permanent; so instead of tape recording the stories or just writing them down for myself, I wrote their stories on construction paper folded to make a book-like pamphlet. And because I believe that part of the process is stepping back and reflecting on what has been done so far, I repeated the words as I wrote them and read the story so far when the telling faltered. At the end, I reread the story again and asked if the author wished to give the story a title. Title and author went on the cover page. Typically, I took story dictation in a semipublic place. Other children could wander over and listen.

Of course, I am not the first psychologist to study children's storytelling. Pitcher and Prelinger (1963) analyzed story content in terms of psychoanalytic theory. Applebee (1978) charted developmental stages in story structure. Brian Sutton-Smith (1981) studied how plots become more involved with age. My interest was in storytelling as a creative episode.

First of all, let me say that the 5-year-old children had no trouble understanding what I was inviting them to do when I asked for a story. This is not surprising. Earlier I mentioned that the very existence of a medium for creative work depends on culture and that each culture provides examples of its media for children. All the children I worked with had heard many stories. In addition, video is now a major narrative form for young children. Even video games have the form of a narrative adventure. In addition, children have experience with two related narrative activities: They tell about events in conversations and, in pretend play, they create imaginary happenings.

In the 3-year-olds, some early stories were little more than an extension of play. R. D.'s first story was "Superman went falling" and he acted it out as he said it. R. E. jumped up and down as he said, "The big thing was jumping. Whoa!" In one 3-year-old's class, few children spontaneously accepted my invitation to dictate stories, so I listened for words I could write down as part of a story. C. F. was wearing a hat and said as part of pretend play, "I'm going home." I said, "Why? I'll write it as a story." C. F. replied, "Cause I'm from home and I don't have a mom. Sometimes I have my mom. I just don't know what time my mom comes home. That's a story." "Is that the end?" "Yes." (By the way, children usually are very clear on when their stories are at the end.) I reread C. F.'s story to him and asked him what he wanted to call it. His title was, "I'm Going Home."

I visited P. G. in the block corner who told me he built a large city. I asked him to tell me about it and that I would make his words into a story. P. G. said, pointing to a section near a police car, "A police station. A bad guy comes in. There were fire engine stations. Then a house." He paused. I asked, "Is your story over?" "No. Then it was a school. Then there was a world. That's all." At the end of the day, P. G. asked, "Where's my story?"

If a child told me about an event, I asked if I could write it as a story. J. I.'s first story was exactly what she just told me about: "Johnny Boy touched dog doodoo." But even the 3-year-olds within a week or two got a sense that storytelling is an activity different from fantasy play and different from telling. The next time I visited, J. I.'s story was, "Once upon a time, Johnny Boy touched dog doodoo. The end."

Storytelling soon takes a shape different from telling or

play. I was watching three children playing with liquid corn-starch, mucking around in the goo, talking to each other, and creating fantasies. C. F., the child who told the "I'm going home" story two weeks before, was one of them. The conversation went like this:

C. F.: Oh slime, get this off my toothbrush. This is my cake. My cake is yuck with slime.

Other Child 1: My cake too.

Other Child 2: I'm making a chocolate cake.

C. F.: This is my hat and it's slimy.

Other Child 2: Kaakaa my peepee.

C. F.: Slime on my toothbrush.

Other Child 1: Kaakaa my bathroom.

C. F.: My poopoo is hairy.

Other Child 1: Get out of my bathrooom.

C. F.: Here's my Kaakaa. Here's my peepee. Yucky...Get off my brother's head.

Soon after, C. F. dictated this story: "Slime is coming down the chimney. All the people wake up from the sound and they see if it's in the fireplace and it is. And they get real scared and real mean."

Note the differences between the fantasy play and the story. The story is a narrative, with a sense of place, cause and effect, and characters other than self. Note also that we do not see pure indulgent pleasure in slime, Kaakaa, and peepee. The slime has turned ominous. He gives us the reactions of people in general to slime—becoming frightened and becoming mean. The story medium allowed the child to represent and master reality as well as participate in free-floating, socially constructed fantasy with two other children.

And lest I should forget that this was a very meaningful activity to him, he kept reminding me. When I reread the story to him, he completed each line of the story as soon as I said the first word of it. When I told "Slime" at story time, he smiled. When his mother came to pick him up, his first words to her were, "I wrote a story."

So both in the older 3-year-olds' class and in the kindergarten, story dictation became a choice children could make during free play. Over three-quarters of the children selected storytelling as a free play activity at least once and a number of them became regular storytellers. Frequently, children lined up to tell stories and I had to give them numbers. I had many opportunities to see how the creative episode in storytelling unfolds.

The Creative Episode in Storytelling

Most children do not know what their stories are going to be at first. They intend to tell a story but do not have a particular story in mind. There are some exceptions. One 5-year-old heard me tell a story about a bird monster. The following week he told me a story that began: "The monster ate the clock. The people called the police. The monster ate the telephone." His mother said he had been waiting all week to tell me the story.

More typically, after the child has asked to tell a story and I ask, "How does the story start, he or she looks off saying "Ahh..." or "I have to think." After a while the story begins. Some children tell about a real event that happened—about a camping trip or about a sister who kicked. But most tell fantasy stories. The most frequent beginnings are "Once," or "There was once" or "Once upon a time"—showing they have learned our cultural conventions There is great variation on what comes next: Once upon a time there was a mouse; once there was a little girl; once upon a time there were three monsters; once upon a time there was blue grass; once we went to the duck pond; one day there was Jumbo. Stories begin with a character from a known tale, with an animal, with people, with places, or with imaginary creatures like monsters. Some children interpret the request for a story as a request to retell a story. In fact, some want to use the story to reinstate a story they love. Three-year-old K. J. dictated: "Cinderella. There was a mean stepmother and a mean step girl." I reread the story. She added, "And there was Cinderella."

I permit a retelling once or twice and then ask for a story they make up themselves. But starting with a given character does not mean shackling the imagination. Like the two young artists I spoke of, young storytellers often weave together material from many sources both real and imagined. Jumbo, Muppet Babies, the big bad wolf, and Mommy and Daddy can appear in the same story. Among the kindergartners there is sometimes a true integration of disparate elements. G. A. listened to another child tell a story about a video game. He wanted to tell a similar story, which I discouraged because I wanted to hear one he made up himself. Then he suggested a story with the title, "When I Went Camping." I don't usually keep discouraging a child's suggestions, but this was the story he had told me the previous week. G. A. told me, "This is a different story about when I went camping." So I put pen to paper and he began narrating a video game about kung fu. I despaired of getting an original story, then G. A. said, "And on the second level, there's a secret passage that goes to the fifth level, the camping level. On the camping level, you have to sleep overnight there. Then, in the morning, I punched the Big Boss and killed him forever. Then I rescued the Princess and Great Knight forever." G. A. managed to meet my request for a new story and his own intentions to tell about both a video game and camping.

Now in the course of storytelling, children may get stuck. Very occasionally—only twice in the course of recording hundreds of stories—they just leave. But most children do not. Once they have committed themselves to storytelling, they want to go on until they sense they have finished. Sometimes they say, "I have to think." In the process of thinking, they discover some tricks to keep a story going. One trick is the use of the ordinary events of everyday life: A. K.'s Muppet Babies left the big bad wolf and "went home and had dinner and went to sleep and had breakfast and lunch." Another favorite strategy children use when they are stuck is to weave in events from the present. L. R. said, "Once upon a time," then we heard the crash of blocks. She added, "There was a blockroom." When A. K.'s moppet baby story faltered, she looked around and said, "Then they go to school and make a picture." Sometimes children tell me they don't know what they want to say next. I try to help them by rereading what they have written so far. If that does not help, I try to give them heuristics by saying, "What happened next?" or "Tell me what happened to the horse" or "Tell me more about the horse." Sometimes I tell them to shut their eyes, imagine the story, and see what happens next.

I knew the adult creative process is both a joy and a frustration and there are moments of getting stuck; but for the most part, storytelling was a very happy activity for the children, sometimes totally transforming prior mood. Most children smiled in the telling and sometimes they laughed outright. I categorized the elements that made them laugh: the unexpected, misbehavior, and the taboo are three of them. One 3-year-old laughed as she asked me to write Elizabeth Headnose as the author. One child told of a magic pond that could talk, walk away, disappear, and come back. The blockroom story I mentioned earlier was told with great gusto. "Once upon a time there was a blockroom, with hundreds of blocks made of candy. And all the children who were in the blockroom builded them and licked them. Until the Martians came and destroyed them and ate them. Then one day the Martians came back and said, 'I'm sorry,' and throwed up on the children."

Throwing up, being spanked, waking up babies, spilling things, kissing trash were all occasions for laughter. T. A. laughed as she told about a bad baby and then said, "And the baby's name was Mrs. Doyle." Then she pictured the father, Mr. Doyle, spanking the Mrs. Doyle. It was great fun to play with the role reversal.

Just as the young visual artists had a joint interest in the form and contents of their drawings, the young authors showed joint interest in form and content as well. And discoveries about story form made them laugh. A child asked to tell a story at cleanup time. I said it would have to be a short story. His story was, "Once there was an ugly, ugly house. The end." And he laughed. One 3-year-old, in looking around the room as she told her story, put one of her classmates in the story. "Then Caroline came." She laughed and called out, "Hey Caroline, I put you in my story." One of my favorites started out as a retelling of a shopping trip C. L. took with her mother: "Mommy came into the store. Then Mommy came out of the store. And then she came in the store." At that point she started to laugh. And laughingly she continued, "She came back out of the store. Then she came right back in a store. And then she came out of a store." C. L. realized she could go on forever this way; only my limiting her to the bottom of the page ended the hilarity of this child's discovery of an infinite pattern.

Many children, in the process of storytelling, centered on what they were doing. Sometimes I could almost pinpoint the beginning of centration. The author of the monster story wrote a story that included a new kind of video game, one he called "Evil in Pizza." He began to pace as he invented the rules, such as, if you collect the pizza with the chain on it you die, but if you don't, you get seven pizzas to eat whenever you want. I had no doubts but that he was totally centered on the story he was telling.

As the children became engaged, the stories flowed more freely. At times I was amazed at how this free reign allowed the children to tell the truth about their concerns. Sometimes the concerns were undisguised. A 3-year-old for whom English was a second language dictated: "I fell down. I feel bad. I had medicine. I feel better and I sleep."

Sometimes, especially in the kindergarten, concerns were more disguised. The week I was teaching about Freud's Oedipus complex to my college students, D. J. told this story:

Once upon a time there was a little rabbit. Know why the rabbit was so sad? He didn't have a home. He saw a badger and asked the badger if he could move in with him and the badger said, "NO YOU CAN'T." He growled and growled to say, "You can't move in with me." The rabbit hopped along and hopped along and hopped along until he came to another badger. And then the mother badger said, "Do you have a home?" And the rabbit said, "No I don't." So the mother badger said, "Would you like to move in with me?" And the bunny said, "Sure. I never had a home." And then Mrs. Badger said, "I am going to take you back to Mr. Badger because that's where I live and he's been so greedy to you and I'm going to tell him he doesn't have a home." And that's the very end. They lived happily ever after.

Note that this is a skillful, well-formed story that uses both the conventions of storytelling and the narrative rules of cause and effect.

M. M. was a little girl who typically told only happy stories. One day, she began her story in a typical way: "Once upon a time, there lived two cats. They lived with a big dog. And they were friends. And they lived in a little house in the woods. And the little woman lived inside the little house in the woods." Then, untypically, M. M. got stuck. I told her to close her eyes and listen as I reread what she wrote. She listened very intently, and then, for the first time in storytelling confronted a concern: "One day the little old woman was very old and very sick. So she died. Then the big dog and the two cats lived alone. The end."

T. A. told a series of stories about mean or misbehaving children; here's the last one in the series:

> Once upon a time, when I was little, I threw up. [Big smile.] My mommy said it wasn't all right. My mommy sent me to my room. But I went to the kitchen to get a cup with some orange juice in it. I carried it carefully to my room. It spilled. [Another smile.] My mommy said it wasn't all right. She said, "I'll give you one more chance and if you don't behave, I'll throw you in the trash masher." Then suddenly I got bigger because I drank so much milk. And then I learned to behave. And my mommy loved me so much she wouldn't throw me away. The end.

These stories capture the truths of children's wishes and concerns and fears in ways that I wouldn't have believed possible if I hadn't heard them myself.

So I became witness to creative episodes in storytelling. But did the children know themselves as creators? Were they aware of their words as their own? I found evidence that they did and they were. They corrected me quite insistently when I did not read back the words that they intended. I mistook a volleyball game for a football game and was corrected. A little girl told me her sister felt a little mad and I misheard it as bad and she corrected me. I was amazed at the lengths to which children would go to make sure I got the right word. A kindergartner said something that sounded like "Playdough" to me. She went and got a book about shadows off the shelf to show me that she meant shadow. A boy kept saying something that sounded like "lots" to me. He took me by the hand, led me outside, and pointed to rocks. A girl said, "Once upon a time there was a board." I repeated that. She said, "No, board, tweet, tweet, tweet." Once I got it right, the children smiled with pleasure as I reread their stories, some-times saying the words with me. When I gave them their stories to put in their cubbies or the take-home box, many took their stories to another adult and asked to have them read again. On joining their playmates, I heard several say, "I just wrote a story." And day's end, they asked for their stories. Often they greeted their parents by saying, "I wrote a story."

The last phase of the creative episode is sharing the work. I wondered what a public reading of the stories a week later would mean. Would they recognize their own stories? I found out quickly that they did. One little girl looked extremely puzzled as I read what I had announced as her story. Then I realized I had attributed another child's story to her. Children were very aware of which words were theirs. Public readings of their stories were times of self-consciousness. Some just loved the attention and were exuberant; others were more shy and ambivalent. They smiled coyly and hid themselves in some way, looking away, covering their ears, and covering their heads. In fact, some went from overt pleasure to hiding, then to pleasure, to hiding, then to pleasure, and back to hiding, and then back to pleasure.

One of my major surprises was how much the children enjoyed other's stories. The 3-year-olds laughed for a full minute when I announced the author of a story as Elizabeth Headnose. Children are often influenced by each other's stories as adult writers are and sometimes develop traditions. Funny stories released other children to be funny. And there are other influences as well.

In one kindergarten, storytelling started out to be the activity of many girls and two rather quiet boys. Then one of these quiet boys told the following story: "Once upon a time, [a] knight found a tent...But there were bombs in there. Then they exploded, but the knight didn't die. But there were fires all around him. But his suit was so strong, he can't die."

This story taught the listeners that child-written stories could present pictures of strength, invincibility, and victory. Thereafter, stories of adventure, of karate and football games and winning video games became very popular among the boys. The boys started telling as many stories as the girls. J. K.'s story started a tradition in the medium.

An unplanned result of making children's words into written language was advancement in literacy. One 3-year-old girl dictated, "I had a cat named Kickin. Kickin ran away." After several of us had read her story to her, she asked me to show her where the story said "ran away." I showed her. She then spent several minutes pointing at the words and repeating them to herself.

Sometimes, the introduction of a creative medium allows a child who seems quiet and ordinary to shine. T. A. never stood out in kindergarten. She got along well with the other children, but there seemed to be nothing exceptional about her. The classroom provided the opportunity for learning to write through invented spelling, but T. A. had almost no sense of phonics and her attempts were among the least skillful. Most of the children in the classes I worked with dictated a story at least once; the average was about six. T. A. did not dictate a story the first time it was offered as an activity. In the second session she dictated a story that was a clear imitation of one she had just heard. But thereafter, storytelling became an activity she would choose

above all others. She dictated at least one story every time I
visited, and on the rare days it was possible, after every child who
wanted to dictate had a turn, she dictated a second. I found in her
stories something similar to what I heard from the mothers of the
children who were drawn to visual art beyond the usual casual,
happy interest. She kept changing both the content and the
forms of her stories. Her early stories were about a brother who
was either mean or nice to his sister, then there were a series of
misbehavior stories, often with Mrs. Doyle as the bad baby, and
then she experimented with stories that were told entirely in
dialogue. At the end of the semester, she was telling very simple,
beautifully formed stories in which a wish was fulfilled. Each
story she told had a stylistic innovation even as the content kept
changing. Clearly, she was drawn to the possibilities of the
medium and enjoyed trying out different ways of telling a story.
The other children enjoyed her stories too, laughing uproariously
at the humor that peppered them all. This quiet child so easy to
overlook and underestimate became recognized by her peers, her
teacher, and perhaps also by herself as an exceptional storyteller.
(Doyle, 1990)

   Is book making an activity that parents can scaffold for their
children at home? Quite by accident, I learned that Martin
Bloom, not in his role as social psychologist and conference
planner extraordinaire, but in his role as grandfather, invented a
way of doing storytelling with his grandson from the time the
child was 3. He sewed pages together to make a book, took
dictation, and then suggested that his grandson illustrate it. The
boy's father also took dictation. Here is an early storytelling
episode from when Paul was only 3. Bloom and his grandson Paul
were sitting on a dock fishing, and Paul dictated this story:

> Beady Bear got up and saw how still the lake was. He saw
> a fish and also his mom and dad in the water. They swam
> till they got tired...The next day they went whaling
> instead of fishing. And they caught whales. [Grandfa-
> ther question: How did they reel them in on little poles?
> Paul continued, picking up on the word "reels".] They

reeled in 150 whales. They had them for dinner. [The boy's father joined them and explained how many days it would take to eat one whale: 225,000 years.]

I am sure Paul enjoyed his father's and grandfather's participation, but the logic of amounts and weights were not really a part of his real world yet. His own imaginary world as it unfolded was more compelling, and he felt so safe and secure that he dared to follow his inner voice without hesitation. So Paul completed the story as he saw it: They ate all the whales they caught in Maine (M. Bloom, personal communication, January, 2000).

Paul, now 6, tells long sagas and it is clearly an activity he enjoys. It allows him to picture human relations in a fantasy way, express frustration, and be victorious despite those who try to thwart him. It also allows him to integrate themes from many parts of his life. He has books and videos in which a train is the main character. Trains are also important in his everyday world, he has ridden them and his parents commute to work on them. In one of his stories there was a train, upset because neither the Redline tunnel nor the Greenline tunnel would give it shelter from the rain. As it started to get wet, it decided to make a building over itself in 1 second or less, laughing as it did. (M. Bloom, personal communication, January, 2000) This is only one adventure in a much more complex tale of rebuff and revenge, a tale told with great narrative excitement and skill.

In Conclusion: The Creative Paradox and its Implications

The creative process, when you try to list its attributes, seems very paradoxical. But if we consider the creative process as an episode in time and follow its course in children and adults, the contradictions do not seem quite so contradictory: The creative process involves freedom and spontaneity; it requires intention, concentration, and commitment. It engages the primitive and the emotional, skill and thought. It calls on fantasy and inventiveness; it demands honesty and a pull to truth. It is an expression of self; it cannot take place without forgetting the self. It is a joy; it brings anxiety and frustration. It is its own reward; it needs support and encouragement from others. As the creative episode weaves its way through time, in and out of the several worlds the creator inhabits, each of these seeming contradictions finds a place.

The ways in which we can support and facilitate children's creativity may seem contradictory as well, but again, if we consider creativity in terms of episodes, the various kinds of supports helpful at different points in the creative episode become clearer. Children need introductions to symbol systems and their power to create meaning; typically this involves adult-structured activities such as reading books and looking at pictures together. But children also need opportunities to "listen to their inner voices," to allow their intentions to structure representational activities such as pretend play and drawing. Some activities, such as storytelling in young children, require a special kind of help from an adult—scaffolding the activity without taking away the child's sense that he or she, not the adult, is the creator. The autonomy of the child at work needs to be respected and trusted; supporting unusual uses of a medium, showing sensitivity to a child's engagement when a child needs to make a transition, and allowing children to solve problems on their own—all these are ways of showing respect and trust. On the other hand, sometimes frustration causes children to abandon their imaginary worlds; at those times, gentle hints and helps can put the creative episode back on course. Children often sense when they have completed what they set out to do, and then typically seek to share their work. Children grasp when what they have done is taken seriously. They feel additional satisfaction when an adult notices features that a child intended to put in the work and when the work is given an honored place in their social world.

Because the creative episode engages so many different, apparently contradictory aspects of a child or an adult, facilitation of the creative process is an amazing way to accomplish many goals at the same time. Since Freud we have understood that the creative process can give shape to emotional issues and concerns, and that it takes trust to give oneself the freedom to do so. Today, we understand that to represent in a medium is not just pure expression, but also a way to get perspective. Each medium provides the tools for incorporating particular kinds of perspectives; representation clarifies and teaches as well as expresses; the world as well as the self fascinates and puzzles children; and the whole process depends on the intentions of an active agent. So the pleasures of creation include not only catharsis, not only clarification, but also the pleasures of constructing all sorts of representations, of learning skills and making discoveries in form and content, the satisfactions of fulfilling one's own intentions, and gaining respect and understanding from others.

I'd like to close with the paradox of self in the creative process. While a person is engaged in the creative episode, no longer inhabiting the everyday world but in a world of one's own imagination, the personal, self-conscious, frightened, vulnerable, conflicted, confused self of everyday life is no longer part of experience. Yet that very trip into the imaginary world can help to transform the self, and when we facilitate creative episodes, we help to set in motion the processes that can lead to self-transformation and enlarged understanding.

My first example comes from pretend play. A 4-year-old girl, who had recently become an older sister, picked up a toy iron and put it on a toy ironing board. She looked around and spotted a baby doll. She put the doll on the ironing board and gleefully began ironing the doll. After about a minute, she began to say something. I moved closer to listen. She was saying, "Ouch. Ouch." Soon after, she moved to a rocking chair, and began to rock the baby. The medium of pretend play allowed her to be both the ironer and the ironed, to experience the situation from two different points of view, and so to enlarge her understanding.

My final example comes from a storytelling experience that embodies many of the features of the creative episode in children. T. was a new student; she had just moved into the area, so her first day of kindergarten meant entering midsession. As she and her mother came in, her eyes were full of tears. She was moaning softly, "I want to go home, I want to go home." Her mother asked her to wait there for just a few minutes while she went to the school office. Then, for today, they would go home. Tiffany looked very sad, but I noticed that she listened as another child dictated a story. I moved toward Tiffany slowly, stooped down, and asked her if she would like to tell a story. Tiffany barely nodded. When I asked, "How does the story start?" Tiffany looked away. I waited for what seemed an eternity; then she said, "Once upon a time...once upon a time there was a little mouse." Pause. "And the mouse loved her mommy very much." Tiffany paused again. "Is that the end?" I asked. Tiffany said no, but not anything else. I said, "Let me read you what you have so far. 'Once upon a time there was a little mouse. And the mouse loved her mommy very much.' What comes next?" Tiffany finished with a burst, "And the mommy loved the little mouse and hugged her and kissed her." Tiffany paused again. I again reread and asked, "Is that the end?" "Yes," she said. I invited Tiffany to draw pictures in her book and she sat down at the coloring table. She drew a mommy mouse and had just started a baby mouse when her mother came back. "Okay, Tiffany" she said, "We can go home now." "I can't," Tiffany answered, hardly looking up, "I'm too busy."

References

Applebee, A. N. (1978). *The child's concept of story*. Chicago: University of Chicago Press.

Czikszentmihalyi, M. (1990). *Flow: The psychology of optimal experience.* New York: Harper & Row.

Czikszentmihalyi, M. (1996). *Creativity: Flow and the psychology of discovery and invention.* New York: HarperCollins.

Doyle, C. (1973). Honesty and the creative process. *Journal of Aesthetic Education, 7*(3), 43–50.

Doyle, C. (1976). The creative process: A study in paradox. In C. Winsor (Ed.), *The creative process* (pp. 6–15). New York: Bank Street College.

Doyle, C. (1989, August). *Young children as authors: The creative process in first stories.* Paper presented at the meeting of the American Psychological Association, New Orleans, LA.

Doyle, C. (1990, August). *Motivations of young authors: Why Rachel told so many stories.* Paper presented at meeting of the American Psychological Association, Boston, MA.

Doyle, C. (1998). The writer tells: The creative process in the writing of literary fiction. *Creativity Research Journal, 11,* 29–36.

Doyle, C. (1998). *You can't catch me.* New York: HarperCollins.

Faulkner, W. (1959). Interviewed by J. Stein. In M. Cowley (Ed.), (1959), *Writers at work: The Paris Review interviews* (pp. 119–141). New York: Viking.

Feldman, D. H. (1980). *Beyond universals in cognitive development.* Norwood, NJ: Ablex.

Franklin, M. B. (1983). Play as the creation of imaginary situations: The role of language. In S. Wapner and B. Kaplan (Eds.), *Toward a holistic developmental psychology* (197–220). Hillsdale, NJ: Erlbaum.

Freud, S. (1925). The relation of the poet to daydreaming. In (J. Riviere, Trans.) *Collected papers.* (Vol. 4, pp. 173–183). London: Hogarth. (Original work published 1908)

Gardner, H. (1983). *Frames of mind: The theory of multiple intelligences.* New York: Basic Books.

Gardner, H. (1993). *Creating minds.* New York: Basic Books.

Guilford, J. P. (1959). Three faces of intellect. *American Psychologist, 14,* 469–479.

Nager, N., and Shapiro, E. K. (Eds.) (2000). *Revisiting a progressive pedagogy: The developmental interaction approach.* Albany, NY: State University of New York.

Penrose, R. (1981). *Picasso: His life and work* (3rd ed.). Berkeley: University of California Press.

Pitcher, E. G., and Prelinger, E. (1963). *Children tell stories: An analysis of fantasy.* New York: International University Press.

Porter, K. (1963). Interview by B. Thompson. In G. Plimpton (Ed.), *Writers at work: The Paris Review interview. Second series* (p. 139–163). New York: Viking.

Pound, E. (1963). Interview by D. Hall. In G. Plimpton, (Ed.), *Writers at work: The Paris Review interview. Second series* (pp. 35–59). New York: Viking.

Schutz, A. (1962). *Collected Papers: Vol. 1.* The Hague, Netherlands: M. Nijoff.

Steinbeck, J. (1989). *Working days: The journals of the* Grapes of Wrath. (R. DeMott, Ed.). New York: Viking.

Sutton-Smith, B. (1981). *The folkstories of children.* Philadelphia, PA: University of Pennsylvania Press.

Wallace, D., and Gruber, H. (Eds.). (1989). *Creative people at work.* New York: Oxford University Press.

Wallach, D., and Kogan, N. (1965). *Modes of thinking in young children: A study of the creativity-intelligence distinction.* New York: Holt, Rhinehart, and Winston.

Wells, C. G. (1986). *The meaning makers: Children learning language and using language to learn.* Portsmouth, NH: Heinemann.

Werner, H. (1948). *The comparative psychology of mental development.* New York: Science Editions.

Wilford, S. (1998). *What you need to know when your child is learning to read.* New York: Scholastic.

Winner, E. (1996). *Gifted children: Myths and realities.* NY: Basic Books.

Acknowledgments

I would like to thank the director of Sarah Lawrence's Early Childhood Center, Sara Wilford, for welcoming me to the Early Childhood Center and being a helpful colleague and friend throughout the project. I would also like to honor the gifted teachers I worked with at the Early Childhood Center: Jean Harris, May Kanfer, Marcia Levy, Sarah Matthews, Lorelle Phillips, Susan Schwimmer, and Sonna Schupak. I am grateful to Elizabeth Johnston for sharing her experiences with the artwork of her son, Ross, and for her generous help in creating figures and slides. Margery Franklin, my colleague and fellow explorer in many areas of mutual concern, has been a continual source of inspiration and support; her sharing of her experiences with her son David and his artwork was one of many, many ways she contributed to the work reported here.

Chapter 4

Promoting Creativity, Giftedness, and Talent in Young Children in Preschool and School Situations

Alice Sterling Honig

Teachers of preschoolers and young grade school children often remark on the marvelous "creativity" of young children's drawings, dramatic play, and invented language. Children show imaginative use of color, themes, and flights of fancy in their language. One preschooler remarked to her mother in passionate disappointment as her quarters in a coin machine produced only a tiny piece of candy, "They highered the money and they smallered the candy bar." When I showed a home insurance advertisement (with some men pulling a sofa out of a house window and looking around furtively) to a 4-year-old and asked him to tell me about this picture, he regarded it intensely and then burst out indignantly, " Teacher! Them be thiefers!" And indeed, the whole purpose of that ad was to make readers worry about thieves so that they would be galvanized to purchase household insurance.

Many children who have produced awesomely splendid drawings and clay work in early childhood seem to "lose" creative responses to problems and to lose creative dramatic expression and art ability as they move through the school system. A mystery. By their tests of creative or divergent thinking, Torrance and Gupta (1964) have revealed what they call the "fourth grade slump in creative behavior." "What are all the possible things Mother Hubbard could have done when she found no bones in the cupboard for her dog" proved easy for young children but "extremely difficult for many fourth graders" (p. 6).

Teacher Interest in Promoting Creativity

When I once asked a group of teachers in training whether they had ever considered the challenge that early child care should produce intellectually gifted and creative children, most were surprised. Primary goals of child care personnel are so often directed to keeping children safe and healthy. Early Childhood educators teach preschoolers cognitive tools, such as shape and color names, to prepare children for success at entry to elementary school. Further goals include encouraging more prosocial and less aggressive peer interaction in the classroom. Much of the focus of intervention programs of the last decades has been on preventing school failure and dropout among children who have not had rich life experiences, such as trips to the zoo or museums and daily story reading times. Because they spend much effort to remediate or to introduce basic literacy and numeration skills in early grades, teachers may have less opportunity to think specifically about the deep importance of nurturing children's gifted and creative behaviors.

Defining Creativity

Teachers and recreation counselors involved with young children vary in their definitions of creativity (Brown, 1989). Some call it "an innate style of boundless, individualistic, divergent thinking" (Palladino, 1997, p. xiii). I would suggest that the definition of creativity focus on the process of divergent thinking (Dowd, 1989, p. 233). Creativity is associated with breaking up of old ideas; making new connections; enlarging the limits of knowledge; the making of sudden, astonishing new connections; and, in Duckworth's (1996) felicitous phrase, "the having of wonderful ideas." Torrance (1970) defines creative thinking as adventurous, getting away from the obvious and commonplace, a successful step into the unknown and unexplored. He has explained:

I regard creativity as a special kind of problem solving...the product of [this] thinking has novelty and value...[and] requires high motivation and persistence and is unconventional in the sense that it requires modification or rejection of previously accepted ideas.

Learning through creative and problem-solving activities, in addition to recognition, memory, and logical reasoning, requires such abilities as evaluation (especially the ability to sense problems, inconsistencies, and missing elements), divergent production (e.g., fluency, flexibility, originality, and elaboration), and redefinition. (p. 2)

Some of the correlates of creativity may be troubling to teachers. "Hyperfocus" on a process or project of great personal interest may make the child difficult for a teacher to reach with more mundane information, such as the homework assignment for tomorrow. Other children may daydream a lot about their adventures as a great superhero in their private mental comic strip. The diverse thinker may "whirl with ideas and images" and seem almost hyperactive and restless in the classroom (Palladino, 1997, p. 22).

When creative children behave in self-absorbed ways, they may even ignore rules for courtesies in the classroom. The teacher or recreation counselor has to struggle to remain a source of calm strength and kind reassurance as well as firm insistence on keeping a safe space for all the children. The adult also has to focus on the strengths and unique qualities of each child, even when the child's creative responses result in experiments that exasperate, for example, squeezing all the paint tubes together to produce a muddy mound of paint, with the result being that the other children have no paint to use.

Techniques to Promote Creativity

What skills and techniques shall adults use in group care to enhance creativity in varied domains?

The Socio-Emotional Domain

Perhaps of greatest urgency is teacher creativity in helping children toward more mature solutions to the emotional tasks of early childhood. For each caring adult is a mirror wherein each child learns the worth of the self and the self's ideas. Adults need to be particularly creative in their generous use of *specific praise*, their positive descriptions of student work and efforts and ideas (Goetz, 1981; 1989) rather than criticism. Self-monitoring and *self-reflectivity* are powerful tools to keep adults focused on the uniqueness of each child and on the pedagogical challenge to nurture trust and creativity in each child. An internal locus of control has been associated more with creativity in kindergarten girls, although not for boys (Cohen & Oden, 1974).

Many teachers hold classroom group meetings to get children thinking about any tensions or tussles among themselves, so that the children can generate solutions of their own. These are ideas often promulgated by A. S. Neill in his unique school in England. Neill drew upon all the social problem solving creativity of the children to manage their own problems, such as setting a rule about the hour of the evening when another child in the dormitory could no longer play blasts of a trumpet because that would keep other youngsters awake.

Creativity and Empathy for Others: Are They Related?

Many teachers take an active role in promoting empathic understanding of others' feelings. Creative art or music often emerges from solo activities by children. However, creative *social* play responses become impossible when a child cannot grasp how another youngster feels.

> When he was threatening a younger child in an after-school program by cornering her under the stairwell with a bat raised on his shoulder, Corrie (a foster child who had been severely abused the first years of his life), told the recreational counselor who rushed over at hearing the little girl's cries, "But I was only holding my

bat on my shoulder. I wasn't hurting her." Corrie is not able to understand the younger child's point of view. He wants to play with her but cannot grasp how his actions seem threatening rather than playful.[1]

Bibliotherapy: A Tool for Teachers

Creative use of bibliotherapy energizes children to think up ways to cope with their own personal troubles as they listen to how the child in the story is coping. Read books that stimulate children's ability to enter into the adventures of others, to re-create scenes and scenarios. Such books often help heal a worry or hurt or resentment in a child faced with difficult family situations, such as divorce quarrels or the death of a pet or simpler sorrows, such as parental inattention, as in the wonderfully illustrated book reflecting a young boy's complaint, "My mother never listens to me" (Sharmat, 1984). Jerome is a child who creates fantastic scenarios to get his mom's attention. He tells her about a mom who wouldn't take her nose out of a book and so the king took her nose and put it in a freezer! He warns his mom there is a huge giant creeping up in back of her. He dangles the possibility that he will invite all the neighborhood kids in for lunch so that he can teach them a new dirty word he has learned. Kids who have ever felt impatient with their parent's long telephone conversation or attention to a visiting relative will revel in the creative ways that the boy devises to try to engage his mom. In the end, his simple but magic request for a kiss does bring his mom into full and affectionate attentiveness.

The rhythmic musicality and piled-up repetitive absurdities in some stories allow children to identify with hard work to succeed and with feeling that their efforts are important. Petya, the tiny beetle, last in a series of family helpers trying hard together to pull an enormous turnip out of the ground, reflects to himself with satisfaction that evening as everyone enjoys the cooked vegetable, "How strong I am!" (Parkinson, 1986). Stories can confirm the importance of their energies and talents for even the littlest children.

Adults Need to Learn the Secrets of Promoting Divergent Thinking

Divergent thinking is essential for intellectual and social creativity. However, teacher guidance is a "necessity" for promoting children's learning and creativity (Torrance, 1970, p. 10). Trusted caregivers are particularly important for sustaining children's motivation and passion for in-depth learning. One teacher technique is to encourage kids to keep on *generating new hypotheses* and to avoid premature closure on evaluations.

Teachers advance complex thinking when they support children's awareness of and ability to become *comfortable with ambiguities*. This is a more difficult task with early preoperational children since they tend to think in rigid categories (such as all-good or all-bad). Preschoolers need training and explicit help in seeing that it is possible to hold two contradictory ideas or feelings at the same time. Real-life examples can assist in this work.

> Joey, an older toddler, was so glad to be invited and to go and eat birthday cake at Amy's birthday party. He also felt quite grumpy and sad that he did not have the wonderful Thomas the Tank Engine toy that Amy received as a birthday present at that party.[1]

Five-year-olds may still find it difficult to hold two categories in mind even when they are not opposed.

> Dana's daddy was driving me to the airport. I told her in the car how happy I was that her daddy could chauffeur me by driving his car so that I could get to the airport in time to catch my plane. "Can a man be a daddy and a chauffeur too at the same time?" I then asked her. "Of course not. That's silly," she answered quite assuredly. [1]

Give children digestible experiences in playing with ideas that may be ambiguous or uncertain. If you help children in practical, easy ways to hold contradictory or opposite ideas and feelings at the same time, this will also help them self-discipline more creatively. Shure's (1995) Interpersonal Cognitive Problem

Solving or I Can Problem Solve program, commonly known as ICPS, gives teachers language tools to encourage this kind of divergent thinking. The following is a brief list of some ICPS ideas for positive discipline that empower a child to think creatively about his or her behaviors.

One feeling or idea IS/IS NOT the same as another person's (your best friend wants to go bike riding; you want to play checkers). Some feelings and wishes are the *same* as those of others; some are *different*. A friend may want to play the same game as you *some* of the time, but not *all* of the time. You can do some actions *now* or *later*. Some actions occur *before* and others *after* (Johnny hit his brother *after* his brother knocked down his block tower). One idea could be a good idea or *not* a good idea (Is hitting another child a good idea for getting back your toy?). What *might* happen next? IF one child hits his playmate, then the other *might* hit back. Help children think of the *consequences* of actions and of *alternatives*—other ideas they could carry out to resolve social tussles. (Honig, 1996, p. 9)

Shure's ICPS system counts on stimulating children's own creativity (rather than the use of adult power assertions) to find solutions to their squabbles and disagreements. If-Then thinking sharpens reasoning skills and sparks a child's own creative solutions to conflicts. If I do *X*, then what will happen next? Will the block tower topple? Will Johnny kick me back?

Encouraging Child Cooperation Creates a Climate for Creativity

The prevalence of inclusive classrooms with a wider range of child typicality and atypicality has impelled teachers in recent years to come up with creative solutions to facilitate children from very different intellectual or education levels working together. Some schools use Aronson's (1978) *Jigsaw Method*. Students are assigned to six-member teams. Each student is given 1/6 of the material to be learned for a presentation. One group, for example, may work on Columbus' voyage, another on the settling of the West. Each of the children in each jigsaw group becomes an expert on a small portion of the material studied, yet each member of the group is tested on the topic material which they have all shared and discussed with each other. In a way, this peer teaching of each other, with each child being an "expert" on a small piece of the assignment, empowers all the children to become more innovative contributors to the collective presentation. When I tried this technique with college students studying language development theorists, one group arranged their presentation as a mock radio show, pretending to quiz famous professors, such as Dr. Chomsky (role played by a student). Another student came with a chimpanzee mask on and was quizzed on the "show" as to what he had learned from his interactions with another famous linguist! The group working together produced more ingenious "reports" than previous term papers assigned to individuals.

Happily, teacher efforts to create a prosocial classroom often spark creativity among the children (Sapon-Shevin, 1986). *Cooperative telling of tales* involves one child starting a story; then each player in turn adds a little portion to continue the story. Children may be asked to use their bodies to create various shapes, such as letters or geometric forms.

Creative thinking is implicit in many of the cooperative games suggested by Orlick (1978). In his game of Big Snake, the children stretch out on their stomachs and hold the ankles of the person in front of them to make a two-person snake. This dyad slithers over on its belly to connect up to make a four-person snake and so on. The children have to figure out how the snake could slither up a mountain or figure out a way to flip over the whole snake on its back without losing its parts.

Sharpen Children's Verbal Tools to Promote Creative Thinking

Aphorisms, metaphors, and similes are rich verbal tools to promote divergent thinking.

> A 4-year-old heard his mom talking on the phone to his daddy, who then turned with a disappointed face and said, "Jamal, honey, we need to eat supper alone tonight.

Daddy is all tied up at the office." Jamal promptly burst into tears.[1]

Some children need a lot of help to understand the symbolic nature of metaphors.

Grade school teachers can stimulate such thinking by asking children to gather metaphors and similes from family members and bring them to class. The whole class may become energized by their discussion of the meanings of sayings such as:

- You are always splitting hairs

- He is as slow as a pig in a poke

- One swallow doesn't make a summer

- Penny wise, pound foolish

- The apple does not fall far from the tree

- You can lead a horse to water but you can't make him drink

- Don't look a gift horse in the mouth

- You are the apple of my eye

- She could sell me the Brooklyn Bridge

- The rosy-fingered dawn

- Don't make a mountain out of a molehill

- There's something fishy about his story

- Where there's smoke, there's fire

- That baby's nose is as cute as a button

Talk about metaphors, similes, and aphorisms. Encourage children to create their own similes. Some 4-year-olds can tell you that the clouds look like fluffy cotton, for example.

One way to introduce the difference between literal versus symbolic talk in class is to provide Amelia Bedelia books for children to read (Parish, 1963). Cheerful Amelia Bedelia is a wonderful cook. Hired as a housekeeper, she interprets literally whatever she is asked to do by her employers. Thus, she cuts out cute clothes to "dress the chicken"; she "draws the drapes" with a crayon on a piece of paper; she dusts the furniture carefully with dusting powder! As children giggle over each of Amelia Bedelia's misinterpretations, they become more aware of language as a tool to express oneself imaginatively as well as literally. The more metacognitive skills children can acquire, the better able they will be to gain creative insights and interpret symbolic subtleties in stories and novels.

Socratic or open-ended questions are a splendid way to get children's thinking juices flowing. Divergent questions function as instigators, activators, and organizers of mental operations (Sigel & Saunders, 1979). Socratic questions help a child distance psychologically from the here and now. They offer the chance to retrieve items from memory, contrast and compare ideas, transform or rearrange elements or things into a new sequence at the will and choice of the child. Comparisons, choices, the entertaining of new ideas, and the formulation of personal responses to them are all part of the ferment of creative thought we so fervently want to engender in children. Although divergent thinking skills are so essential to creativity, research reveals that teachers overwhelmingly (85%) use convergent rather than divergent questions with preschoolers (Honig & Wittmer, 1982).

If given the opportunity to keep a journal of their own and to sketch, doodle, and write responses to quixotic and challenging Socratic questions, grade school children can become more assured in drawing on their own rich and wonderful ideas. Myers and Torrance (1965; 1966) created books chock-full of open-ended questions for which children are encouraged to think up answers. Here is a sampling of open-ended questions to inspire children's creativity:

- What could happen if it *always* rained on Saturday?

- What if cars never wore out?

- If you saw a moose in your backyard chewing your mother's favorite flowers, what would you do?

- Why don't we wake up with our hair neat and combed?

- What would happen if a cow and a bee and clover got together?

- Can you think of some other interesting get-togethers?"

- What could happen if cats could bark when they wanted to?

- What could happen if all the shoes in the world were the same size?

When some questions are too difficult for children, that may be because they have had little experience in the real world with the creatures named (some city children have never seen a cow or clover). Be sure to tailor your imagination-provoking questions to the current experiential knowledge of some of the children.

When possible, take the children on a field trip or show them a video or have a farmer come to class and talk about the creatures that some children only know about verbally from singing verses of "Old McDonald Had a Farm."

Humor Promotes Divergent Thinking

Humor is a great tool for teachers. Humor has orderly developmental stages (Honig, 1988). Even toddlers carry out jokes physically. A young toddler stuck her bare foot in her papa's cylindrical tennis ball container and announced "Shoe!" in great glee. An older toddler pretended to make a milk mustache out of a piece of white paper.

Verbal joke making sometimes starts between 2 and 3 years of age. Toddler: "Daddy, 'oggies go meow meow." "No honey. Doggies go 'woof woof'." After a few more valiant attempts to woo her father with her first created joke, this toddler succeeded. She rolled on the floor with laughter when he finally replied: "Oh of course, honey. And kitty cats say 'woof woof'!"

Try simple "knock knock" jokes with young preschoolers. Vary your tones: "Order in the court!" "Sure your honor. Ham and cheese on rye!" is a favorite of grade school children.

After I had gone through a series of easy jokes while visiting with an Australian 9-year-old, he asked, "Want me to tell you one?" I agreed with enthusiasm and he asked me: "What do you get when you pour hot water down a rabbit hole?" When I gave up, he replied triumphantly, "Hot cross bunnies!" Linguistic tongue twisters and humorous jokes using double meanings of words lighten the school atmosphere and may earn you back some jokes the children can share with you.

Puns, awful and easy to groan at, enliven lesson plans with elementary school children. Math problems and history lessons seem easier when children catch on to puns, grin, and view their "lessons" as less grim emotionally. For example, in "Sir Cumference and the First Round Table" (Neuschwander, 1997) characters such as Lady Di of Ameter and their son, named, of course, Radius, can make learning geometry a more creative learning experience, especially for children who are scared of math terminology and operations.

Writing a silly story is another exercise that can free up a child who is reluctant to write more than a sentence or two. If the "assignment" is left open for the child to choose, then she or he may be more assured that whatever is imagined will be a fine story to write. Before some children, often criticized for spelling errors or messy papers, are willing to undertake such an assignment, they need to develop trust that you truly will accept their silly names, ideas, and crazy plots. Encourage the children to draw pictures to illustrate their stories.

Enlist Curricular Components to Engage Children's Creativity

Making Music. Singing and making music with instruments, creating lyrics, and changing well-known lyrics have always been a preschool domain in which young children experience much pleasure. Grade-school age children, much to the dismay of adults, have even excelled at creating scatological rhyming verses of songs that children have shared for generations. An oldie every summer camper has learned begins: "I took my girl to a baseball game..." and continues on: "Country boy, country boy sitting on the grass; Along came a bumble bee and stung him in the...Ask me no questions, I'll tell you no lies..." and so on. Children giggled as they sang these "creative" lyrics well out of earshot of their teachers or parents.

Making music does not have to involve either unprintable lyrics of years ago or of today's CDs. Many folk songs and rhymes spark offbeat images and notions: "Oh Suzannah, oh don't you cry for me; for I'm going to Alabama with my banjo on my knee. The day I left it rained so hard; the weather it was dry; the sun so hot I froze to death, Suzannah don't you cry!"

Enjoy belting out such musical absurdities with children. Get them to talk about what is silly in the song. Encourage them to make up further absurd rhyming couplets for simple songs, such as "Mr. Froggy went a courting and he did ride, a sword and pistol at his side." This interminable song allows a child to add her own couplets about the guest list at Mr. Froggy's wedding with Miss Mouse. "Next came in was Mr. Moth and he did bring the table cloth" could be one contribution. Creating silly songs and adding rhymes to familiar songs stimulate children's play with language rhythm and rhyming sounds. This creativity is in contrast to passive listening to favorite CD albums or to slavish imitation of rock stars in lieu of creating music on one's own.

Folk music collections provide a rich source for rollicking songs with poignant and mischievous imagery that grade school children will enjoy. An old New York State canal boat song about rising waters (a patent absurdity on the canal!) offers the captain's impudent solution to the barge's "precarious" position: "The cook she was a grand old gal and she wore a bright red dress; We hoisted her upon the mast as a signal of distress, as a signal of distress!"

Toddlers particularly relish chants and songs that have accompanying body and hand motions. "The Wheels on the Bus Go Round and Round? is a favorite in preschool. Kids grin as they sing out the verse where "The babies on the bus go 'wah wah wah' all through the town."

Artwork.   Easel and finger painting while listening to classical music, drawing, clay work, making potato prints, slithering cornstarch goop between fingers—these are just a few of the art activities that are already staples in many early childhood classrooms. In addition, children love to make mudpies, sift sand through sifters, and experiment with pouring water out of fruit juice cans with pinholes at different levels. Plastic art activities and water play are emotionally satisfying as well as suggestive of creative uses as children become absorbed in play with these materials.

However, just because an adult sets up art projects in a classroom does not mean that these projects intrinsically will be furthering child creativity. A teacher had set up easels and given a large brush to each young preschooler. "Remember, you need to draw a blue circle," she reminded each child as she went around adjusting smocks and providing each child with a jar of blue poster paint. Lorene dabbed blue on her paper. In dreamy pleasure she watched the patch of blue on her paper. Then she redipped her brush and watched wide-eyed as the blue of her initial swath deepened in color and great drips of blue paint slowly crept down the easel paper. She was creating a deeper tint of blue. Absorbed in her small creation, she was startled when the teacher coming near remarked, "Remember you are supposed to draw a blue circle, honey." Seeing with the child's eyes, we can appreciate the discovery of how layering more and more color changes the intensity of the color and the amount of drip. Teacher sensitivity to the power that a child's discoveries can make (whether in art or science, or dramatic play, for example) best unlocks the passionate commitment and delight that are a bedrock requirement for creativity.

Sometimes a teacher needs to think about how a picture feels to a child as well as how it looks. A preschooler had drawn a vehicle on a street. Then he smeared brown paint all over the picture he had drawn. When I asked about this, he stared at his picture and said, "That was the ambulance that took my daddy to the hospital." His creative response to express his mood and feelings resulted in a picture scribbled over with sorrowful brown color, rather than presenting the literal drawing of an ambulance. The sensitive teacher surely does not exclaim "But look, now you have ruined your nice picture."

Dance, Drama, Puppetry, and Movement. Some little
folks need to be in intense active movement a lot of the time.
For them, it might be wise to encourage dance and movement
as often as possible (Benzie, 1987; Chenfeld, 1995). Ask parents to help by sewing up edges on huge squares of gauze and
rectangles of nylon in wonderful colors. Then put on slow
dance music, such as the Skater's Waltz, and let the children
dreamily create patterns of whirling color in space while they
make up movements to the music.

Children learn to represent by using their bodies in space.
Toddlers love to try to hop like a bunny; preschoolers might like
to try to move like a turtle, a dragonfly, or an elephant; grade
school children are sophisticated enough to form a group to act
out the parts of an old rumbling washing machine about to fall
apart. Ask the children whether they can use their body motions
to represent emotions, such as joy or scared feelings, or mad
feelings or surprise:

> A young toddler was finishing his bath. Fascinated by
> the swirling water, as his father let the water out of the
> tub, he started curling and twisting his chubby little
> body to reproduce the graceful motions of the water
> gurgling down the drain. His dad let him "dance" the
> water pattern before lifting him out for a towel rub and
> pajama dressing.[1]

Bodily grace is one of the ways in which some children show
their special talents. Ask children, "Show how you would be a
raindrop or a kite by dancing like one; by singing about what
would happen to you if your were one; by drawing what you
think would happen to you if you were one? (Myers & Torrance,
1965, p. 7).

While working with disadvantaged children ages 6 through
14, Torrance (1970) overcame their fear of creative dramatics and
role playing by use of "Magic Net," a piece of nylon net 36" x 72"
in various colors. In his Creative-Aesthetic Approach, Torrance
gave several children each a piece of the net and asked them to
choose some role—a person, animal, or other being that they

wanted to become. Then, he asked them to wear the net and in turn to stand, walk, and dance like the designated creature he or she had chosen. The use of Magic Net impelled children toward more fluency and originality in creating dramatic scenarios.

> Next, the entire group would begin making up a story, using the roles chosen by the children with the "Magic Nets." The role players then enacted in pantomime the story as it was told by the audience...The problem of the actors was to interpret through movement or pantomime the actions related by the storytellers." (pp. 3-4)

One child wanted to play a bear but was too timid to play the role she had chosen. When Torrance engaged some peers to be other bears with her, she was able to be successful and even act as a scary bear. For teachers who may not have prior experience in using creative drama strategies in the classroom, activities for 3- to 13-year-olds are available with step-by-step procedural guides (Kelner, 1993).

Ewart (1998), a Scottish primary school teacher, has introduced techniques for teachers to work with children in making imaginative and magical puppets and screens, writing plays, and using shadow puppetry. Pleydell & Brown (1999) describe an experiential program to explore ideas and situations through story dramatizations that includes the use of props and strategies for adapting to special needs.

Create Classroom Time for Imagination Games

"Just Imagine" games permit children to take off on flights of fancy that require them to retrieve from memory, compare and contrast, and make connections between disparate bits of information (Honig, 1982; Lane, et al. 1982). Myers & Torrance (1965) showed children from low-income households an interesting picture of a pond and asked the children to imagine that they could enter into the life of the pond and become anything they wanted to be. The children later drew murals of their imaginative pond life scenarios and discussed their paintings and the problems of painting animals in a pond with water that may cover up the animal you choose to represent.

At rest time, after a quiet period, you might let the children conjure different imaginary scenarios (DeMille, 1976), such as being a fly busily walking across the ceiling. What are they looking for? How do the children on their cots look to the fly from an upside down vantage point on the ceiling? Try reading *I Want to Paint My Bathroom Blue* (Kraus, 1956) about a boy who has a vivid imagination. On the outside walls of his house he conjures a huge picture of his mother blushing because her children are each cheerfully poking both feet deep down into a freshly baked cake.

Ask children to pretend. "You can become any animal you want to. Which animal would YOU choose. Tell me what you would do all day long as that animal. What kinds of games would you play with friends if you were that animal?"

Pretend voyages are something all the children enjoy in the series of books about the teacher, Mrs. Frizzle, and her classroom in *The Magic School Bus* stories. Mrs. Frizzle takes her class on wonderful trips of imagination, deep under the seas or up into space or to strange lands (Cole, 1986). These imaginary voyages stretch children's ability to wonder, to imagine, to create new scenarios and experiences through the awesome "trips" in the Magic School Bus.

Some creativity games, such as the "One Goes Back" game, help a child learn more clearly who she or he is, and what are her or his personal preferences and reactions. Suppose you were given these three objects: "Which one of the three would you give up, if you had to give one back? Why? What could you do with the other two things? Could you use them together?" (Myers & Torrance, 1965 p. 23)

The "Uses" game (Torrance & Gupta, 1964) draws on children's ability to conjure up lots of usual and unconventional uses for objects, such as a tin can, paper clip, cardboard tube from a paper towel, paper bag, bell, or any other ordinary item. When I gave some men's old ties to 6-year-olds, they pretended to use them for seat belts while taking an airplane trip; they used them as lion tamer whips as if they were circus masters; they pretended the ties were slithery snakes crawling on the floor. Give children the chance to play out their imaginative scripts with inexpensive props and then enjoy your peek into the window of their creative conjuring.

A Strong Knowledge-Base Undergirds Creativity

Knowledge and experience form a rich loam from which creative ideas can flower in the group. Without a strong knowledge-base, even a gifted child may not be able to experiment creatively with science ideas and materials. Part of a teacher's work in promoting creativity has to be to enlarge and enrich children's knowledge of the world. A narrow knowledge-base ill prepares a child to participate in all the creative adventures a teacher is prepared to offer in the classroom.

Some 4-year-olds can recite the multisyllabic names of a plethora of dinosaurs. There are 6-year-olds who have traveled abroad with their families and seen other peoples' homes, clothes, and lifestyles. They have heard the music of other lands and peoples. Visiting a museum, seeing dinosaur skeletons, and watching a sea anemone unfold near a sea-salt suffused New England shore all provide grist for creating imaginative scenarios. Children with poor reading skills who have not read about King Arthur or the imaginary realms of *The Hobbit* (Tolkien, 1996) may only be able to fall back on the two-dimensional violent villains of TV, such as Ninja turtles(Honig, 1998). Then, perhaps in the classroom, with real kicks and pretend guns made of fingers or wooden blocks, children who have been exposed to such programs may imitate what they have seen superheroes act out violently on the screen.

Creative Scenarios May Serve Children's Deeper Psychological Needs

Why do some children play out the same scenario—being a mommy of many little babies or a cape-flying Superman? The same scenario may serve deep psychological needs for self-protection against too many perceived threats to a child's emotional integrity. Paley (1990) vividly describes such a preschooler who needed with great determination to be, to crash, and to repair a helicopter day after day, month after month. Other children are open to such multiple sights, sounds, and ideas that they are not able to listen to the teacher; they cause uproars and commotion. Sometimes their astonishing mental connections, their need to be doing or dreaming rather than studying, and their unconventional responses throw off a teacher who is trying to get through a class syllabus. These children need a calm, steady teacher who recognizes and redirects distracting behaviors and yet values the intense interests and insights these children sometimes produce. If some creative children do have Attention Deficit and Hyperactivity Disorder, commonly known as ADHD, the teacher must work with parents as they explore with their pediatrician and with a trained professional in making a decision whether to use medication to permit the child to focus on lessons and settle into seat work, so that he or she achieves success in schoolwork as well as in creative self-initiated pursuits. This is a parental decision and teachers will want to be kept informed of any medications. Not only do teachers want to spark creativity in kids; they also need to protect a classroom from the chaos that such "Edison Trait" kids, as Palladino (1997) calls them, can create. There is an old characterization of some folks as hunters and others as farmers. Some children need the slow careful attention of the farmer to do classroom work. Instead, that child, full of impulsive energy, is a hunter in a farmer's world. Sometimes judicious use of medication allows that child to focus on learning and to show real creativity in classroom accomplishments.

Imaginary Parties Create a Happy Indoor Climate During Severe Winters

Plan together with children to create indoor imaginative scenarios to lift the mood of the children during dark winter days. Get children brainstorming together to create a plan to actualize the special scenario. During dark days of winter when sleet and ice make it difficult to take the children out even for a half-hour walk, try creating a summer picnic in the child care setting. Use a tan large muslin sheet on the floor. Spread seashells and maybe a few handfuls of sand in shallow plastic tubs of water. The children can prepare a variety of sandwiches (although bologna and peanut butter and jelly may not be a teacher's idea of creative cooking!) and slices of fresh peeled cucumber and apple. Ask parents to send some summer wear so the preschoolers can change into swimsuits and carry towels. Have a small plastic swimming pool on a linoleum floor or on a large plastic drop cloth. After the children splash awhile, they can dry themselves with their beach towels. Other activities could be making sand pies and sorting seashells on the edge of a "sand" sheet. If you ask around, parents may be willing to donate seashells collected on trips for this special imaginary beach scene. Then the children can learn the names of seashells they discover that you have strewn about on the sand sheet. They can put seashells into groups, such as clams, snails, etc. Three-year-olds and 4-year-olds are fascinated by making decorations with seashells as well as by sorting them and will constantly ask you their names. Thus, children create a seashore and picnic experience of their very own in their own way in their own classroom, regardless of what the weather outside "dictates." Creative dramatic programming "out of season" can also serve to help children realize how some rules are very important to obey all the time, such as "not running into the street after a ball."

Promote Poetry to Prominence in the Classroom

Read poetry! Brain researchers emphasize how important it is to wire in neural pathways with variety and richness of language interactions. "Use it or lose it" seems to be the rallying cry for brain development during the first years of life and "Cells that fire together wire together" (Healy, 1994; Nash, 1997). Andrews (1988) notes that exposing children to poetry encourages them to problem solve and to ask what is coming next. Even toddlers experiment with rhymes in their cribs. "Oogy, woogy, poogy" murmured a tiny one in sing-song experimentation with sounds while she hung on to her mother's hand as they walked along.

When the world of poetry is opened for grade school children, they often produce wonderful personal writing. Younger children will ask over and over for special poems to be read aloud (Gable, 1999). Introduce poems that tickle a child's fancy and dreams (Hale, n.d.; McCord, 1961; Merriam, 1988). With older children try the outrageously funny poems in "The Sheriff of

Rottenshot" (Prelutsky, 1994).

Challenge children to talk about why a poem is funny or silly or sad or puzzling. Try this humorous and rollicking poem from Eve Merriam's (1985) book *Blackberry Ink*:

Bella had a new umbrella
Didn't want to lose it,
So when she walked out in the rain
She didn't ever use it.
Her nose went sniff,
Her shoes went squish,
Her socks grew soggy,
Her glasses got foggy,
Her pockets filled with water
And a little green froggy.
All she could speak was a weak **Kachoo**!
But Bella's umbrella
Stayed nice and new.

Encourage children to figure out why riddles are funny. Even older toddlers (who understand the form but not the double meanings for some "Knock-knock jokes") like to create their own riddles. A 2 1/2-year-old to whom I was reading some silly poems asked me this riddle, "Do you know why cats can't ride bicycles?" I thought about this for a while and then asked her for the answer. "Because they have no tush!" she replied, grinning triumphantly. (Tush is Yiddish for buttocks.)

Celebrate Creative Writing

Treat initial creative writing attempts as wonderful chances to experiment with ideas and sequences. Do not denigrate "sloppy" writing and do allow pencil and eraser use freely in order to let a child's thinking juices flow without fear of teacher disapproval of a messy paper.

I asked a very serious 10-year-old child, whose parent was overly controlling about requiring "perfect" writing in school papers, to read aloud some riddles and write down why each one was funny. One riddle was: "How do you stop a dog from barking in the back seat of a car?"

Answer: "Have him sit in the front with you." (Cerf, 1964, p. 3)

The child wrote: "Because the dog will bark in the front seat too." What a beautiful smile he gave me as he creatively responded to this riddle. The child's teacher calls all "messy" homework papers "slumpy-dumpy" papers and the parent has learned to apply this term to the child's work. Now, worried, the parent wonders why this child no longer is willing to try to write a long book report. He told me he is so afraid to "mess up." "I press so hard on the paper because I feel tense," he confided. He is afraid to make a "mistake" in spelling or in his writing.[1]

Sometimes we squash creative writing in schoolchildren simply by being unaware of how difficult writing utensil hand control and neat writing can be for some children. A simpler solution might be to allow a grade school child to use the computer for all long compositions, in order to free up a child who can use the delete or cut and paste computer buttons with assurance that his or her finished book report will look just fine.

Children need opportunities to be inventive in writing stories and poems. They need to have opportunities to brainstorm for rhymes and accurate words that reflect their vision. They need to try their hand at rewriting endings for stories they have already read. Some children might enjoy creatively thinking up new titles for familiar and favorite tales. Forecasting plots, synthesizing diverse elements in a story—these are skills that the teacher may have to assess accurately and offer quite specific help to further the child's ability to move along the road to autonomous creativity in writing.

Allow very young children just learning orthography to experiment freely with invented spelling. Allowing very young children to invent their spelling frees them to try early writing long before they have correct lexicon spelling ability. "HRS LV HR" (horses live here) was the fine title a 5-year-old wrote with elan over his picture of pinto horses among the sagebrush and cacti in a wild west setting.

Try Classroom Arrangements That Enhance Child Creativity

Arrange classroom opportunities for creative adventuring. Provide enough blocks and space for a safe block corner and enough cars and tracks for creating highways and bridges and traffic jams. Have easels already out and smocks with plastic flexible neckbands easy for youngsters to put on themselves. Save orange juice cans for poster colors so that when the cans get messy they are easy to replace. The Constructivist classroom allows children more choices of activities. Fewer time constraints for how long children can spend at an activity open a path for creative juices to flow unfettered by a classroom clock.

Although story reading times and circle "Show and Tell" times are wonderful ways to increase social cohesiveness and shared experience in the classroom, be aware of the implications of requiring all children to participate together for other planned activities. Children may be discovering creatively on their own something not part of your specific lesson plan. If outdoors all the children are playing a circle game such as "Put your right foot in and turn yourself about" and Jolene wants to create a sandcastle and dig vigorously and peacefully, a flexible teacher is not threatened by this personal child choice. Nor does a "different" behavior choice of itself signify that there is a social problem. For example, some very friendly children have deep needs to create with blocks and have the block buildings "saved" for tomorrow rather than torn down so the blocks can be neatly stacked away for today. Perceptive adults handle such individual creative needs in ways to nurture a child's vigorous growth toward sustained creative enterprises rather than squash budding initiatives.

Reflect on how to strike a balance between teacher guidance and children's decisionmaking so that needs for learning and creativity are constructively met (Koestner et al. 1984). "Guide [the child] by providing a responsive environment. It is my belief that this approach will lead to the controlled kind of freedom which seems to be necessary for productive, creative behavior" (Torrance, 1970, p. 15).

Dramatic Play Spaces. An indispensable classroom ingredient for preschool play is the housekeeping corner. Teachers and children respect and treasure the dramatic play corner. In rich variety, dress-up clothes are heaped in baskets. Teachers may be challenged by how much to guide or not intervene in dramatic play scenarios. One 4 1/2-year-old girl stomped over to her teacher after another playmate had wandered into the house-keeping corner, sat down, and demanded, " Bring me a beer, woman!" When we explained to her that he must have heard that kind of talk from a man to someone in his life, and that some men do make demands like that to women, the plucky girl retorted, "Then I ain't ever getting married!"

Can rigid, stylized, dramatic play be considered creative in any way? Chasing peers, some preschoolers play "monster" with guttural cries as other children screech and run away in pretend or real fear. The repetitive "monster" play requires no surprise scripts or fanciful variations on a theme. Yet the teacher who wants to promote creativity needs to help connect the stereotyped behavior of a given young child with the larger world of imaginative dramatic play in the preschool. Vivien Paley (1990), in her richly perceptive musings on how to grow into being a wiser and more effective supporter of all children's talents, describes the role of the teacher. Teachers need to be constant observers and learn about each child's unique style, fears, strengths, and use of fantasy. In her book *The Boy Who Would be a Helicopter* (1990), Paley describes how she tape records children's fantasy play stories and then dialogues with co-teachers to better understand how to support the emotional flowering of each child. She describes her daily technique of taking down dictated child stories. Every day, in a special tape-marked play place on the rug, she reads each child's story and has that child invite classmates to act out that personal scenario. No child can add to the scenario without the express permission of the child whose story is being acted out. Through this daily magic "ritual," Paley creates a climate of safety and acceptance among the children. In a dialectic sense, this teacher creation frees the children from the fear of aloneness and of being misunderstood. They do not have to create rigid spaces in which to play out single repetitive themes. The children extend bridges of communication and inclusion for each other in their dramatic themes. The teacher's invitation to create a story, acceptance of each story, and each dramatic role play allows the children to extend their social caring as well as their ability to construe bridging roles between play themes. Thus, Paley's work teaches us that by perceptive noticing of children's repetitive themes and how they serve to buffer a young child against anxiety (whether over a new baby sister or over the fact of being in a strange new classroom with lots of unknown persons) and by questioning the children to better understand their dramatic themes and wishes, the teacher can elicit more creative and socially participatory responses from an isolated or a shy child.

Power Relations in the Classroom Affect Creativity

How power relations among teachers and students are organized and how space and time and materials are made available for children to choose in classrooms seems to make a difference in child creativity. Developmentally Appropriate classrooms, commonly known as DAP, as described in detail in materials prepared by the National Association for the Education of Young Children (Bredekamp & Copple, 1997) are more likely to promote children's genuine eagerness to explore materials and relationships without fear of disapproval from teachers or peers.

Teacher-dominated classrooms are less likely to lead to children's increased creative expression (Borgman, 2000). Schemp, Jeffers, and Zaichowsky (1983) tested 208 children from first through fifth grade who were in physical education classes that either had teacher-dominated decisionmaking or an atmosphere where teachers encouraged students to share in decisionmaking. The shared decisionmaking group scored significantly higher on creativity, motor skills, and self-concept and they scored higher on positive attitudes.

Other Experiential Domains Where Teachers Can Encourage Creativity

To the list of art or story domains where some children will shine in creativity, we need to add other domains, such as cooking, nurturing younger children, solving social spats among peers, making a shy or a disabled child feel included and welcome in the group, turning cartwheels. A wider lens helps teachers notice and validate creative functioning in domains other than those traditional in early childhood settings.

Encourage Collections. Some children are like wonderful squirrels as they hoard smooth stones that have taken their fancy. Children trot home from an outing with a bird feather they found on the ground, a few rocks, a golden or scarlet autumn leaf or a berry, and even a frog surreptitiously captured as a treasure to hide under a sibling's covers that night! One 4-year-old had a positive genius for discerning tossed away beer bottle caps. He collected pocketfuls! A child's collecting interests need to be nurtured and admired. Of course, children need to be taught that they may not harm a creature to "collect" it. But children who find dead beetles or flies can be encouraged to collect and to read about these creatures or objects.

Support children's interest in collecting—rocks, leaves, found bird feathers, seashells, stamps. Encourage youngsters to delight in something that intrigues them but may repel you. A 3-year-old found an earthworm in the play yard at our Center. In awe of its mucus-wreathed body glistening on her plastic shovel, she lifted it triumphantly for the teacher to see. "Yuck!" called out the young teacher. "Put that thing down. It is time to come in and wash up for lunch," she added cheerfully. If Elena wants to learn everything about earthworms or Andrew wants to learn more about itchy skin, or Doretta wants to know all about plumbing and sewer pipes or if Tommy wants to learn how come noses drip in cold weather, then teachers should be ready to help them unearth resources and pictures and materials to satisfy this wonderful creative thirst to know.

Decrease "Consumer Gimmees" Through Emphasis on Creativity

Creative programming has auxiliary benefits for children. When teachers value ideas and talents, artistic efforts and dramatic play efforts, they may decrease the pervasive gimme-gimme, consumer purchase orientations that dominate some children's thinking. "My dad took us for two hours to Wal-Mart on Sunday," reported a 10-year-old child from a divorced family, "and he didn't buy us anything—just a can of tuna fish," she added scornfully. By emphasizing art and movement and music rather than commercial toys, teachers "help to unlock children's creative juices and make store-bought purchases pale in comparison." (Holst, 1999, p. 21). Explore nature by going on nature walks and identifying wildflowers and weeds. Admire when the children notice natural treasures (such as beetles scurrying under an upturned rock, odd-shaped marble or other mineral incrustations in boulders along a path, the earliest shoots of a spring wildflower such as pokeweed). During outdoor "discovery" walks, teachers can actively *notice talents* of different children. One child hears different birdcalls. Another identifies trees by their rough or smooth or shaggy bark. Teachers are crucial mentors who increase children's exhilaration with the natural world rather than exclusive preoccupation with the world of store-bought things.

Partner with Parents to Enrich Creativity in Children's Lives. Parents are primary adults in a child's life. A challenge for teachers is how to make an alliance with families in order to help them find and recognize their child's special "gifts." Sometimes reaching out will require creative techniques, such as phoning each family every few weeks to tell something positive and special about each child.

Primary Prevention and Creativity

What are the Connections between Creativity and Mental Health in Early Childhood?

Fueled by shock at student violence in schools and a lack of civility in many classrooms, a great deal of interesting and creative work on how to galvanize prosocial behaviors for classrooms and whole schools has been carried out over the past decade. As teachers become more thoughtful about the necessity to pay attention to the mental health of children as well as their accomplishments in academic subjects, more of these innovative programs may become implemented in school systems (Harrison, 1976; Honig & Wittmer, 1992).

Students who are afraid of writing or of mathematics, and who are turned off by book reading assignments, cannot bring to the classroom the creativity gifts they may well have. The more a teacher's responses establish firm foundations of trust and admiration for each child, the more free to be herself or himself each child will feel. Authenticity is one profound sign of good mental health. Primary prevention requires that teachers receive far more training than is usual in recognizing mental health blocks to early learning and creativity. The daydreaming child, the class clown, the aggressive bully, the smirking child who tries to curry favor with the "powerful" person, the teacher, by constant tattling, all need specialized and acutely sensitive handling. The perceptive teacher frees each child to become deeply comfortable and deeply engaged in the work of learning, so that each child's creativity will emerge in domains reflecting the child's gifts. Prevention of emotional difficulties in young children is a first-class way to promote their ability to become fully engaged with early learning.

What Directions are Creativity Research, Practice, and Policy Going in the Next Decade?

Research into how to stimulate creativity in children flourished more 30 years ago than today (Glover et al., 1989; Torrance, 1960, 1964, 1971, 1979). Problems of classroom discipline, interpersonal violence, children unable to read and write at grade level, integration and management of children with differing levels of disabilities into classrooms—these issues have been of far more concern in recent decades than society's interest in how to promote creativity. Research on enhancing creativity in low-creative, bright children by providing 10 weekly sessions, which included role-playing, creative writing, open discussion, and artistic expression, did not show strong gains at the end of the sessions (Sisk, 1972). Use of a delayed-post-test research design might better address the possibility of finding later "sleeper effects" of training. But fostering creativity still retains an element of mystery.

A challenge for colleges of education is how to find time in the syllabus to focus on promotion of creativity in the classroom. What changes in coursework could be implemented to help adults gain more insights and perspective on their own responses to child creativity and curricular expertise in promoting creativity? It is certainly not easy for some adults with responsibility for a group of youngsters to take a playful perspective on young children's experimentation that may disrupt a classroom (Koestner et al., 1984). A mature teacher struggles to hold discrepant ideas about a child who is both disruptive to the classroom and also an interesting little fellow who has been acting out some vigorous ideas. Taking the creative attitude toward discovering the gifts and needs of each individual child is a challenge for new teachers. The challenge for college trainers is to enroll young teachers in preparatory programs where they will learn both to create an atmosphere in the classroom that permits and tolerates experimentation and also to set up formal special times when children, unafraid, can share their experiences together. Such preparation needs to provide more specific supervised practice for teachers to optimize creativity in the preschool and kindergarten curriculum (Tegano, Moran, & Sawyers, 1991).

Calm shepherding of and perceptive support for children who are exploring and experimenting in sometimes messy and novel ways, as they analyze or synthesize with materials while gaining a rich knowledge-base, requires a kind of teacher wisdom that may well benefit from mentoring programs. A seasoned teacher can provide support for new teachers in the classroom. "Creative behavior cannot be summoned at the will of the teacher or 'ordered by numbers'" (Torrance & Gupta, 1964, p. 18).

On a positive note, currently there are many multicultural materials available that focus on recognition of ways of fostering creativity with minority children (Greenberg, 1992; Marfey, 1998) and gifted children (Morelock & Morrison, 1996). The wonderful classroom processes and uses of community resources implemented by the Reggio Emilia program in Italy (Gandini,

1994) have done much to stimulate American preschool educators in expanding their ideas of artwork in the classroom. Ideas for teachers to apply Gardner's theory of multiple intelligence in classroom practices are available (Phipps, 1997). Interest in play as the medium par excellence for children to work out important themes for their lives creatively continues to receive excellent support in the literature for teachers (Isenberg & Jalongo, 1997).

For creativity in the domain of science learning, many resources focus on the use of children's questions to awaken new ideas (Gallas, 1995). Environmental sensitivities have led to the creation of curricular materials that emphasize using the natural ecology of the schoolyard to further children's explorations of the environment (Harlan & Rivkin, 2000). Multicultural sensitivities have resulted in the creation of materials in Spanish as well as English to promote preschool science (George et al., 1995).

Certainly Developmentally Appropriate Practices, or DAP, guidelines specified by the National Association for the Education of Young Children (Bredekamp & Copple, 1997) have energized many preschool teachers to examine their own work and move toward more creativity-affirming practices. Interpreters of child development theories have worked hard to promote "constructivist classrooms" based on Piagetian concepts of equilibration and the fundamental necessity for hand-on experiences (Kamii & DeVries, 1980), which give a central role to children's creation of concepts based on their own experimentation and out-loud thinking through of problems and solutions.

Vygotsky's theory has become more widely disseminated and gives a powerful affirmation to the creative role of the teacher. Vygotsky's notion of the "zone of proximal development" centralizes the role of the adult in helping a child advance toward greater understandings and skills. Teacher training must take up the challenge of how to clarify this creative role for adults who will be working in classrooms and with recreational groups (Honig, 1999).

A straightforward way to assist teachers in transforming their ideas to permit a passion for creativity to flourish would be to supply a generous portfolio of specific activities for use with young children. Amabile (1989), DeMille (1976), and Hendricks & Wils (1975) describe simple physical awareness activities for stretching the body and mind, working with dreams, and using guided imagery and Sufi stories with children to help them expand awareness of their inner powers to be creative. Some of the stretch and relax exercises would also be wonderful to reduce children's tensions from the rushed lives they often experience at home. Centering and calming the children through these exercises will allow them to use their energies for creativity rather than emotional and intellectual defenses against their stress. The creativity games devised by Torrance and Gupta (1964) (and described in earlier sections) are excellent for implementation by teachers.

A rich supply of workbooks and curricular guides are currently available for helping children become aware of the consequences of their own actions and thinking processes. Some of the programs, such as "Think Aloud" (Camp & Bash, 1985), use dramatic play areas and tagboard strips with animal pictures to help children learn how to deal with difficult feelings and situations. Suppose a child in the classroom is leaning back and tipping her chair and that makes another student mad. What plan could the upset student make? Has the student seen someone else respond in a different way besides acting out mad feelings in such a situation? This program promotes children's creativity in thinking of all possible consequences of inappropriate behaviors. One scenario involves asking the class, "How many different consequences...might happen if you throw a ball in the house?" (p. 193)

Some new techniques are available for older children and adults to free up their thinking and get creative ideas flowing. In his book *The Mind Map Book*, Buzon (1990) encourages students to draw, doodle, create diagrams, sketch radiating lines, make up comic book blurb bubbles, and other techniques as aids to free association around a topic that the student needs to write about. The resultant verbal plus spatial productions confirm how much a student really does already know about a topic and what ideas have blossomed forth on the branches of the radiating lines that connect the central topic to the student's musings and associations. This game-like technique might be useful with overly constricted youth who are too worried about messy papers or not being competent enough to write a long report.

Recent theoretical work has clarified aspects of creativity and/or intellectual functioning in children. Gardner's (1983) ideas about multiple intelligences mean that many youngsters have specialized gifts, more in one area than another. In the Japanese tale of Crow Boy (Yashima, 1983), all the children ridicule a poor peasant child who comes to the village school. The teacher does nothing to intervene, but gradually becomes aware that this boy has a strange and unique gift the others do not have. He can imitate crows and call them down from the skies. Only when the teacher observes, notices, reflects, and cares about the unique talent of this ostracized child can the teacher begin to make creative efforts to change the classroom climate toward respect for each child.

Sternberg's (1985) triarchic theory of intelligence has teased out components of intellectually creative functioning. What verbal and performance components must the child use in solving various kinds of problems and how will he or she decide how to combine these into an overall strategy? How does the child represent information? How well has the child figured out how to trade off speed for accuracy in handling a complex intellectual problem? Sternberg emphasizes the importance of the child's response to novelty and the importance of using what he calls "automatization" of component operations to smooth the solution of problem-solving tasks. For a child to learn how to solve analogies, for example, Sternberg identifies component skills she or he must learn: encoding, making inferences, mapping concepts from one domain to another; application of rules generated from mapping; comparisons of word and concept meanings; justification reasoning to defend one's conceptual thinking; and ability to produce an overt response to a creative problem, such as solving an analogy of the type: Lawyer is to Client as Teacher is to (?). When several answer choices are offered (Principal, Student, Custodian), the child must galvanize all the component process skills in solving the analogy.

How Can We Promote Creativity in Society?

A difficult challenge for society is how to promote the creativity, talents, and giftedness of all citizens, regardless of color, social class, national origin, or gender.

Gender and Creativity. Gender issues in creativity are certainly complex. Creativity is a gift that flourishes among young children. However, boys are frequently allowed more freedom of movement, more permission to cross streets and roam further in neighborhoods, more indulgence for climbing and jumping and expressing the exuberance of their body creativity in sports and games. Girls are not pictured as often as adventurous characters on television shows or on television commercials. Thus, teachers and recreational counselors need to craft new ideas to permit equal flourishing of creativity among boys and girls.

Stories that feature creative heroines are one technique adults can use. For young children, the story of the paper bag princess shows the gumption and ingenuity of a girl who cleverly bests a dragon to rescue the boy with whom she often plays tennis (Munsch, 1980). The young princess pretends to admire the dragon's fire breathing and asks for demonstrations over and over until the dragon runs out of fire and it is safe for her to go into his cave and rescue the boy. However, the boy snubs her. Since her regular clothes were singed off by the dragon's breath of fire, she had hit upon the idea of using a paper bag as temporary clothing. The young man's contemptuous response to her disheveled, sooty appearance leaves this creative young lady determined to go her own way. Female "creativity" may not be appreciated by younger (or older) males. Counselors and teachers need to sustain the self-esteem of girls whose creative and spunky ideas are "put down" by others in the group.

The Importance of Fairy Tales. The use of fairy tales has been urged as a means of helping children focus on their identity and come into a realization of their own powers of self-healing (Thomas, 1999). Bettleheim (1976) eloquently explained that for a fairy tale to enrich a child's life,

> it must stimulate his imagination; help him to develop his
> intellect and to clarify his emotion; be attuned to his

anxieties and aspirations, give full recognition of his difficulties, while at the same time suggesting solutions to the
problems which perturb him. (p. 5)

In the fairy tale of Hansel and Gretel, Gretel's imaginative
ideas save the day. She cleverly provides a skinny bone for Hansel
to thrust through the bars so the witch believes he is still not
fattened up enough for her to roast and feast upon. It is important
for teachers to search out materials where girls are heroines and
save the day or think up wonderful solutions for life problems.
Girls will identify with the heroines in such stories. This form of
"bibliotherapy," as it were, can provide role models for girls who
are marching to a different drummer, especially in groups where
cliques appear to value expensive clothes or makeup over sterling
ideas and gems of insights!

In the story "Rachel the Clever" (Sherman, 1993), a king
boasts at an inn that he would only marry a woman who was as
clever as he. The innkeeper, in turn, boasts of his daughter
Rachel's ability to solve riddles. So the story begins:

"I don't like liars", the king told the innkeeper. "I will ask
you three riddles. If your daughter can solve them, you
will be rewarded, but if she fails, you shall lose your inn.
First, what is the fastest thing? Second, what is the
richest thing? Third, what is the dearest thing?" Sadly
the innkeeper went home to his daughter, Rachel, and
told her what the king had said. Rachel smiled. "You
won't lose the inn, Father. Go to the king and tell him
that Thought is the fastest thing, life-giving earth is the
richest thing, and Love is the dearest thing." (p. 44)

Rachel's quickness of intellect and her quirky ways of analyzing
and responding to challenges are tested and proven several times
throughout this tale. At one point the king demands that she bring
him a gift that is not a gift. Rachel brings two doves and at the instant
of her handing them over to the king the doves fly away.

Such stories can inspire young girls to want to be imaginative
and creative in thinking up solutions to life problems even when

this means they may differ from others. Preteen girls are more vulnerable to self-discouragement when they perceive that their ideas are not valued as much as those of boys (Gilligan, et al., 1990).

Creative Activities Can Buffer Children Against Stress. Mental health issues are rampant in many families with heavy stresses due to poverty, inappropriate communication patterns, or divorce. When children are scared or worried because of family troubles or health problems in the family, their creativity may be very subdued. By stereotypic actions, children try to cope with fears and yet they may box themselves into rigid "solutions." One preschooler, whose divorcing parents were fighting a great deal in the home, lay on the floor of the child care center and turned the pages of Maurice Sendak's *Where the Wild Things Are* (1991) over and over. The monsters in that book were safely within the pages. He could control those monsters by closing the book. He also drove a small toy car through the dollhouse to the opposite side and let the car crash onto the floor. Then he retrieved the car and repetitively carried out the same motions. Because of fierce troubles at home, he confined his play to symbolic, "safe" actions he could control and replay over and over.

A challenge for counselors and parents is to use their own creativity to find "magic" ways to empower children to face their own worries and deal courageously with them. Stories provide one such technique. The crafting of classic tales subtly gives children the possibilities of

> conjuring up *inner* possibilities—that is to say, the grati-
> fication of (sometimes impossible) desires and the pro-
> visional working through and mastery of basic fears by
> means of fantasy, mental adventure and magical trans-
> formations. (Spitz, 1999, pp. 10-11)

Creating and reading stories with children that show children dealing positively and with ingenuity with threats to their well-being provide models of coping skills that give courage and inspire children. In *Something from Nothing,* whenever Joseph's mother wants to throw out a treasured piece of clothing (made initially by his grandpa from scraps from his precious baby blanket) Joseph counts on his Grandpa's creative sewing skills to come to the rescue. At the end of the story, Joseph also learns to be creative on his own when no scraps of fabric are left (Gilman, 1993).

Brett (1986) created the *Annie Stories* to help her young daughter cope with anxious feelings and release more imaginative ways to handle tense situations, such as a scary tiger in a bad dream, or dealing with the first day of kindergarten. In one Annie story, Brett told her daughter she would give her an invisible secret ring and "when you have it on, you cannot be harmed. So if something frightening is happening to you in a dream, you just need to remember that you have your dream ring on and that you are protected" (p. 39). There are social situations for which a child needs to create personal emotional solutions. Annie stories about a child much like the child the adult is caring for can be crafted as a powerful tools to embolden the child and release creative coping energies in the domain of socioemotional challenges.

Conclusions

The tools to promote our own creative ideas in order to support young children's creativity are available everywhere. Perhaps we simply need a clarion call to "pick up the tools and use them with good will!"

Endnote

1. These anecdotes are either the author's personal anecdotes or come from the author's case notes as a therapist. The names of the children have been changed.

References

Amabile, T. M. (1989). *Growing up creative: Nurturing a lifetime of creativity*. New York: Crown Publishers.

Andrews, J. H. (1988). Poetry: Tool of the classroom magician. *Young Children, 43*, 17–25.

Aronson, E. (1978) *The jigsaw classroom*. Beverly Hills, CA: Sage.

Benzie, T. (1987). *A moving experience: Dance for lovers of children and the child within*. Tucson, AZ: Zephyr.

Bettelheim, B. (1976). *The uses of enchantment*. London: Penguin.

Borgman, J. (2000, Winter). Respecting the creativity in our children. *Montessori Life*, 42–43.

Bredekamp , S., & Copple, C. (1997) (Eds.). *Developmentally appropriate practice in early childhood programs* (Rev. ed.). Washington, DC: National Association for the Education of Young Children.

Brett, D. (1986). *Annie stories*. Victoria, Australia: Penguin Books.

Brown, R. T. (1989). Creativity: What are we to measure? In J. A. Glover, R. R. Ronning, & C. R. Reynolds (Eds.), *Handbook of creativity* (pp. 3–32). New York: Plenum Press.

Buzan, T. (1990). *The mind map book*. New York: Dutton.

Camp, B. W., & Bash, M. A. (1985). *Think aloud: Increasing social and cognitive skills: A problem-solving program for children*. Champaign, IL: Research Press.

Cerf, B. (1964). *Animal riddles*. New York: Random House.

Chenfeld, M. (1995). *Creative experiences for young children* (2nd ed.). Orlando, FL: Harcourt Brace.

Cohen, S., & Oden, S. (1974). An examination of creativity and locus of control in children. *Journal of Genetic Psychology, 124,* 179–185.

Cole, J. (1986). *The magic school bus at the waterworks*. New York: Scholastic.

DeMille, R. (1976). *Put your mother on the ceiling: Children's imagination games*. New York: Viking Books.

Dowd, E. T. (1989). The self and creativity: Several constructs in search of a theory. In J. A. Glover, R. R. Ronning, & C. R. Reynolds (Eds.), *Handbook of creativity* (pp. 233–241). New York: Plenum Press.

Duckworth, E. (1996). *The having of wonderful ideas and other essays on teaching and learning*. New York: Teachers College Press.

Ewart, F. (1998). *Let the shadow speak: Developing children's language through shadow puppetry*. Staffordshire, England: Trentham.

Gable, S. (1999). Promote children's literacy with poetry. *Young Children, 54*, 12–15.

Gallas, K. (1995). *Talking their way into science: Hearing children's questions and theories, Responding with curricula.* New York: Teachers College Press.

Gandini, L. (1994). Educational and caring spaces. In C. Edwards, L. Gandini, & G. Forman (Eds.), *The hundred languages of children: The Reggio Emilia approach to early childhood education.* Norwood, NJ: Ablex.

Gardner, H. (1983). *Frames of mind: The theory of multiple intelligences.* New York: Basic Books.

George, Y. S., Malcom, S. M., Worthington, V. L., & Daniel, A. B. (Eds.) (1995). *In touch with preschool science.* Washington, DC: American Association for the Advancement of Science.

Gilligan, C., Lyons, N., & Hammer, T. (1996). *Making connections: The relational world of adolescent guilt at Emma Willard School.* Cambridge, MA: Harvard University Press.

Gilman, P. (1993). *Something from nothing.* New York: Scholastic

Glover, J. A., Ronning, R. R., & Reynolds, C. R. (1989). *Handbook of creativity.* New York: Plenum Press.

Goetz, E. M. (1981). The effects of minimal praise on the creative blockbuilding of three-year-olds. *Child Study Journal, 11*, 55–67.

Goetz, E. M. (1989). The teaching of creativity to preschool children: The behavior analysis approach. In J. A. Glover, R. R. Ronning, & C. R. Reynolds (Eds.), *Handbook of creativity* (pp. 411–428). New York: Plenum Press.

Greenberg, P. (1992). Ideas that work with young children. Teaching about Native Americans? Or teaching about people, including Native Americans? *Young Children, 47*, 27–30, 79–81.

Hale, B. M. (n.d.). *The elf in my ear.* Brigham City, UT: Blue Creek.

Harlan, J. C., & Rivkin, M. S. (2000). *Science experiences for the early childhood years: An integrated approach* (7th ed.). Columbus, OH: Merrill/Prentice Hall.

Harrison, M. (1976). *For the fun of it: Selected cooperative games for children and adults.* Philadelphia, PA: Nonviolence and Children's Series. Friends and Peace Committee.

Healy, J. M. (1994). *Your child's growing mind.* New York: Doubleday.

Hendricks, G., & Wils, R. (1975). *The centering book: Awareness activities for children, parents, and teachers.* New York: Spectrum Books.

Holst, C. B. (1999). Buying more can give children less. *Young Children, 54,* 19–23.

Honig, A. S. (1982). *Playtime learning games for young children.* Syracuse, NY: Syracuse University Press.

Honig, A. S. (1988). Research in review. Humor development in children. *Young Children, 43,* 60–73.

Honig, A. S. (1996, Fall). Using an "I can problem solve" approach with children. *NYSAEYC Reporter,* p. 9.

Honig, A. S. (1998). Sociocultural influences on sexual meanings embedded in playful experiences. In D. P. Fromberg & D. Bergen (Eds.), *Play from birth to twelve and beyond: Contents, perspectives, and meanings* (pp. 338–347). New York: Garland Press.

Honig, A. S. (1999). Critical issues and research in early childhood education. In H. K. Chiam (Ed.), *Toward excellence in early childhood education: Policies and practices in the 21st century* (pp. 95–117). Selangur Darul Ehsan, Malaysia: Pelanduk Publications.

Honig, A. S., & Wittmer, D. S. (1982). Teacher questions to male and female toddlers. *Early Child Development and Care, 9,* 19–32.

Honig, A. S., & Wittmer, D. S. (1992). *Prosocial development in children: Caring, sharing and cooperation: A bibliographic resource guide.* New York: Garland Press.

Isenberg, J. P., & Jalongo, M. R. (1997). *Creative expression and play in early childhood.* Upper Saddle, NJ: Merrill.

Kamii, C., & DeVries, R. (1980). *Group games in early education: Implications of Piaget's theory.* Washington, DC: National Association for the Education of Young Children.

Koestner, R., Ryan, R. M., Bernieri, F., & Holt, K. (1984). Setting limits on children's behavior: The differential effects of controlling vs. informational styles on intrinsic motivation and creativity. *Journal of Personality, 52,* 233–248.

Kelner, L. M. (1993). *The creative classroom: A guide for using creative drama in the classroom.* Portsmouth, NH: Heinemann.

Kraus, R. (1956). *I want to paint my bathroom blue.* New York: Harper & Row.

Lane, T. W., Lane, M. Z., Friedman, B. S., Goetz, E. M., & Pinkston, E. M. (1982). A creativity enhancement program for preschool children in an inner city parent-child center. In A. M. Pinkston, J. L. Levitt, G. R. Green, N. L. Linsk, & T. L. Rzepnicki (Eds.), *Effective social work practice: Advanced techniques for behavioral intervention with individuals, families and institutional staff* (pp. 435–441). San Francisco, CA: Jossey-Bass.

Marfey, A. (1998). *The miracle of learning: How to inspire children. A multicultural approach to early childhood development.* Albany, NY: Windflower.

McCord, D. (1961). *Every time I climb a tree.* Boston: Little, Brown.

Merriam, E. (1985). *Blackberry ink.* New York: William Morrow and Company.

Merriam, E. (1988). *You be good and I'll be night.* New York: Morrow Junior Books.

Morelock, M. K., & Morrison, K. (1996). *Gifted children have talents too: Multidimensional programmes for the gifted in early childhood.* Victoria, Australia: Hawker Brownlow Education.

Munsch, R. (1980). *The paper bag princess.* Toronto: Annick.

Myers, R. E., & Torrance, E. P. (1965). *Can you imagine? A book of ideas for children in the primary grades* (p. 7, 23). Boston, MA: Ginn and Company.

Nash, J. M. (1997, February 3). Fertile minds. *Time,* 49–56.

Neuschwander, C. (1997). *Sir Cumference and the first round table: A math adventure.* Watertown, MA: Charlesbridge Publishing.

Orlick, T. (1978). *The cooperative sports and games book: Challenge without competition.* New York: Pantheon Books.

Paley, V. (1990). *The boy who would be a helicopter: The uses of storytelling in the classroom.* Cambridge, MA: Harvard University Press.

Palladino, L. J. (1997). *The Edison trait* (pp. xiii, 222). New York: Random House.

Parish, P. (1963). *Amelia Bedelia.* New York: Harper & Row.

Parkinson, K. (1986). *The enormous turnip.* Morton Grove, IL: Albert Whitman.

Phipps, P. (1997). *Multiple intelligences in the early childhood classroom.* Santa Rosa, CA: McGraw Hill.

Pleydell, S., & Brown, V. (1999). *The dramatic difference: Drama in the preschool and kindergarten classroom.* Portsmouth, NH: Heinemann.

Prelutsky, J. (1994). *The sheriff of Rottenshot.* New York: William Morrow and Co.

Sapon-Shevin, M. (1986). Teaching cooperation. In G. Cartledge & J. R. Milburn (Eds.) *Teaching social skills to children* (pp. 270–302). New York: Pergamon Press.

Schemp, P. G., Jeffers, J. T., & Zaichowsky, L. D. (1983). Influence of decision making on attitudes, creativity, motor skills, and self-concept in elementary children. *Research Quarterly for Exercise and Sport, 54,* 183–189.

Sendak, M. (1991). *Where the wild things are.* New York: Harper Collins.

Sharmat, M. W. (1984). *My mother never listens to me.* Niles, IL: Albert Whitman.

Sherman, J. (1993). *Rachel the clever and other Jewish folktales* (p. 44). Little Rock, AR: August House Publishers.

Shure, M. (1995). *Raising a thinking child workbook.* New York: Henry Holt.

Sigel, I., & Saunders, R. (1979). An inquiry into inquiry: Question asking as an instructional model. In L. Katz (Ed.), *Current topics in early childhood education* (pp. 169–193). Norwood, NJ: Ablex.

Sisk, D. (1972). Relationship between self-concept and creativity: Theory into practice. *Gifted Child Quarterly, 16,* 229–234.

Spitz, E. H. (1999). *Inside picture books* (pp. 10–11). New Haven, CT: Yale University Press.

Sternberg, R. J. (1985). *Beyond IQ: A triarchic theory of human intelligence.* New York: Cambridge University Press.

Tegano, D. W., Moran III, J. D., & Sawyers, J. (1991). *Creativity in early childhood classrooms.* Washington, DC: National Education Association.

Thomas, J. (1999). The role of the fairy story in development of a 'sense of self' in young children with identified emotional and behavioural difficulties. *Early Child Development and Care, 157,* 27–50.

Tolkien, J. R. R. (1996). *The hobbit.* London: Harper Collins.

Torrance, E. P. (1962). *Guiding creative talent.* Englewood Cliffs, NJ: Prentice-Hall.

Torrance, E. P. (1964). *Role of evaluation in creative thinking.* Minneapolis, MN: Bureau of Educational Research, University of Minnesota.

Torrance, E. P. (1970). *Encouraging creativity in the classroom.* Dubuque, IA: William C. Brown.

Torrance, E. P. (1971). Identity: The gifted child's major problem. *Gifted Child Quarterly, 15,* 147–155.

Torrance, E. P. (1979). *The search for Satori and creativity.* Buffalo, NY: Creative Education Foundation.

Torrance, E. P., & Gupta, R. (1964, February). *Development and evaluation of recorded programmed experiences in creative thinking in the fourth grade.* Minneapolis, MN: Bureau of Educational Research, University of Minnesota.

Yashima, T. (1983). *Grow boy.* New York: Viking.

Bibliography
Resources for Teachers to Read with Children

Cole, J. (1986). *The magic school bus at the waterworks.* New York: Scholastic.

DeMille, R. (1976). *Put your mother on the ceiling: Children's imagination games.* New York: Viking Books.

Gilman, P. (1993). *Something from nothing.* New York: Scholastic.

Hale, B. M. (n.d.). *The elf in my ear.* Brigham City, UT: Blue Creek.

Kraus, R. (1956). *I want to paint my bathroom blue.* New York: Harper & Row.

McCord, D. (1961). *Every time I climb a tree.* Boston: Little, Brown.

Merriam, E. (1985). *Blackberry ink.* New York: William Morrow and Company.

Merriam, E. (1988). *You be good and I'll be night.* New York: Morrow Junior Books.

Munsch, R. (1980). *The paper bag princess.* Toronto: Annick.

Myers, R. E., & Torrance, E. P. (1965). *Can you imagine? A book of ideas for children in the primary grades.* Boston, MA: Ginn and Company.

Myers, R. E., & Torrance, E. P. (1966). *For those who wonder.* Boston, MA: Ginn and Company.

Neuschwander, C. (1997). *Sir Cumference and the first round table: A math adventure.* Watertown, MA: Charlesbridge Publishing.

Parish, P. (1963). *Amelia Bedelia.* New York: Harper & Row.

Parkinson, K. (1986). *The enormous turnip.* Morton Grove, IL: Albert Whitman.

Prelutsky, J. (1994). *The sheriff of Rottenshot.* New York: William Morrow and Co.

Schenk de Regnieres, B. (1958). *What can you do with a shoe?* New York: Simon & Schuster.

Sendak, M. (1991). *Where the wild things are.* New York: Harper Collins.

Seuss, Dr. (1961). *The Sneetches and other stories.* New York: Random House.

Sharmat, M. W. (1984). *My mother never listens to me.* Niles, IL: Albert Whitman.

Sherman, J. (1993). *Rachel the clever and other Jewish folktales.* Little Rock, AR: August House Publishers.

Yashima, T. (1983). *Grow boy.* New York: Viking.

Chapter 5

Developing Creativity in Children Through the Enrichment Triad Model

Joseph S. Renzulli and Sally M. Reis

How can we develop the creative potential of children? In a time period in which fast is good and faster is better, how can we help children learn to think creatively, and to value opportunities for quiet reflection and creative work of their choice? Today, many educators seem more interested in how to raise achievement scores, rather than how to develop creativity in their students. In the decades since the Enrichment Triad Model (Renzulli, 1976) has been used as the basis for educational programs for high-potential students, an unusually large number of examples of creative productivity have occurred in students whose educational experiences have been guided by this plan. Perhaps, like others involved in the development of theories and generalizations, we did not fully understand at the onset of our work the full implications of this model for encouraging and developing creative productivity in young people. These implications relate most directly to concerns about how we develop creativity, motivation, and task commitment that might have gone unexamined, undeveloped, and unrefined if not for the favorable results reported to us by early implementers of the model. We became increasingly interested in how and why a model that encourages creative productivity in children was working in different schools and how we could provide additional services to promote creativity in more students. Thus began several years of research and an examination of the work of other theorists which brought us to the material presented in this chapter.

The original Enrichment Triad Model (Renzulli, 1976), which was initially field tested in districts in the northeast, was developed to provide children with the opportunity to develop their above-average abilities, creativity, and task commitment and was based on a central premise: If we give children opportunities to become involved in self-selected, creative, productive work in school, this will increase the likelihood that they will emerge as creatively productive adults in whatever area they select as their future work. The model proved to be quite popular and requests were received from all over the country for school visitations and for information on how to implement the model. A book about the Enrichment Triad Model (Renzulli, 1977) was published, and more and more districts began asking for help in implementing this approach.

We became fascinated by the variety of programs being developed by different types of teachers. In some programs, for example, teacher A consistently elicited high levels of creative productivity in students while teacher B had few students who engaged in this type of work. In some districts, many enrichment opportunities were regularly offered to students not formally identified for the program, while in other districts only identified "gifted" students had access to enrichment experiences. We wondered how we could replicate the success of one teacher or one district in implementing the model in diverse districts. For example, how could we help other teachers learn to produce high levels of creative productivity in students like teacher A? And, of course, we became increasingly interested in why the model was working and how we could further expand the theoretical rationale underlying our work: The opportunity for children to engage in creative and productive work in self-selected interest areas increases the likelihood that they will be creatively productive adults.

Two Kinds of Giftedness

Our present efforts to define giftedness are based on a long history of previous studies dealing with human abilities. Most of these studies focus mainly on the concept of intelligence and are briefly discussed here to establish an important point about the process of defining concepts rather than any attempt to equate intelligence with giftedness. Although a detailed review of these studies is beyond the scope of the present chapter, a few of the general conclusions from earlier research (Neisser, 1979) are necessary to set the stage for this analysis.

The first conclusion is that intelligence is not a unitary concept, but rather there are many kinds of intelligence and therefore single definitions cannot be used to explain this multifaceted phenomenon. The confusion about present theories of intelligence has led Sternberg (1984) and others to develop new models for explaining this complicated concept. Sternberg's "triarchic" theory of human intelligence consists of three subtheories: a contextual subtheory, which relates intelligence to the external world of the individual; a two-faceted experiential subtheory, which relates intelligence to both the external and internal worlds of the individual; and a componential subtheory, which relates intelligence to the internal world of the individual. The contextual subtheory defines intelligent behavior in terms of purposive adaptation to, selection of, and shaping of real-world environments relevant to one's life. The experiential subtheory further constrains this definition by regarding as most relevant to the demonstration of intelligence contextually intelligent behavior that involves either adaptation to novelty or automatization of information processing, or both. The componential subtheory specifies the mental mechanisms responsible for the learning, planning, execution, and evaluation of intelligent behavior.

Sternberg's approach emphasizes three aspects of intellectual giftedness: the superiority of mental processes, including metacomponents relating intelligence to the internal world of the individual; superiority in dealing with relative novelty and in automating information processing, which is an experiential aspect relating cognition to one's level of experience in applying cognitive processes in particular tasks or situations; and superiority in applying the processes of intellectual functioning, as mediated by experience, to functioning in real-world contexts, which is a contextual aspect. Sternberg believes that "the outward manifestation of giftedness is in superior adaptation to, shaping of and selection of environments" (1986, p. 9) and would agree with Renzulli (1978, 1986) that it can be attained in a number of ways that may differ from one person to another.

In view of this recent work and numerous earlier cautions about the dangers of trying to describe intelligence through the use of single scores, it seems safe to conclude that this practice has been and always will be questionable. At the very least, attributes of intelligent behavior must be considered within the context of cultural and situational factors. Indeed, some of the most recent examinations have concluded that "[t]he concept of intelligence *cannot* be explicitly defined, not only because of the nature of intelligence but also because of the nature of concepts" (Neisser, 1979, p. 179).

A second conclusion is that there is no ideal way to measure intelligence and therefore we must avoid the typical practice of believing that if we know a person's IQ score, we also know his or her intelligence. The reason we have cited these concerns about the historical difficulty of defining and measuring intelligence is to highlight the even larger problem of isolating a unitary definition of giftedness. At the very least, we will always have several conceptions (and therefore definitions) of giftedness. To help in this analysis, we will begin by examining two broad categories of giftedness that have been dealt with in the research literature: "schoolhouse giftedness" and "creative-productive giftedness" (Renzulli, 1986). Before describing each type, we want to emphasize that:

- Both types are important.

- There is usually an interaction between the two types.

- Special programs should make appropriate provisions for encouraging both types of giftedness as well as the numerous occasions when the two types interact with each other.

Schoolhouse Giftedness

Schoolhouse giftedness might also be called test-taking or lesson-learning giftedness. It is the kind most easily measured by IQ or other cognitive ability tests, and for this reason it is also the type most often used for selecting students for entrance into special programs. The abilities people display on IQ and aptitude tests are exactly the kinds of abilities most valued in traditional school learning situations. In other words, the games people play on ability tests are similar in nature to games that teachers require in most lesson-learning situations. A large body of research tells us that students who score high on IQ tests are also likely to get high grades in school, and that these test-taking and lesson-learning abilities generally remain stable over time (Cronbach & Snow, 1977; Jones & Bayley, 1941; Moffitt, Caspi, Harkness, & Silva, 1993). The results of this research should lead us to some very obvious conclusions about schoolhouse giftedness: It exists in varying degrees; it can be identified through standardized assessment techniques; and we should therefore do everything in our power to make appropriate modifications for students who have the ability to cover regular curricular material at advanced rates and levels of understanding.

Creative-Productive Giftedness

If scores on IQ tests and other measures of cognitive ability only account for a limited proportion of the common variance with school grades, we can be equally certain that these measures do not tell the whole story when it comes to making predictions about creative-productive giftedness. Creative-productive giftedness describes those aspects of human activity and involvement where a premium is placed on the development of original material and products that are purposefully designed to have an impact on one or more target audiences. Learning situations that are designed to promote creative-productive giftedness emphasize the use and application of information (content) and thinking skills in an integrated, inductive, and real-problem-oriented manner. The role of the student is transformed from that of a learner of prescribed lessons to one in which she or he uses the modus operandi of a firsthand inquirer. This approach is quite different from the development of lesson-learning giftedness that tends to emphasize deductive learning, structured training in the development of thinking processes, and the acquisition, storage, and retrieval of information. In other words, creative-productive giftedness is simply putting one's abilities to work on problems and areas of study that have personal relevance to the student and that can be escalated to appropriately challenging levels of investigative activity. The roles that both students and teachers should play in the pursuit of these problems have been described elsewhere (Renzulli, 1977,1982), and have been embraced in general education under the concepts of authentic learning and performance assessment.

Why is creative-productive giftedness important enough for us to question the "tidy" and relatively easy approach that traditionally has been used to select students for gifted programs on the basis of test scores? Why do some people want to rock the boat by challenging a conception of giftedness that can be numerically defined by simply giving a test? The answers to these questions are simple yet compelling. A review of the research literature (Renzulli, 1986) tells us that there is much more to identifying human potential than the abilities revealed on traditional tests of intelligence, aptitude, and achievement. Furthermore, history tells us it has been the creative and productive people of the world, the producers rather than consumers of knowledge, the reconstructionists of thought in all areas of human endeavor, who have become recognized as "truly gifted" individuals. History does not remember persons who merely scored well on IQ tests or those who learned their lessons well.

Howard Gardner's (1983) theory of multiple intelligences, also referred to as MI, and Renzulli's (1978) "three-ring" definition of gifted behavior serve as examples of multifaceted and well-researched conceptualizations of intelligence and giftedness. Gardner's definition of an intelligence is the ability to solve problems, or create products, that are valued within one or more cultural settings (Gardner, 1993). Within his multiple intelligences theory, he articulates at least seven specific intelligences:

linguistic, musical, logical-mathematical, spatial, bodily-kines-thetic, interpersonal, and intrapersonal. Gardner believes that people are more comfortable using the term "talents" and that "intelligence" is generally reserved to describe linguistic or logi-cal "smartness"; however, he does not believe that certain human abilities should arbitrarily qualify as intelligence over others (e.g., language as an intelligence vs. dance as a talent) (Gardner, 1993).

Renzulli's (1978) definition, which defines gifted behaviors rather than gifted individuals, is composed of three components (See Figure 1) as follows:

> Gifted behavior consists of behaviors that reflect an interaction among three basic clusters of human traits—above average ability, high levels of task commitment, and high levels of creativity. Individuals capable of developing gifted behavior are those possessing or ca-pable of developing this composite set of traits and applying them to any potentially valuable area of hu-man performance. Persons who manifest or are capable of developing an interaction among the three clusters require a wide variety of educational opportunities and services that are not ordinarily provided through regular instructional programs. (Renzulli & Reis, 1997, p. 8)

A Change in Direction: From Being Gifted or Creative to the Development of Giftedness and Creativity in Children

In the past, the general approach to the study of gifted persons could easily lead one to believe that giftedness is an absolute condition that is magically bestowed upon a person in much the same way that nature endows us with blue eyes, red hair, or a dark complexion. This position is not supported by the research. For too many years we have pretended that we can identify giftedness and creativity in children in an absolute and unequivocal fash-ion. Many people have come to believe that certain individuals have been endowed with a golden chromosome that makes them

Figure 5-1 *Three-Ring Conception of Giftedness.*
Characteristics that may be manifested in Renzulli's three-ring conception of giftedness are presented in Table 1.

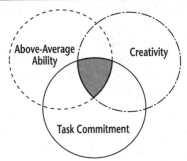

Table 5-1 *Taxonomy of Behavioral Manifestations of Giftedness According to Renzulli's Three-Ring Conception of Giftedness.*

Above-Average Ability (general)
- high levels of abstract thought
- adaptation to novel situations
- rapid and accurate retrieval of information

Above Average Ability (specific)
- applications of general abilities to specific area of knowledge
- capacity to sort out relevant from irrelevant information
- capacity to acquire and use advanced knowledge and strategies while pursuing a problem

Task Commitment
- capacity for high levels of interest, enthusiasm
- hard work and determination in a particular area
- self-confidence and drive to achieve
- ability to identify significant problems within an area of study
- setting high standards for one's work

Creativity
- fluency, flexibility, and originality of thought
- openness to new experiences and ideas
- curiosity
- willingness to take risks
- sensitivity to aesthetic characteristics

(Adapted from Renzulli & Reis, 1997, p. 9)

gifted or creative. This belief has further led to the mistaken idea that all we need to do is find the right combination of factors that prove the existence of this "gift."

Most of the confusion and controversy surrounding the definitions of giftedness that have been offered by various writers can be placed into perspective if we examine a few key questions. Is giftedness or creativity an absolute or relative concept? That is, is a person either gifted or not gifted (the absolute view), or can varying degrees of gifted behaviors be developed in certain people, at certain times, and under certain circumstances (the relative view)? Is giftedness or creativity a static concept (i.e., you have it or you don't) or is it a dynamic concept (i.e., it varies within persons and among learning/performance situations)?

These questions have led us to advocate a fundamental change in the ways the concept of giftedness should be viewed. For 20 years, we have advocated *labeling the services students receive rather than labeling the students*. We believe that our education should shift its emphasis from a traditional concept of "being gifted" (or not being gifted) to a concern about the *development of gifted and creative behaviors* in students who have high potential for benefiting from special educational opportunities. This change in terminology may also provide the flexibility in both identification and programming endeavors that will encourage the inclusion of at-risk and underachieving students in our programs. Our ultimate goal is the development of a total school enrichment program that benefits all students and concentrates on making schools more creative places for talent development in all young people.

Characteristics of Children with High Creative Ability or Potential

Academically gifted and creatively gifted students vary greatly, and most who have studied the area would probably agree with Sternberg and Lubart's assertion that the "academically successful children of today are not necessarily the creatively gifted adults of tomorrow" (1993, p. 12). Individuals with high intelligence may or may not have high creative ability or potential (Davis & Rimm, 1998; Renzulli 1978; Renzulli & Reis, 1985, 1997). There is evidence, however, to suggest a relationship between the constructs. The "threshold concept" discussed by MacKinnon in 1978 describes a base level (an IQ of about 120) of intelligence as essential for creative productivity. Beyond that threshold, there is no relationship between creativity and intelligence as measured by IQ tests (Davis & Rimm; Sternberg & Lubart).

What are the traits that help to define children with high creative ability or potential? Gardner's (1993) conception of a creative individual is one who *"regularly* solves problems or fashions products in a *domain,* and whose work is considered both novel and acceptable by knowledgeable members of a field" (p. xvii). He further believes that creativity should not be regarded as a construct in the mind or personality of an individual, but rather as something that emerges from the interactions of intelligence (personal profile of competence), domain (disciplines or crafts within a culture), and field (people and institutions that judge quality within a domain) (Gardner).

Sternberg and Lubart (1993) view creativity as a type of giftedness in itself, rather than as one dimension of intelligence. They propose that a person's "resources" for creativity allow a process of creative production to occur. Because they believe that six separate resources combine to interactively yield creativity, they find creative giftedness to be a rare occurrence because so many components must interact at once. Sternberg and Lubart's six "resources" succinctly describe many of the traits of creative individuals:

1. *Intellectual processes.* Creatively gifted people excel in problem definition, using insight (selective encoding, selective comparison, and selective combination) to solve problems, and divergent thought as a problem-solving strategy. These intellectual processes of creatively gifted learners are not measured by traditional IQ tests.

2. *Knowledge.* Knowledge of the domain allows one to identify areas where new and novel work is needed. To some extent, knowledge may serve as a hindrance to creativity, as too much of it can limit ability to have fresh ideas.

3. *Intellectual (cognitive) styles.* Creatively gifted people tend to prefer a legislative style (creating, formulating, and planning) and a global mode of processing information (thinking abstractly, generalizing, and extrapolating). Both of these styles are encouraged through approaches such as the Enrichment Triad Model (Renzulli, 1977; Renzulli & Reis, 1985, 1997).

4. *Personality.* Five key personality attributes are important to creative giftedness: tolerance of ambiguity, moderate risk-taking, willingness to surmount obstacles and persevere, willingness to grow, and belief in self and ideas.

5. *Motivation.* A task-focused orientation (drive or goal that leads a person to work on a task, as opposed to a goal-focused orientation (extrinsic motivators, rewards, or recognition which lead people to see a task as a means to an end), often exists in creatively gifted individuals. (See also Renzulli, 1978.)

6. *Environmental Context.* Environmental resources play into creativity as well. Implications for educators include providing surroundings that promote creativity, a reward system for creative ideas, and an evaluation of creative products by appropriate audiences. (See also Renzulli & Reis, 1985, 1997.)

Davis (1992) also provided a list of characteristics of individuals with high creative ability or potential, after reviewing many lists of personality characteristics compiled by researchers (see Table 2). Based on work conducted by Torrance (1962), Smith (1966), and Domino (1970), Davis also compiled a list of traits not uncommon in creative students which may be considered more "negative" (see Table 2). These traits may tend to upset the parents and educators, as well as some of the peers, of creative children, since they lead to behaviors not considered appropriate in traditional classrooms. A challenge exists for educators and parents to identify these characteristics of creativity in children and to channel creative energy into constructive outlets (Davis & Rimm, 1998) by encouraging playfulness, flexibility, and the production of wild and unusual ideas (Torrance, 1962).

In summary, creatively gifted and talented children may exhibit different characteristics than academically gifted children. Those with high academic abilities have the potential to develop creative gifts and talents, yet many creatively gifted students do not necessarily display high academic performance in school.

An Overview of the Enrichment Triad Model and Case Studies of Student Creative Productivity

The Enrichment Triad Model was designed to encourage creative productivity on the part of young people by exposing them to various topics, areas of interest, and fields of study, and to further train them to *apply* advanced content, process-training skills, and methodology training to self-selected areas of interest. Accordingly, three types of enrichment are included in the Enrichment Triad Model (See Figure 2).

Type I enrichment is designed to expose students to a wide variety of disciplines, topics, occupations, hobbies, persons, places, and events that would not ordinarily be covered in the regular curriculum. In schools using this model, an enrichment team of parents, teachers, and students often organizes and plans Type I experiences by contacting speakers, arranging minicourses, demonstrations, or performances, or by ordering and distributing films, slides, videotapes, or other print or nonprint media.

Type II enrichment includes materials and methods designed to promote the development of thinking and feeling processes. Some Type II enrichment is general, consisting of training in areas such as creative thinking and problem solving, learning "how-to-learn" skills such as classifying and analyzing data, and advanced reference and communication skills. Type II training is usually carried out both in classrooms and in enrichment programs and includes (1) the development of creative thinking and problem solving, critical thinking, and affective processes; (2) the learning of a wide variety of specific how-to-learn skills; (3) the development of skills in the appropriate use of advanced-level reference materials; and (4) the development of written, oral, and visual communication skills. Other Type II enrichment is specific, as it cannot be planned in advance and usually involves advanced instruction in an interest area selected by the student. For example, students who became interested in botany after Type I enrichment described above would pursue advanced training by doing advanced reading in botany; compiling, planning, and carrying out plant experiments; and through the exploration of even more advanced methods of training for those who want to go further.

Type III enrichment involves students who become interested in pursuing a self-selected area and are willing to commit the time necessary for advanced content acquisition and process training in which they assume the role of a firsthand inquirer. The goals of Type III enrichment include:

- providing opportunities for applying interests, knowledge, creative ideas, and task commitment to a self-selected problem or area of study;

- acquiring advanced level of understanding of the knowledge (content) and methodology (process) that are used within particular disciplines, artistic areas of expression, and interdisciplinary studies;

- developing authentic products that are primarily directed toward bringing about a desired impact upon a specified audience;

- developing self-directed learning skills in the areas of planning, organization, resource utilization, time management, decision making, and self-evaluation; and

Figure 5-2 *Enrichment Triad Model.*

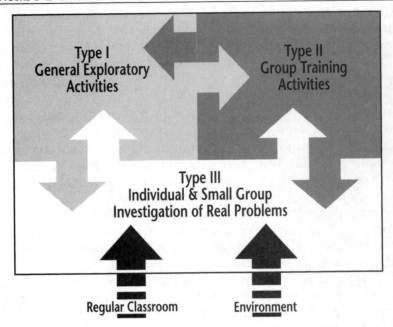

TABLE 5-2 *Positive and Negative Characteristics of Creative Individuals.*

Positive Characteristics

- aware of own creativeness
- independent
- energetic
- keen sense of humor
- artistic
- need for privacy, alone time

- original
- willing to take risks
- curious
- attracted to complexity and novelty
- open-minded
- perceptive

Negative Characteristics

- questioning of rules and authority
- stubbornness
- low interest in details
- forgetfulness
- carelessness and disorganization with unimportant matters

- indifference to common conventions
- rebelliousness
- tendency to be emotional
- absentmindedness

(Davis, 1992)

- developing task commitment, self-confidence, and feelings of creative accomplishment.

Two case study examples of Type III enrichment completed by students are provided in Figures 3 and 4. The first Type III example was completed independently and the second was a group project. The first, a book, was written by a fifth-grade student named Gretchen Anderson who had two major interests: the literature of Louisa May Alcott and cooking. Gretchen read all of Louisa May Alcott's books and identified each time a specific food was mentioned. She researched the recipes of the time that would have been used to make the food (such as buckwheat cakes), field-tested each recipe (including making substitutions for ingredients no longer available), and created an original cookbook entitled *The Louisa May Alcott Cookbook* (Anderson 1985), published by Little Brown. In this Type III example, both the process and the final product involved high levels of creative engagement and clear evidence of creative work.

A second example of a Type III activity involved the creation of a bicycle path in a city in the northwestern United States. The local high school students included a group of avid bikers as well as some students who just believed that automobiles should not own the road. The creative process of having the town council agree to the expenditure took this group of young people through a labyrinth of politics and legal issues, financial machinations, and, finally, a tough vote. The bike path was built and the creative process of political and civil action was a peak experience for these young people.

Research about Creative Productivity in Students

Research conducted by Torrance (1962, 1974) demonstrated that students who were rated highly on creativity measures do well in school and on achievement tests, but are often not selected for gifted programs because their scores are often below the cutoff for admission. Research (Reis, 1981) indicated that when a broader population of students (15–20% of the general population called the talent pool) were able to participate in Types I and II enrichment experiences, they completed Type III products that were as high quality as the products completed by traditionally "gifted" students (the top 3-5%). This research produced the concept of identifying a larger talent pool of students who receive regular enrichment experiences and the opportunity to "revolve into" Type III creative productive experiences.

We recommend that students be selected for participation in the talent pool on the basis of multiple criteria that include indices of creativity, because we believe that one of the major purposes of gifted education is the development of creative thinking and creative productivity in all students. Once identified and placed in the talent pool through the use of test scores; teacher, parent, or self-nomination; or examples of creative potential or productivity, students are observed in classrooms and enrichment experiences for signs of advanced interests, creativity, or task commitment. We call this part of the process "action information" and have found it to be an instrumental part of the identification process in assessing students' interest and motivation to become involved in Type III creative productivity. Further support for this approach has recently been offered by Kirschenbaum (1983) and Kirschenbaum and Siegle (1993) who demonstrated that students who test high on measures of creativity tend to do well in school and on measures of achievement. The process of identifying students for a talent pool eventually led to the practical plan for implementation of the Enrichment Triad in schools: the Schoolwide Enrichment Model.

Delcourt (1988) and Starko (1986) also investigated student creative productivity. Delcourt (1988) investigated characteristics related to creative/productive Type III products both within or outside of school. Selection of students for this study was based upon the quantity and quality of their projects; therefore, giftedness was viewed as being manifested in performances and focused upon the dynamic nature of gifted behavior (Renzulli, 1986). The sample consisted of 18 students in grades 9 through 12 from 4 sites in the Northeast. All sites were located in typical high schools that had Triad programs. A qualitative analysis of

FIGURE 5-3 *Case Study Example of a Type III Enrichment Project Completed Independently by a Fifth-Grade Student.*

The Louisa May Alcott Cookbook

by Gretchen Anderson, Grade 5
Haynes School, Sudbury, Massachusetts

Description of Type III Activity

Gretchen spent a year-and-a-half working on a cookbook that combined vignettes of scenes from *Little Women* and *Little Men* with many authentic nineteenth century recipes for making the foods described in the novels. Cooking was Gretchen's hobby and she became fascinated with the foods mentioned in the novels and learned how to recreate them. Because Gretchen believed that other youngsters would also be interested in these foods, she sent her book to Little Brown & Company. *The Louisa May Alcott Cookbook* was accepted and became the first book contracted by them with a child author.

Teacher's Role and Comments

Gretchen's teacher, Elizabeth D. Beloff, reported that Gretchen's enthusiasm for reading the books and researching the recipes could not sustain her through the writing of each scene and the incredible attention to detail necessary in creating the recipes.

Therefore, Ms. Beloff needed to complete the following steps to help Gretchen complete her project.

1. Vary the assignments
   (e.g., text writing/research/recipe writing).
2. Assign tasks that could be completed in one or two sessions.
3. Break large segments into small parts.
4. Use a system to record accomplishments
   (e.g., weekly or daily check sheet).

Gretchen's teacher also indicated that Gretchen was always able to envision the book but had a problem getting organized. She was able to help her by suggesting ways of organizing information. Particularly useful was a file box to keep recipes and notecards that recorded steps to be taken.

FIGURE 5-4 *Bike Path Project Undertaken by Students in Tigard, Oregon.*

$200,000 Bike Path System

by Sean Sweeney, Brenda Roos, Kim VanDell, Brian Mohr, Gary Gibb, Kevin Hatch, Allison Duchow, Jill Havens, Chris Soberg (Grades 8 and 9)

Fowler Junior High School, Tigard, Oregon

Description and Chronology of Type III Activity

BIKE PATH PROJECT: TIME LINE, OCTOBER 1980 TO JULY 1981

OCTOBER 1980

☐ Arrive at project idea.

☐ Visits from Raeldon Barker, City Administrator in Tigard and Frank Curry, Tigard Public Works Director.

☐ Write to Eugene, Oregon for their master plan—which was then studied.

☐ Write to Beaverton, Oregon for their master plan—which was then studied.

☐ Visit from Washington County Bikeway Planner.

☐ Visit from member of Tigard Park Board.

NOVEMBER 1980

☐ Discovered Tigard's 1974 "Comprehensive Plan for Bicycle/ Pedestrian Pathways."

☐ One part of group focused in on Tiedeman Road, an extremely dangerous street adjoining the junior high school.

☐ The other part of the group decided to revise Tigard's 1974 plan and check community opinion about bike path needs.

DECEMBER 1980

☐ Development of community survey.

☐ Measuring and photographing of Tiedeman Road.

☐ Testing and revising of survey.

☐ Distribution of surveys (about 2,500).

JANUARY 1981

☐ Tallying and analysis of surveys.

☐ Preparation of presentation for Tigard Park Board.

☐ Presentation of findings to Tigard Park Board.

FIGURE 5-4 *Bike Path Project (continued).*

FEBRUARY 1981
- ☐ Development of a three-phase plan for bike paths.
- ☐ First presentation to Tigard City Council (February 17).
- ☐ Presentation to Tigard Rotary.

MARCH 1981
- ☐ Revision of phased plan.
- ☐ Presentations to City Council.
- ☐ Presentation to Tigard Lions Club.
- ☐ Discussion of plan with individual City Council members.

APRIL 1981
- ☐ City Council agrees to place $200,000 serial level on May 19th ballot.
- ☐ Writing of measure and filing with County Elections Department (we thought!).
- ☐ Presentations to parent groups at Fowler, Charles F. Tigard Elementary, and Tigard High School.
- ☐ Preparation of flyer.

MAY 1981
- ☐ Bike-A-Rama at Fowler (May 16th) with prize giveaway and 5-mile-ride on proposed streets.
- ☐ Mapping, producing and posting of lawn signs around Tigard.
- ☐ Printing and door-to-door distribution of flyer (about 6,000).
- ☐ May 19th—ELECTION DAY—
  OUR MEASURE IS NOT ON THE BALLOT!
- ☐ The county conducts an investigation. Findings—no one is at fault, all should share blame for lack of communication.
- ☐ The state conducts an investigation. Their findings to come out in June.
- ☐ In an emergency session May 22nd, Tigard City Council approves placing our measure on the ballot June 30th.
- ☐ We file the measure again in Hillsboro on May 26th.
- ☐ Channel 2 television news station does a story on our project.
- ☐ Down come the lawn signs.

FIGURE 5-4 *Bike Path Project (continued).*

JUNE 1981

- [ ] The Secretary of State's report comes out, placing blame on the Washington County Elections Department (June 4th).
- [ ] Letter writing campaign to all the radio and TV stations in Portland to have public service announcements made.
- [ ] Redesigning of flyer.
- [ ] Printing, stuffing, mailing of new flyer (about 6,000).
- [ ] County elections responsibilities shifted to county administrator (June 9th).
- [ ] Lawn signs repainted and up again.
- [ ] UH-OH! The state says our refiled ballot measure may be invalid because of the ballot's wording (June 18th).
- [ ] At another emergency City Council meeting (June 19th), one sentence is added to our measure to satisfy state requirements.
- [ ] The County Election Coordinator is suspended for two weeks without pay.
- [ ] Channel 8 television news station does a feature on our project.
- [ ] JUNE 30TH—ELECTION DAY. OUR MEASURE IS ON THE BALLOT.

JULY 1981

- [ ] Voter turnout is light, but our measure passes by more than a 2/3 margin.
- [ ] Channel 8 does a follow-up story on our project.
- [ ] Down come the lawn signs. Summer vacation begins.

student interviews, questionnaires, and documents was conducted. Responses from the following question were analyzed: "Having developed several products, how do you think your ability to work on these projects has changed over time?" These responses were separated into the following groups: (a) changes related to improvements in products, or changes related to the skills necessary for product completion (e.g., writing, research methodology), (b) changes in personal characteristics (e.g., patience, self-satisfaction), and (c) changes related to career choices. Results concerning the family, the school, and the individual revealed the following: (1) targeted students do exhibit characteristics similar to those of creative/productive adults; (2) these students can be producers of information as well as consumers; and (3) the learning processes of these students merit closer attention if their abilities are to be better understood by themselves, their parents, and their teachers.

Delcourt (1994) later initiated a longitudinal study in which the same subjects were sent a questionnaire focusing on their interests, educational and professional experiences, career plans, and projects. Results indicated that students maintained similar or identical career goals to their plans in high school and remained in their major fields of study in colleges. College students reported satisfaction completing projects related to their courses or professions since these assignments coincided with their interests and goals. This congruence apparently made their investigations easier to complete. By contrast, 3 years prior to the study they reported little or no relation between personally initiated and assigned high school projects. Some of these young adults were not particularly concerned with high levels of attainment in their careers but rather with good relationships with friends and family. Overall, the young adults who participated in the follow-up study reported being satisfied with their academic and professional choices. Perceptions of their professional success will be sought in a continuation of this longitudinal study. Based upon each student's level of involvement with his or her investigations and the quality of the projects, Delcourt's study supports the concept that adolescents and young adults can be producers of information.

Starko (1986) also examined the effects of the Triad Enrichment Model on student creative productivity. Students who participated in Schoolwide Enrichment Model (SEM) programs for at least four years were compared with students who qualified for such programs but received no services. Questionnaires were used to determine the number of creative products produced by both groups, within school programs and within independent activities outside of school. Information about attitudes and skills associated with creative productivity was also gathered through the questionnaire. Data were analyzed by hierarchical multiple regression, as well as by qualitative analysis of open-ended questionnaire items. Results indicated that students who became involved in independent study projects in the SEM more often initiated their own creative products both *in and outside of school* than did students in the comparison group. A total of 103 students, 58 program students and 45 nonprogram students of similar ability, participated in the study. The group in the enrichment program reported more than twice as many creative projects per student (3.37) as the comparison group (1.4). The group that participated in the enrichment program also reported doing more than twice as many creative products outside of school on their own time (1.03) than the comparison group (.50). Additionally, students who had participated in the enrichment program showed greater diversity in projects and more sophistication in both the creative products attempted and in their description of goals. One student was not just "painting" but "painting and working on a catalogue of my paintings;" others did not simply read about animals but "observed the habits of wild animals and recorded my observations." Other examples from the enrichment group included students who composed music, wrote novels in various genres (romance, mystery, etc.), created a launching system for model rockets, and designed and built model houses and furniture.

In an examination of students who participated in an Enrichment Triad program for almost a decade, Hébert (1993) found several benefits of program involvement. Nine senior high school students from the program underwent extensive interviews concerning their educational experiences 10 years after their involvement in the program. The students selected for the study were chosen because of the number and quality of the Type III products they completed during their elementary Talented and Gifted (TAG) program experience. The interviews with the students about their Type III experiences were transcribed and analyzed for themes. Four major findings from the study provide insightful information for educators who implement programs for high ability students. The findings were: (1) Type III interests of students affect postsecondary plans, (2) creative outlets are needed in high school, (3) a decrease in creative Type III productivity occurs during the junior high experience, and (4) the Type III process serves as important training for later productivity.

The Schoolwide Enrichment Model

The Enrichment Triad Model serves as the theoretical basis for an organizational plan known as the Schoolwide Enrichment Model (SEM), that is used as the basis for many gifted programs, enrichment programs, magnet and charter schools, and theme schools (Renzulli & Reis 1994). In the Schoolwide Enrichment Model, a talent pool of 15%-20% of above average ability/high potential students is identified through a variety of measures including: achievement tests, teacher nominations, and assessment of potential for creativity and task commitment, in addition to alternative pathways of entrance (self-nomination, parent nomination, and such). High achievement test and IQ test scores automatically include a student in the talent pool, enabling those students who are underachieving in their academic schoolwork to be included.

Once students are identified for the talent pool, they are eligible for several kinds of services. First, interest and learning style assessments are used with talent pool students. Informal and formal methods are used to create or identify students' interests and to encourage students to further develop and pursue these interests in various ways. Learning style preferences that are assessed include: projects, independent study, teaching games, simulations, peer teaching, programmed instruction, lecture, drill and recitation, and discussion. Second, curriculum compacting is provided to all eligible students for whom the regular curriculum is modified by eliminating portions of previously mastered content. This elimination or streamlining of curriculum enables above average students to avoid repetition of previously mastered work and guarantees mastery while simultaneously finding time for more appropriately challenging activities (Reis, Burns, & Renzulli, 1992; Renzulli, Smith, & Reis, 1982). A form, entitled the Compactor, (Renzulli & Smith, 1978) is used to document which content areas have been compacted and what alternative work has been substituted. Third, the three types of enrichment experiences in the Enrichment Triad Model, Types I, II, and III Enrichment, are offered to all students; however, Type III enrichment is usually more appropriate for students with higher levels of ability, interest, and task commitment. A new method of providing enrichment through the Enrichment Triad Model, Enrichment Clusters, has also been developed and is discussed as follows.

Newest Directions for the Enrichment Triad Model

Current school reform initiatives have resulted in heightened awareness on the part of administrators and policymakers about the expanded role of enrichment specialists and how enrichment programs can encourage creativity in students. These programs have been the true laboratories of our nation's schools, because they have presented ideal opportunities for testing new ideas and experimenting with potential, creative solutions to long-standing educational problems. Programs for high potential students have been an especially fertile place for creative experimentation because prescribed curriculum guides or traditional methods of instruction do not usually govern such programs. Other developments that had their origins in special programs are currently being examined for general practice. These developments include: a focus on concept rather than skill learning; the use of interdisciplinary curriculum and theme-based studies, student portfolios, performance assessment, cross-grade grouping, and alternative scheduling patterns; and, perhaps most importantly, opportunities for students to exchange traditional roles as lesson-learners and doers-of-exercises for more challenging and creative roles that require hands-on learning, firsthand investigations, and the *application* of knowledge and thinking skills to complex problems.

The present reform initiatives in general education have created a more receptive atmosphere for more flexible approaches that challenge all students, and accordingly, the Schoolwide Enrichment Model has expanded and is currently being used as the basis for schoolwide improvement for all students. A book that describes how this occurs is *Schools for Talent Development: A Practical Plan for Total School Improvement* (Renzulli, 1994). A key component of this approach has been the application of the Enrichment Triad Model for all students in regularly scheduled opportunities called Enrichment Clusters.

Enrichment Clusters

Enrichment clusters are nongraded groups of students who share common interests, and who come together during specially designated times to pursue these interests. Like extracurricular activities and programs such as 4-H and Junior Achievement, the main rationale for participation in one or more clusters is that *students and teachers want to be there.* All teachers (including music, art, physical education, and such) are involved in teaching the clusters. Their involvement in any particular cluster is based on the same type of interest assessment that is used for students in selecting clusters of choice. Community resource persons should also be invited to organize enrichment clusters. The model for learning used with enrichment clusters is based on an inductive approach to the pursuit of real-world problems rather than traditional, didactic modes of teaching. This approach, referred to as enrichment learning and teaching, is designed to create a learning environment that places a premium on the development of higher order thinking skills and the authentic application of these skills in creative and productive situations. The theory underlying this approach is based on the work of constructivist theorists such as Jean Piaget, Jerome Bruner, and John Dewey, and applications of constructivist theory to classroom practice. Enrichment clusters are excellent vehicles for promoting cooperativeness within the context of real-world problem solving, and they also provide superlative opportunities for promoting self-concept. A major assumption underlying the use of enrichment clusters is that *every child is special if we create conditions in which that child can be a specialist within a specialty group.*

Enrichment clusters are organized around major disciplines, interdisciplinary themes, or cross-disciplinary topics (e.g., an electronic music group or a theatrical/television production group that includes actors, writers, technical specialists, costume designers, and such). The clusters are modeled after the ways in which knowledge utilization, thinking skills, and interpersonal relations take place in the real world. Thus, all work is directed toward the production of a product or service.

Enrichment clusters are not intended to be the total program for talent development in a school, but are instead a major vehicle for stimulating interests and developing creative potential across the entire school population. They are also vehicles for staff development in that they provide teachers an opportunity to participate in enrichment teaching, and subsequently to analyze and compare this type of teaching with traditional methods of instruction. In this regard, the model promotes a spill-over effect by encouraging teachers to become better talent scouts and talent developers, and to apply enrichment techniques to regular classroom situations. Enrichment clusters are used by some schools on a one-half a day per week basis and in other schools they meet each day. At the Webster Elementary School in St. Paul, Minnesota, for example, a broad array of interdisciplinary clusters are offered daily. At the Southeast School in Mansfield, Connecticut, enrichment clusters are offered two afternoons a month, and are taught jointly by teachers and parent volunteers. An example cluster is called "Flight School," and has been organized by the superintendent of schools who is a licensed pilot.

The Benefits of Enrichment Opportunities

The best way to summarize the opportunities provided through the Enrichment Triad Model is by the following four principles:

1. Each learner is unique, and therefore, all learning experiences must be examined in ways that take into account the abilities, interests, creative potentials, and learning styles of the individual.

2. Learning is more effective when students enjoy what they are doing; therefore, learning experiences should be constructed and assessed with as much concern for enjoyment as for other goals.

3. Learning is more meaningful and enjoyable when content (i.e., knowledge) and process (i.e., thinking skills, methods of inquiry) are learned within the context of a real and present problem; therefore, attention should be given to opportunities to personalize student choice in problem selection, the relevance of the problem for individual students at the time the problem is being addressed, and authentic strategies for addressing the problem.

Some formal instruction may be used in enrichment learning and teaching, but a major goal of this approach to learning is to enhance knowledge and thinking skill acquisition gained through formal instruction with applications of knowledge and skills that result from students' own construction of meaning.

The ultimate goal of learning that is guided by these principles and by the Enrichment Triad Model is to replace dependent and passive learning with independence, opportunity for creative productivity, pursuit of individual interest and engaged learning. We hope that as schools adopt this model, they can be transformed into places for talent development through creative learning opportunities.

References

Anderson, G. (1985). *The Louisa May Alcott cookbook*. Boston: Little Brown & Co.

Burns, D. E. (1992). *SEM network directory*. The Talent Development Program, The University of Connecticut, Storrs.

Cronbach, L. J., & Snow, R. E. (1977). *Aptitudes and instructional methods*. New York: Irvington.

Davis, G. A. (1992). *Creativity is forever* (3rd ed.). Dubuque, IA: Kendall/ Hunt Publishing Company.

Davis, G. A., & Rimm, S. B. (1998). *Education of the gifted and talented* (4th ed.). Boston: Allyn and Bacon.

Delcourt, M. A. B. (1988). *Characteristics related to high levels of creative/ productive behavior in secondary school students: A multi-case study*. Unpublished doctoral dissertation, University of Connecticut, Storrs.

Delcourt, M. A. B. (1994). Characteristics of high level creative productivity: A longitudinal study of students identified by Renzulli's three-ring conception of giftedness. In R. F. Subotnik & K. D. Arnold (Eds.), *Beyond Terman* (pp. 401–436). Norwood, NJ: Ablex.

Domino, G. (1970). Identification of potentially creative persons from the Adjective Checklist. *Journal of Consulting and Clinical Psychology, 35*, 48–91.

Gardner, H. (1983). *Frames of mind*. New York: Basic Books.

Gardner, H. (1993). *Frames of mind: The theory of multiple intelligences* (10th anniversary ed.). New York: Basic Books.

Hébert, T. P. (1993). A developmental examination of young creative producers. *Roeper Review: A Journal on Gifted Education, 16*, 22–28.

Jones, H. E., & Bayley, N. (1941). The Berkeley Growth Study. *Child Development, 12*, 167–173.

Kirschenbaum, R. J. (1983). Let's cut out the cut-off score in the identification of the gifted. *Roeper Review: A Journal on Gifted Education, 5*, 6–10.

Kirschenbaum, R. J., & Siegle, D. (1993, April). *Predicting creative performance in an enrichment program*. Paper presented at the Association for the Education of Gifted Underachieving Students Sixth Annual Conference, Portland, OR.

MacKinnon, D. W. (1978). *In search of human effectiveness.* Buffalo, NY: Creative Education Foundation.

Moffitt, T. E., Caspi, A., Harkness, A. R., & Silva, P. A. (1993). The natural history of change in intellectual performance: Who changes: How much: Is it meaningful? *Journal of Child Psychology and Psychiatry, 34,* 152–156.

Neisser, U. (1979). The concept of intelligence. In R. J. Sternberg & D. K. Detterman (Eds.). *Human intelligence* (pp. 179–189). Norwood, NJ: Ablex.

Reis, S. M. (1981). *An analysis of the productivity of gifted students participating in programs using the revolving door identification model.* Unpublished doctoral dissertation, The University of Connecticut, Storrs.

Reis, S. M., Burns, D. E., & Renzulli, J. S. (1992). *Curriculum compacting: The complete guide to modifying the regular curriculum for high ability students.* Mansfield Center, CT: Creative Learning Press.

Renzulli, J. S. (1976). The enrichment triad model: A guide for developing defensible programs for the gifted and talented. *Gifted Child Quarterly, 20,* 303–326.

Renzulli, J. S. (1977). *The enrichment triad model: A guide for developing defensible programs for the gifted and talented.* Mansfield Center, CT: Creative Learning Press.

Renzulli, J. S. (1978). What makes giftedness? Re-examining a definition. *Phi Delta Kappa 60,* 180–184.

Renzulli, J. S. (1982). What makes a problem real: Stalking the elusive meaning of qualitative differences in gifted education. *Gifted Child Quarterly, 26,* 147–156.

Renzulli, J. S. (1986). The three ring conception of giftedness: A developmental model for creative productivity. In R. J. Sternberg & J. E. Davidson (Eds.), *Conceptions of giftedness* (pp. 53–92). New York: Cambridge University Press.

Renzulli, J. S. (1994). *Schools for talent development: A practical plan for total school improvement.* Mansfield Center, CT: Creative Learning Press.

Renzulli, J. S., & Reis, S. M. (1985). *The schoolwide enrichment model: A comprehensive plan for educational excellence.* Mansfield Center, CT: Creative Learning Press.

Renzulli, J. S., & Reis, S. M. (1994). Research related to the Schoolwide Enrichment Model. *Gifted Child Quarterly, 38,* 2–14.

Renzulli, J. S., & Reis, S. M. (1997). *The schoolwide enrichment model: A how-to guide for educational excellence* (2nd ed.). Mansfield Center, CT: Creative Learning Press.

Renzulli, J. S., & Smith, L. H. (1978). *The compactor.* Mansfield Center, CT: Creative Learning Press.

Renzulli, J. S., Smith, L. H., & Reis, S. M. (1982). Curriculum compacting: An essential strategy for working with gifted students. *The Elementary School Journal, 82,* 185–194.

Smith, J. M. (1966). *Setting conditions for creative teaching in the elementary school.* Boston: Allyn and Bacon.

Starko, A. J. (1986). *The effects of the revolving door identification model on creative productivity and self-efficacy.* Unpublished doctoral dissertation, The University of Connecticut, Storrs.

Sternberg, R. J. (1984). Toward a triarchic theory of human intelligence. *Behavioral and Brain Sciences, 7,* 269–316.

Sternberg, R. J., & Davidson, J. E. (1986). *Conceptions of giftedness.* New York: Cambridge University Press.

Sternberg, R. J., & Lubart, T. I. (1993). Creative giftedness: A multivariate investment approach. *Gifted Child Quarterly, 37,* 7–15.

Torrance, E. P. (1962). *Guiding creative talent.* Englewood Cliffs, NJ: Prentice-Hall.

Torrance, E. P. (1974). *Norms-Technical manual: Torrance tests of creative thinking.* Bensenville, IL: Scholastic Testing Service.

Chapter 6

Creative Adaptation to Life Adversity: Deriving Meaning from the Past and Expectations for the Future

Peter A. Wyman and Emma L. Forbes-Jones

Although scholars in many disciplines have studied creativity across a range of human activities, researchers of risk and resilience have not often focused on ways in which individuals use creative thinking in adapting to adverse life conditions. In this chapter we focus on creative thinking in two spheres: (1) among at-risk adolescents, examining relationships between their expectations and their development; and (2) among parents of at-risk children as a mechanism of adaptation to the task of parenting.

This chapter reports on two studies of creative thinking that were conducted among a racially diverse group of youth and parents. Our investigations centered on how individuals use cognitions to construct and modify internal working models in ways that promote positive adaptation. The participants were selected from an ongoing longitudinal study within the Rochester Child Resilience Project (RCRP), a 12-year investigation of risk and protective factors among families and children exposed to multiple, chronic adversities such as poverty, family separation, and violence. (For references to this research see Cowen, Work & Wyman, 1992; Parker, et al. 1990; Wyman et al., 1992; Wyman et al., 1999). In the sections to follow we first review the concept of resilience and several primary processes of resilience within development are outlined (Wyman et al. 2000). Concepts from *creative realism* (Finke, 1995) are considered; this theory focuses on the application of creative ideas to enhance life conditions and well-being. Hypotheses and findings from the two studies of adaptation are presented along with considerations about how interventions might use knowledge of *creative cognition* to enhance children's development.

The first study presented in this chapter focused on a group of parents whose children were ages 7 to 9. The study examined ways in which they attributed positive meaning to their own negative childhood experiences of being parented in constructing useful models for parenting their own children. Understanding this process can enhance knowledge of how some parents develop parenting competence in the absence of their own positive caregiving experience, or even, in some cases, their exposure to maladaptive parenting. The second study focused on a group of 13- to 15-year-old youth. The study examined: (a) their expectations for the future (e.g., educational attainment, employment), and (b) the relationship between these expectations and school functioning, social adjustment, and problem behaviors of these youth. These relationships were examined within the cohort as a whole, and also within groups of youth demonstrating different functional patterns of adjustment. This approach is part of a larger effort to explore how children establish and maintain constructive goals under adverse conditions (Wyman et al., 1993).

Resilience and Adaptation

To conceptualize how creative thinking can enhance adaptation requires a framework for understanding the interaction of life adversities and development. Extensive research has investigated how individuals achieve adaptive functioning under challenging conditions. The roots of this research go back several decades (Cicchetti & Garmezy, 1993) and include studies that identify factors (e.g., family conflict, violence) that increase children's risk for maladjustment (Johnson, 1986; Rutter, 1983). Correspondingly, early investigators of children in poverty and children exposed to traumatic conditions such as war and natural disaster found that some showed highly competent development under conditions that affected most other children negatively (Elder, 1974; Epstein, 1979; Moskovitz, 1983; Pavenstedt, 1965).

Interest in understanding this seemingly paradoxical development catalyzed studies examining how children become competent in "unhealthy" environments (e.g., Cowen et al. 1990; Garmezy et al., 1984; Rutter et al., 1975; Sameroff et al., 1987; Werner & Smith, 1992; Wyman et al., 1991). These studies have focused primarily on identifying children's resources and aspects of their environments that antecede or co-occur with sound developmental outcomes under adversity (Masten & Coatsworth, 1998; Wyman et al., 1999). A more recent research focus has been on understanding factors that relate to children's recovery from maladjustment (Greenbaum & Auerbach, 1992; Quinton et al., 1993).

Early conceptualizations of resilience attributed positive adaptation to exceptional characteristics of individual children (Baldwin et al., 1993). However, subsequent research has shown that more complex formulations are needed. It is evident that characteristics associated with resilience occur both in children and across many different systems in the context of a child's life. These resources can be classified as:

- *Child-centered characteristics*, including typical affective style and cognitive and social competencies. For example, children's temperament qualities that favor positive, stable mood and adaptability have been shown to moderate the negative effects of stressors on children (Werner & Smith, 1982, 1992; Wyman et al., 1991). Among older children, intelligence and other child-based characteristics such as internal locus of control, positive problem-solving strategies, and positive expectations for the future are linked with positive adjustment in the presence of chronic life stressors (Cowen et al., 1992; Hoyt-Meyers et al., 1995;

Luthar, 1993; Masten et al., 1988; Parker et al., 1990; Werner & Smith, 1982; Wyman et al., 1993).

- *Relational and structural characteristics of families* and other intimate systems in which children develop. The protective effects of children's involvement in emotionally responsive relationships (with parents, extended family members, mentors) was an important finding in first generation studies of resilience (Baldwin et al., 1993; Egeland et al., 1993; Masten et al., 1990; Werner & Smith, 1982; Wyman et al., 1991, 1992, 1999). The extent to which families and other structured groups meet children's age-appropriate relational needs is central to how well children adjust to specific stressors, such as parental divorce, as well as to adjustment in the context of multiple stressors (Masten, 1994; Masten & Coatsworth, 1998).

- *Community and macrosystem resources.* These factors refer to the quality of educational institutions, and characteristics of neighborhoods, such as availability of positive models and mentors for children (Sampson et al., 1997; Werner & Smith, 1982).

A child's adaptation to adversities has been demonstrated to be impacted by characteristics of the child and the social environment. However, children rely on different resources to enhance adaptation, depending on their constellation of strengths, vulnerabilities, and developmental history. Cicchetti and Rogosch's (1997) vivid description of such differences stressed that different resources were associated with positive adaptation for at-risk children with or without histories of neglect or abuse. Whereas relationship resources figured prominently in resilience among children without neglect or abuse histories, for those with histories of abuse or neglect, positive adaptation was more likely to be associated with personal mastery and competence. It appears that children who had experienced neglect or abuse were not as likely to draw on relationships as a source of comfort, or as a vehicle for experiencing mastery in the context of adversity.

Findings that children use different self-righting capacities raise important questions for studies of resilience. First, what are the principal, different methods used by children and adults in achieving resilience? Which methods involve the creative use of cognition? Second, what processes alter individuals' experiences with adversities to promote well-being? Although primarily intended to describe the development of children, processes that promote resilience also apply to aspects of adaptation by adults.

Developmental Processes and Resilience

Wyman et al. (2000) proposed that children's personal and social resources promote self-righting capacities by: (a) protecting against, or moderating, the negative effects (cognitive, affective, physical) of adversities, and (b) promoting ongoing mastery of developmental tasks. Life adversities can threaten well-being and interfere with developmental tasks, thus altering the relationship between the individual and his or her environment. Both chronic adverse conditions (e.g., ongoing family conflict) and acute stressful events (e.g., exposure to violence) induce distress in children and others, initiating changes at the physiological, psychological, and social levels of functioning. Adversities can also undermine the necessary developmental "scaffolds" (e.g., safe, stimulating environments) that children (and adults) require for competent development (Masten & Coatsworth, 1998). However, when individuals have sufficient resources to meet such environmental challenges, they can be successful in adapting to these circumstances (Cicchetti & Rogosch, 1997).

Resources can protect against adversities in many ways. Children's cognitive competencies or characteristic coping strategies, for example, can influence how they experience or interpret adversities (e.g., the extent to which they feel responsible), and whether their distress escalates or is managed constructively. Parents and other adults can also serve protective functions by

- limiting children's exposure to the damaging aspects of stressful conditions,

- helping children to regulate their distress, and

- promoting children's understanding of adversities in ways that attenuate distress and fears.

Protective effects can also include cognitive changes in the internal representation of an adversity.

In addition to stress protection, children's resources, including their own competencies and interpersonal supports, play a crucial role in how ongoing developmental tasks are mastered. In early childhood, these tasks include physiological and affective regulation, and the development of attachment relationships (Masten & Coatsworth, 1998). In families where adversities have diminished or destroyed effective interpersonal relationships (through separation, dysfunction), the ability of the child to draw on constructive adult models in the broader social context can promote academic and social development. Developmental transitions are opportunities for children (and adults) to renegotiate their behavioral organization. Youth who form new intimate relationships in young adulthood, for example, can alter previous relationship patterns and, in addition, other areas of adjustment such as conduct can be positively affected (Pickles & Rutter, 1991; Quinton et al., 1993).

Creative Realism and Creativity in Adaptation

Creative realism (Finke, 1995; Finke, Ward & Smith, 1992) is concerned with the practical application of creative thinking. Creative realism focuses on how the integration of innovative ideas with real-world conditions can create concepts that have a novel, positive impact on an individual's well-being. A major tenet of this theory is that individuals use creativity in addressing many everyday life problems. For example, an individual may devise a new way to complete a tedious chore, resulting in saving time and resources, or discover new routes for travel to work, to make that task more efficient and enjoyable. Conversely, when individuals generate ideas that address realistic problems but lack creative inspiration they are unsatisfied and less likely to use practical ideas in effective ways.

One goal of creative realism is to describe processes and structures that underlie the effective synthesis of creative thinking and real-world conditions (Finke et al., 1992). Two concepts from this theory regard the qualities of ideas that effectively bridge creativity and realism. The first concept is *imaginative divergence,* which describes how ideas excite the imagination and foster exploration; that is, they diverge from an individual's conventional thinking in a way that stimulates further creativity. Effective creative ideas are also described by the concept *structural connectedness,* which refers to the integration of creative ideas with established concepts or with prior experience. The theory proposes that innovative ideas that can be applied to existing concepts or experiences, or which can build on them, are more likely to stimulate positive change and growth (Finke, 1995).

The concepts of imaginative divergence and structural connectedness provide parameters to gauge creative cognitions and how individuals apply and integrate these ideas when dealing with life adversities. For example, imaginative divergence of ideas may stimulate engagement in constructive problem solving. Structural connectedness of ideas, however, may be needed to anchor ideas to experiences or behavior. Without this connection to behavior or experience, creative ideas may not be effective in promoting adaptation.

Creativity and Resilience: Modifying Working Models

One way individuals can apply creative cognitions to promote resilience is through the process of constructing and modifying the *working models* that guide their interactions with the environment. The concept of working models has proven useful in conceptualizing how individuals distil and internalize experiences within the social and physical worlds (Bowlby, 1969). Conceptualized as a series of "if-then" propositions involving the self, and the self in relation to others, working models influence how individuals perceive and interpret events, develop plans, and forecast the future.

A core concept of working models is that they are *dynamic* mental structures that are modified over time (Bowlby, 1969, 1988). Bretherton (1991) suggested that working models can be modified by how individuals conceptualize their experiences, including how they challenge and evaluate these working models. Thus, working models are not passive products of experience (i.e., what "happens" to people); rather, working models can be shaped by how individuals interpret and reinterpret their experiences. These processes may be considered creative acts because they can involve innovations in thinking and conceptualizing.

Although usually associated with parent-child relationships, working models apply to a broad range of representations. In the studies that follow we examine aspects of parents' models of caregiving behavior and future expectations of youths. We will examine the imaginative divergence of these models, insofar as they depart from experience and appear to manifest the impact of creative thinking. In the study of youth expectations, the structural connectedness of models relates to how youth expectations are integrated with their behavioral competencies.

Study 1: Creativity and Working Models of Parenting

Background

Parents living in conditions of chronic stress face formidable challenges that include economic concerns and threats of violence. In addition, a disproportionately large number of parents who are poor report histories of childhood abuse and/or neglect (Belsky, 1980). Research with adults has demonstrated that how individuals cognitively and emotionally integrate earlier relationship experiences is related to their current social and emotional functioning, including their parenting behaviors (George, Kaplan, & Main, 1985; van Ijzendoorn & Bakersmans-Kranenburg, 1996). This research has also shown that some parents demonstrate emotionally responsive caregiving despite a wide range of prior relational experiences (e.g., Pearson, Cohn, Cowan, & Cowan, 1994). Thus, parents show considerable plasticity in how they develop the internal structures that organize caregiving behavior, which is consistent with the concept of internal working models as dynamic (Bowlby, 1969, 1988).

Less attention has been given to understanding how parents attribute meaning to their prior relationship experiences in forming models for parenting their own children. Parents can, for example, view their own relational experiences as confirmatory of parenting models. Conversely, parents can view prior experiences with their own parents as inadequate or negative exemplars, and use these experiences of unmet needs as a vehicle for constructing different models guiding interactions with their own children.

Goals and Hypotheses

Previously, Wyman et al. (1999) found that parents' (retrospective) views of the emotional quality (e.g., warmth, hostility) of their own childhood parenting experiences did not predict their 7- to 9-year-old children's quality of adaptation. Many parents in the sample reported histories of childhood neglect or abuse. However, parents' perceptions of *how* their childhood relationships had influenced their current parenting goals and behaviors did predict their children's quality of adjustment. Children whose parents reported that their relationship experiences had motivated them to be aware of, and attendant to, their children's emotional needs were demonstrating more positive adjustment (based on independent raters) than peers. This study focused on a subgroup of parents from the prior study (Wyman et al., 1999) who reported negative emotional quality in their own childhood relationships, and examined their creative thinking in the process of constructing effective working models for parenting their children.

A first study goal, preliminary to the primary study goal, was to examine relationships between parents' emotional quality of childhood caregiving (EQ-CC) and several indicators of their own current well-being. To test the theory that these internalized relational models influence self-perceptions and expectations (George et al., 1985), parents' perceptions of warm, responsive prior relationships were predicted to be related to positive mental health, self-esteem, and social support.

The second, primary study goal was to examine parents' attributions of meaning to negative childhood caregiving experiences, focusing on a subgroup of parents who reported poor EQ-CC (i.e., low warmth, high aggression-rejection). We hypothesized many parents in this subgroup would ascribe positive value to their adverse experiences in motivating them to be effective parents. We also identified salient features in the content of parents' narratives.

Study Sample

This study drew on a subset of a cohort of 7- to 9-year-old urban children and families (Wyman et al., 1999). The sample was racially diverse (55% African American, 27% white, 16% Latino, and 2% other race). This study focused on parents whose children were classified as either competent-resilient (n = 69) or maladjusted (n = 53), based on high exposure to stressors and concordance of adjustment ratings. Subjects were predominantly poor (i.e., approximately 50% reported prior year family income below $15,000), and reported high chronic exposure to life stressors (including economic problems, family turmoil, separation, death, and illness). Interviews were conducted with each child's designated "primary caregiver" (Wyman et al. 1999), 90% of whom were children's biological mothers. Nearly two-thirds of these primary caregivers were head of a single-parent household, and approximately 30% had never married.

Measures

Measures used in this study are described in Table 1. Two measures assessed parents' perceptions of (EQ-CC).

On the Parental Acceptance-Rejection Questionnaire (Rohner, Saavedra, & Granum, 1983), parents identified their own main caregiver when between the ages of 6 to 12, and then responded to items about that relationship (e.g., "Enjoyed having me around him/her;" "Hit me, even when I didn't deserve it."). An interview measure of EQ-CC (Wyman et al., 1991) was obtained. Because the two measures of EQ-CC were highly correlated, they were combined to form a total EQ-CC score, with higher scores reflecting more warmth and acceptance, and lower scores indicating rejection and hostility. This total score was intended to reflect internalized models of relationships with childhood caregivers, distinct from the literal history of that relationship (van Ijzendoorn & Bakersmans-Kranenburg, 1996).

Parents also completed an interview measure regarding perceptions of how their own childhood experiences of being parented had impacted how they raised their own children. Higher scores reflected perceptions of a positive impact, including perceptions of efficacy in achieving goals of positive parenting. Parents also completed standardized measures of mental health, self-esteem, and social support, and reported on their number of years of education.

Results

Emotional Quality of Childhood Caregiving: Prediction of Parents' Well-Being. A first set of analyses tested the hypothesis that perceived EQ-CC would be associated with parents' current well-being. Parents' EQ-CC scores were not correlated with education or corrected family income, and therefore the latter variables were not controlled for in subsequent analyses. As predicted, EQ-CC scores correlated positively and significantly with parent global mental health ($r = .31$, $p \leq .001$), self-esteem ($r = .37$, $p \leq .001$), and social support ($r = .45$, $p \leq .001$).

Parents' Perceived Impact of Childhood Caregiving on Parenting Practices. The overall relationship between EQ-CC and perceived impact on parenting was first examined and found to be modest ($r = .23$, $p < .01$). In other words, parents who reported more positive childhood caregiving experiences (more warmth-affection and less rejection-hostility) were more likely to report that those relationships had positively affected their own parenting of their children.

TABLE 6-1 *Study 1 Measures.*

MEASURE	REFERENCE	DESCRIPTION
EQ-CC (emotional qualtiy-childhood caregiving)		
Parental Acceptance-Rejection Questionnaire	Rohner, Saavedra, & Granum (1983)	Measures (a) warmth-affection, (b) neglect-indifference, and (c) aggression-hostility.
Interview measure	Wyman, Cowen, Work, & Parker (1991)	Provides a narrative in response to open-ended question.
PERCEIVED IMPACT ON PARENTING		
Interview measure	Wyman et al. (1991, 1999)	Measures parents' perceptions of impact of childhood experience on how they raise their own children. Open-ended question.
PARENT PSYCHOSOCIAL RESOURCES		
Global mental health	Berwick et al. (1991)	Measures frequency of dysphoric affect and anxiety in last year.
Self-esteem	Rosenberg (1965)	Measures global self-esteem
Social support	Wyman et al. (1991)	Measures access to and satisfaction with instrumental and emotional support.
No. of years of education		

The variability in perceived impact scores was examined for a subset of parents who reported negative EQ-CC (i.e., bottom 50% percentile). Approximately 20% of these parents reported significant emotional deprivation, physical abuse, or problems in childhood related to parental substance abuse. The distribution of scores on the interview measure of perceived impact (Wyman et al., 1991) for this subgroup is summarized in Table 2. The figure shows that 37.7% of parents in this low EQ-CC group reported that their childhood caregiving experiences had oriented them *positively* to be aware of their children's emotional needs and respond to those needs, and many believed they had achieved that objective.

Illustrative Parent Narratives. Examples of parents' narratives are useful in illustrating the variations in how parents constructed parenting goals. For example, some parents described limited success in surmounting their experiences. As a case in point, a mother of a 10-year-old girl described her childhood as follows:

> It wasn't good. I was an abused child, on the streets a lot. In a lot of homes. I didn't have a good relationship with anybody in my family. There's a saying. "Abused kids are abusing parents." I try to fight that a lot.

In response to questions regarding how her childhood experiences influenced her parenting of her daughter, she said,

> It did a lot. I try to do the opposite, but there's times I hear my mother in me. It scares me, like 'get the hair outta your eyes'. 'Look at you!' Nagging.

This mother's concerns about her parenting voice and its potential impact may have been warranted. Her daughter was evidencing multiple problems, including aggression with peers and signs of nascent depression.

Other parents described how they had derived meaning from their own hardships to promote constructive parenting goals. A father of a 9-year-old boy in the study well-illustrated this phenomenon.

TABLE 6-2 *Distribution of Scores on Perceived Impact of Childhood Caregiving on Parenting.* (Low Emotional Quality Subsample, n = 61)

Score	Characteristic Response	Frequency	Percent
-2	Repetition of maladaptive parenting	8	13.2
-1		12	19.7
0	Neutral impact, or equal negative and positive	18	29.4
+1		15	24.6
+2	Orientation to achieve nurturant parenting and efficacy in accomplishing that goal	8	13.1

> My mother and father separated. My father held me back in school. I had no regular hours of sleeping, dinner, other things. At times, I hate my father. He caused many problems I have today. It upsets me that I have a learning disability, self-esteem problems. It's hard for me to trust some people, relate to some people.

When asked how his own childhood experience had influenced how he was raising his son, this father said:

> First of all, I wanted him to have things I never had: be happy, have confidence. No matter how mad I get, always love him and show it. No matter what he wants to do to improve himself he can do.

This father had sole custody of his son, who had experienced inconsistent parenting in early childhood from his mother, who had substance abuse problems. Independent evidence (including teachers and the child's self report) suggested that this father's goals for his child were being realized. As a third grader, the boy was demonstrating sound social and scholastic adjustment.

The concepts from creative realism, presented earlier in this chapter, are useful in considering this father's narrative. First, the father's narrative demonstrated imaginative divergence; that is, construction of his goals for parenting and for his son diverged from his own experience and were inspiring to him. Thus, this father's narrative construction was creative. A second property of useful creative ideas is structural connectedness, which describes the value of creative ideas being linked to experience or prior structures. In fact, this father's narrative suggested that his parenting goals, while divergent and inspiring to him, were indeed connected to his prior experience. His own experience with lack of encouragement was useful to him in initiating encouragement with his child.

Summary: Creativity and Parent Working Models

This study investigated parents' constructions of meaning from their own primary childhood caregiving relationships. A specific focus in this study was on a subset of parents within this highly stressed cohort who reported high neglect and aggression and low warmth in their relationships with their own primary caregivers. Of considerable interest was the finding that many of these parents attributed positive value to their adverse relational experiences as motivating them to be effective parents. It is likely that deriving positive meaning from adversity and developing competent parenting behaviors are co-occurring processes.

In reporting on the next study, we turn to another form of internalized models, youths' future expectations, which can also be influenced by creative thinking.

Study 2. Youth Working Models: Resilience and Future Expectations

Background

Positive future expectations have been viewed as a potentially important feature of resilience among youth. In their pioneering study of resilient youth, Werner and Smith (1982) described a resilient child as one who "works well, loves well, and *expects* well" in the context of significant adversity. Their description implies that a child's positive expectations can help him or her to overcome the difficult odds that chronic adversity creates. However, the lack of systematic assessment or tracking of youths' future expectations in Werner & Smith's (1982, 1992) study restricted such conclusions.

Studies of hopelessness and optimism have demonstrated meaningful associations between these constructs and children's psychological well-being and physical health (Beck, Kovacs, & Weissman, 1975; Kazdin, Rodgers, & Colbus, 1986; Wetzel, Margulies, Davis, & Karam, 1980). However, studies of optimism and hopelessness have not focused on children's conceptualizations of their future lives, either globally or in specific role domains (e.g., education, employment), or on how children's future expectations change with maturation.

We propose that a child's positive future expectations, in the context of significant life adversity, can be understood as a creative use of cognition. Moreover, positive future expectations can be viewed as an exemplar of creative realism because these conceptualizations of self relate to youth positive adaptation. Although we have found a child's expectations for the future are linked to prior experiences (e.g., relationships with parents) (Wyman et al., 1993), those expectations also reflect children's constructions of models that draw on a child's cognitive capacities, such as in the use of abstract thinking.

Wyman et al. (1992, 1993) developed a measure assessing children's future expectations, in the context of the RCRP. The Children's Future Expectations measure assesses a child's expectations for

- the successful handling of problems,

- education,

- relationships,

- avoidance of legal trouble,

- overall happiness, and

- the likelihood of having interesting things to do.

The measure also includes an interview question (i.e., "What do you think your life will be like when you grow up?" followed by domain specific prompts, e.g., "Do you think you'll finish school?"), to assess children's active construction of future. The measure demonstrated adequate psychometric properties in a sample of 10- to 12-year-olds (Wyman et al., 1993).

Initial findings from research using the Children's Future Expectations measure were in line with a conceptual model outlining how expectations relate to children's adaptation to adversity (Wyman et al., 1992, 1993). Among a sample of 10- to 12-year-old, at-risk, urban youth, positive expectations were, as predicted, associated with children's affect regulation (i.e., lower anxiety), self-representations of competence, and behavioral and social adjustment in school (Wyman et al., 1993). Children with positive expectations also demonstrated higher scholastic achievement scores. Significantly, a 2.5 to 3 year follow-up evaluation found that children's early positive future expectations predicted sound social-emotional adjustment in school and a more internal locus of control at ages 12 to 14, above and beyond initial levels of those variables (Wyman et al. 1993). Children's future expectations at ages 10 to 12 did not predict their levels of behavior and learning problems at ages 12 to 14.

The preceding findings suggested that children's positive expectations can promote positive adaptation by providing them with constructive goals and supporting their engagement in age-appropriate, constructive tasks. The study to follow examined the role of future expectations in individual adaptation during adolescence, both for a group of at-risk adolescents as a whole, and for youth demonstrating different patterns of adaptation. The concept of structural connectedness from creative realism was used to develop hypotheses about differences in how expectations of the youth would serve adaptation.

Goals and Hypotheses

A first study goal was to examine how the future expectations among this group of 13- to 15-year-old highly stressed adolescents related to different domains of their adaptation. Based on our model proposing that positive future expectations promote engagement in constructive developmental tasks (Wyman et al., 1993), we hypothesized that more positive future expectations scores would predict

- greater competencies (i.e., school engagement, social competence), and

- fewer problem behaviors (i.e., delinquency behaviors, substance use).

A second study goal had two dimensions. The first was to identify groups of youth in the sample showing different patterns of adjustment. Based on prior studies of adolescent development (e.g., Cairns & Cairns, 1994), we expected to identify subgroups of youth characterized by

- peer popularity, coupled with relatively high problem behaviors (substance use, delinquency behaviors);

- poor social-emotional adjustment, coupled with low problem behaviors; and

- highly competent school and social adjustment, coupled with low levels of problem behaviors.

This second study goal is an example of a "pattern-based" approach (e.g., Seidman et al., 1998), useful for identifying distinct pathways in development (Cicchetti & Rogosch, 1997). Drawing on the concept of structural connectedness, we hypothesized that positive future expectations in these youth would have greater adaptive value if they were anchored with experience. Operationally, this viewpoint translated into the hypothesis that positive future expectations of youth would be more strongly linked to competencies (e.g., school engagement), and negatively to problems, for youth demonstrating adaptive adjustment patterns, in contrast to youth with maladaptive adjustment patterns. For youth demonstrating maladaptive adjustment patterns, highly positive expectations may not provide realistic goals for sustaining motivation and engagement in age-appropriate tasks. Instead, for maladapted youth, particularly those engaged in delinquency and other problem behaviors, positive expectations might reinforce bravado and risk taking, rather than sustaining motivation for constructive activities.

Study Sample

Of an original group of 199, 7- to 9-year-old children in the RCRP, 167 were followed-up as eighth or ninth graders (ages 13 to 15). The subject population was highly mobile and had dispersed extensively over the intervening 6-year period. One youth had died, and several others had left their homes and could not be located. Approximately two-thirds of the sample (n = 118) remained in their original urban school district (Rochester City Schools), while the remaining youth had relocated in approximately 50 different communities, several outside of New York State.

Measures

Youth and parents participated in a comprehensive assessment, including youth and parent interviews and the collection of school record data. This present study drew on a portion of the data collected. Table 3 summarizes the measures for this study.

The youth measures included future expectations and several measures of school behavior, social-emotional adjustment, and the current presence of problem behaviors. Parents reported on youth adjustment and delinquency behaviors. A teacher measure was used to assess youth competence and problem behaviors.

Results

Descriptive analyses were conducted first to summarize the current life conditions of the youth and families in order to place the main findings in a more accurate context. These descriptive analyses drew on several measures not described in Table 3.

Life Context of Sample. Nearly one-third of families reported total yearly incomes below $15,000. An additional 15%

TABLE 6-3 *Study 2 Measures.*

MEASURE	REFERENCE	DESCRIPTION
YOUTH		
Future expectations	Wyman, Cowen, Work, & Kerley (1993)	Modified from Childrens' Future Expectations
YRS (Youth rating Scale)	Hightower et al. (1987)	Self-report of youth (a) rule compliance, (b) school interest, (c) peer social skills, and (d) anxiety
Alcohol/Drug Use Scale	Wills, Vaccaro, & McNamara (1992)	Recent use of mind-altering substances.
Delinquent behaviors	Elliott, Huizinga, & Ageton (1985)	Measures (a) minor delinquency, (b) street delinquency, and (c) serious delinquency.
Global mental health	Berwick et al. (1991)	Frequency of dysphoric affect and anxiety.
PARENT		
P-YRS (Parent-Youth Rating Scale)	Hightower (1994)	Parent report of youth (a) acting out, (b) shyness-anxiety, (c) frustration tolerance, and (d) peer sociability.
Youth delinquency behaviors	Cowen et al. (1997)	Frequency of 8 behaviors used to diagnose conduct disorder.
TEACHER		
TCRS (Teacher Child Rating Scale)	Hightower et al. (1986)	Teacher report of youth (a) acting-out behavior, (b) shyness-anxiety, (c) learning problems, (d) frustration tolerance, (e) task orientation (f) peer social relationships, and (g) peer assertiveness.

reported incomes between $15,000 and $20,000. Parents reported high rates of serious adversities (e.g., close family member arrested or in jail; substance abuse problems) during the preceding 5 years. Fifty percent of study parents reported eight or more stressors (out of 32 possible). Many youth reported that they had been victims of violence, such as being robbed (31%), threatened with a weapon (21%), or shot or shot at (7%). Many also reported that family members had been victims of violence. Most striking was the fact that 24% of youth reported that a family member (including extended family) had been murdered. These data highlight the fact that participants in the RCRP sample continued to experience many, often profound, life adversities since originally evaluated at ages 7 to 9.

Future Expectations at Ages 13 to 15. Despite chronic exposure to ongoing adversity, most youth reported optimistic, positive expectations for the future. The item average on the measure of future expectations was 3.34 (out of a maximum of 4.0). Because future expectations of youth were not related to gender, family income, or parent education levels, those variables were not controlled for in subsequent analyses. Although we had not established hypotheses about differences among different ethnic groups, significant differences were in fact found. African American youth had significantly higher average future expectations than White youth. Average expectations for Latino youth were directionally higher than Whites, and lower than African Americans, but not significantly so.

Future Expectations and Youth Adjustment

Primary Adjustment Domains. Three domains of youth adjustment were identified in factor analyses with the study measures.

- *School Competence*, consisting of six subscales from the teacher-rated Teacher-Child Rating Scale (T-CRS) (high scores on Frustration Tolerance, Peer Sociability, Task Orientation, and Assertive Social Skills; and low scores on Acting Out and Learning Problems).

- *Social-Emotional Competence*, which included three youth self-ratings of mood and peer relations (lower Youth Rating Scale [YRS] Anxiety, higher YRS Peer Social, and higher Brief-Mental Health Inventory scores) and two parent ratings of youth adjustment (high Parent Youth Rating Scale [P-YRS] Peer Social, low P-YRS Shy-Anxious).

- *Problem Behaviors*, consisting of three youth ratings of behavior (higher substance use and delinquency behaviors, and lower YRS Rule Compliance), and three parent ratings of youth behavior (higher delinquency and P-YRS Acting-out scores, and lower P-YRS Frustration Tolerance).

For the full youth sample, future expectations of youth correlated positively with their *Social-Emotional Competence* ($r = .31$, $p < .001$) and *School Competence* ($r = .16$, $p < .05$) ratings, and negatively with *Problem Behaviors* ($r = -.30$, $p < .001$). The School Competence factor was based on ratings by classroom teachers, and the Problem Behaviors factor included both parent and youth ratings. Thus, youth ratings of future expectations related meaningfully to perspectives of independent raters, albeit only modestly in the case of teacher ratings.

Future Expectations and Patterns of Adjustment. Cluster analysis (based on *School Competence, Social-Emotional Competence,* and *Problem Behaviors)* was used to identify groups of youth demonstrating different patterns of adjustment (using youth scores on the three adjustment factors). Selection of an optimal cluster solution, using a k-means iterative clustering procedure, was based on convergent criteria (Rapkin & Luke, 1993), including

- minimal within-cluster correlations on profile variables (reflecting homogeneity of clusters), and

- replicability of the chosen cluster solution by repeating the iterative solution on two stratified random halves of the total sample.

Four adjustment clusters were identified. Figure 1 depicts each cluster group's average factor scores, relative to the total sample mean. Because of missing data, 152 of 167 youth could be classified. Cluster 1 youth demonstrated higher than average school and social-emotional competence, and few problem behaviors (*n* = 39). These youth were designated *Manifold Competent*. Cluster 2 youth (*n* = 49) had average school competence and somewhat above average levels of social-emotional competence and problem behaviors. These youth were labeled *Popular-Moderate Problem Behaviors* based on positive peer relationships and mood, coupled with moderately elevated levels of substance use, delinquent behaviors, and under controlled behaviors. Cluster 3 youth (*n* = 32), designated *Anxious-Withdrawn*, were characterized by average school competence, below average social-emotional competence (i.e., high anxiety-depression, fewer peer competencies), and few problem behaviors. Cluster 4 youth (*n* = 32) had low school and social-emotional competence and high problem behavior scores. The term *Manifold Problems* was used to describe these vulnerable youth. Cluster groups had comparable proportions of males and females, and of racial groups.

Differences in Future Expectations by Cluster Membership. Cluster groups differed significantly on average levels of future expectations, $F(3, 151) = 3.99$ ($p \leq .009$). *Manifold Competent* youth ($M = 38.97$) reported more positive future expectations than either the *Anxious-Withdrawn* ($M = 36.88$) or the *Manifold Problems* ($M = 34.91$) groups. The *Popular-Moderate Problem Behaviors* group did not differ in expectations from the other groups.

We next examined relationships among future expectations and adjustment domains separately for each cluster group. For these analyses we set a *p* value ≤ .10 (to reject the null hypothesis), because of relatively small numbers within each cluster. Table 4 summarizes future expectations-adjustment correlations, separately for the full sample and each cluster group. For the *Manifold Competent* group, expectations predicted fewer problem behaviors. For youth designated *Popular-Moderate Problem Behaviors*, expectations predicted positive social-emotional adjustment. For youth designated *Anxious-Withdrawn*, positive expectations pre-

FIGURE **6-1** *Youth Adjustment Clusters (ages 13–15).*

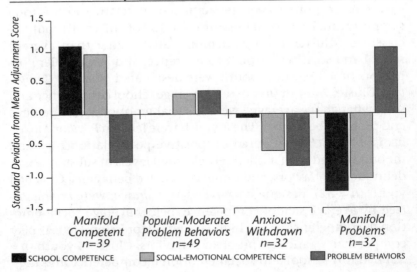

dicted few problem behaviors and better social-emotional adjustment. Conversely, for youth designated *Manifold Problems*, positive expectations were associated with less school competence, but not significantly with any other adjustment domain (although related directionally to better adjustment). Although these findings are limited by the small *n*s in each cluster group, they are of interest because they demonstrate differences in processes of adaptation among youth with different adjustment profiles.

Illustrative Youth Narratives

The structured future expectations measure used in this study did not incorporate youth narratives. However, these narratives are pertinent to the present study in two respects. First, they underscore how each youth's conception of future is an active construction, which reflects the interweaving of life experience with imaginative thinking applied to common themes (i.e., career,

TABLE 6-4 *Future Expectations—Adjustment Correlations for Total Sample and for Each Adjustment Cluster.*

VARIABLES	TOTAL SAMPLE	MANIFOLD COMPETENT	POPULAR-MODERATE PROBLEM BEHAVIORS	ANXIOUS-WITHDRAWN	MANIFOLD PROBLEMS
Future expectations & school competence	.16**	-.05	.16	-.15	-.34*
Future expectations & social emotional competence	.31***	.10	.28*	.34*	.29
Future expectations & problem behaviors	-.30***	-.28*	-.13	-.47***	-.27

$* p < .10; ** p < .05; *** p < .001$

family). Second, these narratives illustrate the variability in future conceptions among this group of adolescents in terms of optimism versus pessimism, realism versus wishfulness, and global versus differentiated goals.

Few youth expressed clear pessimism or forecast negative life outcomes. More common was difficulty in reporting a vivid future. In response to an initial question (i.e., "What do you think your life will be like when you get older?"), a 14-year-old boy answered, "I have no clue. Who could guess what could happen. I'm hoping I could get a job and have a family and stuff...I don't want to have more than four kids." This youth's narrative suggests a disavowal of expectations—not unexpected given how many of these youth's lives had been deeply and adversely affected by uncontrollable violent events. More common, however, were highly wishful future expectations. A 15-year-old girl's response to the same initial question: "I'm gonna be rich and happy. I'm gonna have a good job and lots of kids and a husband and a big house. And I'm gonna have a forest-green sports car."

Many other youth responses indicated significant prior thought, and consideration of steps required for accomplishing goals. A 14-year-old boy's answer to the question about what his future will be like when he gets older: "I think it will be good. I hope so. Yes. Umm, I want to be a lawyer and a judge. I'm hoping to make it that far, and if I don't, I want to be a teacher, because I know I can do that, because I've student-taught. I plan on being happy." The narrative from a 15-year-old girl also reflected prior thought, evidenced by her unremitting certainty. In response to the initial question, she said, "Good. I'm going to finish school and go to college." ("Will you find a job you want?") "Yes, in business management or in a recording studio." ("Will you be close to other people?") "Yeah, but I'm going to have just one kid." ("Do you think you'll be happy?") "Everyone's sad about something."

Summary: Creativity and Future Expectations

Findings from Study 2 are best viewed in light of the life conditions of this racially heterogeneous cohort of 13- to 15- year-olds. Most were poor when they entered the RCRP as 7- to 9-year-olds, and many continued to be poor. All were selected initially because of high exposure to life stressors in early childhood. Follow-up information showed that this high exposure to adversities was chronic. Most youth continued to experience high levels of family stressors, including parent separations and conflict, and exposure to violence outside the home.

The present findings on relations between future expectations and adjustment are both complex and provocative. For the group as a whole, positive expectations were associated with better adjustment, although only modestly when adjustment was based on teacher ratings of school competence. The *Manifold Competent* group reported the most positive expectations. *Manifold Problems* youth reported expectations similar to *Popular-Moderate Problem Behaviors* and *Anxious-Withdrawn* youth. However, positive expectations among youth with multiple problems may reflect a bravado or defensive denial of current problems and therefore may not be linked to positive adaptation processes, as would be suggested from the concept of structural connectedness. For youth with multiple problems, positive expectations predicted lower school competence. This finding underscores the value of considering differing pathways of risk and resilience.

Creative Adaptation: Future Directions

One goal of this chapter was to explore how children and parents use cognitions in the process of actively adapting to their environments. Studies of resilience have drawn on concepts such as "risk factors" and "protective factors," which imply stable structures, not dynamic processes. Those concepts (i.e., risk and protective factors) have not been easily translated into understanding how individuals actively draw on resources and engage with adversities in ways that can promote mastery and competence. Findings from this chapter suggest that youth's creative thinking about their future lives, and parents' creative conceptualizations about their past relationships, are linked in meaningful ways to their adaptations. Future research can help to clarify how creative adaptive processes are stimulated productively in some individuals, but not in others, and to what extent these cognitive processes are linked to actual behavioral changes.

Studies of resilience have underscored how developmental transitions can promote adaptive changes. Another goal for future research is to explore how developmental and life transitions can initiate creative thinking. The experience of becoming a parent may stimulate individuals to reexamine and reconstruct the models that underlie parenting behaviors. Likewise, developmental transitions in cognition, such as the emergence of formal operations, may promote new and creative thinking about the future as youth discover the capacity to use complex abstractions to enrich conceptualizations of their futures.

An array of interventions is currently available to enhance social and emotional competencies in children (Durlak, 1997). Many of these interventions are applied in the context of school classroom or small group settings and thus have the capacity to reach larger numbers of children than is possible within individual formats. Interventions such as these can gainfully explore how creative adaptive processes can be stimulated to promote useful ways of interpreting problems and of constructing goals. Interventions that can excite imaginative processes may be helpful in engaging individuals in processes of change. However, imaginative processes may not be useful unless they are integrated with experiences or with life conditions in ways that can stimulate effective actions. For example, the present findings suggest that interventions to promote positive future expectations in youths may be most useful if they facilitate realistic future expectations and goals.

Interventions that seek to enhance imaginative, realistic future expectations must also account for the great variability in youth conceptions of future. Garbarino (1999), for example, found that many severely traumatized or disordered youth have truncated or severely limited expectations for the future. For such youth, interventions would have to take into account the effects of complex developmental processes, resulting in impaired cognition or disinvestment in the concept of future.

One author of this chapter (EF-J) is currently developing and implementing a conflict resolution intervention in third grade classrooms of an urban elementary school. Although not yet fully evaluated, this intervention may have components that are promising for enhancing adaptive future expectations. The intervention includes activities intended to encourage children to think creatively about their futures. In small groups, children are asked to generate ideas about what they want to be when they grow up, and to write down and illustrate these choices on poster boards. Group facilitators assist the children in devising "steps" (e.g., "stay in school") to reach their goals. Children are then encouraged to break down steps into further smaller steps (e.g., "do my homework"; "stay out of fights"). Children create steps individually and as a group, the latter to facilitate group cohesion.

Later, group facilitators encourage children to identify obstacles to their steps (e.g., "You have a lot of homework and have to take care of your little brother"), and to identify solutions. The goal is to promote structural connectedness at a level appropriate to a child's developmental stage. Many of the children, when first asked to choose careers, will select "basketball player" or "movie star." Although the leaders are careful not to discourage or demean those goals, children are encouraged to consider other options as well (e.g., "most people have more than one thing they want to be"). Often, when children are encouraged to devise steps to attaining goals, their choices became less fantasy-oriented. Teachers of classrooms participating in this pilot intervention rate the program highly.

The youth and parents who have shared intimate knowledge of their lives with us have taught us much about coping and adaptation. From parents we have learned how creative approaches to understanding past adversities may be used to construct effective parenting goals. The children we have observed periodically from early elementary school into high school have demonstrated how positive expectations for the future are sustained despite ongoing exposure to adversity, including for many loss of family members to violence. Lucretius wrote that "nothing can be created from nothing." However, many of the parents and youth in our at-risk cohort have created something out of what may seem like very little, deriving valuable meaning from past deprivations and generating hope from despairing conditions.

References

Baldwin, A. L., Baldwin, C. P., Kasser, T., Zax, M., Sameroff, A., & Seifer, R. (1993). Contextual risk and resiliency during late adolescence. *Development and Psychopathology, 5,* 741–761.

Beck, A. T., Kovacs, M., & Weissman, A. (1975). Hopelessness and suicidal behavior: An overview. *Journal of the American Medical Association, 234,* 1146–1149.

Belsky, J. (1980). Child maltreatment: An ecological integration. *American Psychologist, 35,* 320–335.

Berwick, D. M., Murphy, J. M., Goldman, P. A., Ware, J. E., Barsky, A. J., & Weinstein, M. C. (1991). Performance of a five-item mental health screening test. *Medical Care, 29*, 169–176.

Bowlby, J. (1969). *Attachment and loss: Vol. 1. Attachment.* New York: Basic Books.

Bowlby, J. (1988). *A secure base: Parent-child attachment and healthy human development.* London: Routledge.

Bretherton, I. (1991). Pouring new wine into old bottles: The social self as internal working model. In M. Gunnar & L. A. Sroufe (Eds.), *Minnesota Symposium on Child Psychology: Vol. 26. Self processes in development* (pp. 1–41). Hillsdale, NJ: Erlbaum.

Cairns, R. B., & Cairns, B. D. (1994). *Lifelines and risks: Pathways of youth in our time.* Cambridge, MA: Cambridge University Press.

Cicchetti, D., & Garmezy, N. (1993). Milestones in the development of resilience. *Development and Psychopathology, 5*, 497–783.

Cicchetti, D., & Rogosch, F. A. (1997). The role of self-organization in the promotion of resilience in maltreated children. *Development and Psychopathology, 9*, 797–815.

Cowen, E. L., Work, W. C., & Wyman, P. A. (1992). Resilience among profoundly stressed urban children. In M. Kessler & S. E. Goldston (Eds.), *The present and future of prevention: In honor of George Albee* (pp. 155-168). San Francisco, CA: Sage Publications.

Cowen, E. L., Wyman, P. A., Work, W. C., Kim, J., Fagen, D. B., & Magnus, K. B. (1997). Follow-up study of young stress affected and stress resilient urban children. Development and Psychopathology 8, xxx–xxx.

Cowen, E. L., Wyman, P. A., Work, W. C., & Parker, G. R. (1990). The Rochester Child Resilience Project (RCRP): Overview and summary of first year findings. *Development and Psychopathology, 2*, 193–212.

Durlak, J. A. (1997). *Successful prevention programs for children and adolescents.* New York: Plenum.

Egeland, B., Carlson, E. A., & Sroufe, L. A. (1993). Resilience as process. *Development and Psychopathology, 5*, 517-528.

Elder, G. H., Jr. (1974). *Children of the Great Depression.* Chicago: University of Chicago Press.

Elliott, D. S., Huizinga, D., & Ageton, S. S. (1985). *Explaining delinquency and drug use.* Beverly Hills, CA: Sage.

Epstein, H. (1979). *Children of the Holocaust.* New York: Penguin Books.

Finke, R. A. (1995). Creative realism. In S. M. Smith, T. B. Ward, & R. A. Finke (Eds.), *The creative cognition approach* (pp. 303–326). Cambridge, MA: MIT Press.

Finke, R. A., Ward, T. B., & Smith, S. M. (1992). *Creative cognition: Theory, research, and applications.* Cambridge, MA: MIT Press.

Garbarino, J. (1999). *Lost boys: Why our sons turn violent and how we can save them.* New York: The Free Press.

Garmezy, N., Masten, A. S., & Tellegen, A. (1984). The study of stress and competence in children: A building block for developmental psychopathology. *Child Development, 55*, 97–111.

George, C., Kaplan, N., & Main, M. (1985). *Adult Attachment Interview.* Unpublished manuscript, University of California, Berkeley.

Greenbaum, C. W., & Auerbach, J. G. (1992). The conceptualization of risk, vulnerability, and resilience in psychological development. In C. W. Greenbaum & J. C. Auerbach (Eds.), *Longitudinal studies of children at psychological risk: Cross national perspective* (pp. 9-27). Norwood, NJ: Ablex Publishing Cooperation.

Hightower, A. D. (1994). Parent Child Rating Scale. Rochester, NY: Primary Mental Health Project.

Hightower, A. D., Cowen, E. L., Spinell, A. P., Lotyczewski, B. S., Guare, J., C., Rohrbeck, C. A., & Brown, L. P. (1987). The Child Rating Scale: The development and psychometric refinement of a socioemotional self-rating scale for young school children. *School Psychology Review, 16*, 239–255.

Hightower, A. D., Work, W. C., Cowen, E. L., Lotyczewski, B. S., Spinell, A. P., Guare, J. C., & Rohrbeck, C. A. (1986). The Teacher-Child Rating Scale: A brief objective measure of elementary children's school problem behaviors and competencies. *School Psychology Review, 15*, 393–409.

Hoyt-Meyers, L. A., Cowen, E. L., Work, W. C., Wyman, P. A., Magnus, K. B., Fagen, D. B., & Lotyczewski, B. S. (1995). Test correlates of resilient outcomes among highly stressed 2nd and 3rd grade urban children. *Journal of Community Psychology, 23*, 326–338.

Ijzendoorn van, M. H., & Bakersmans-Kranenburg, M. J. (1996). Attachment representations in mothers, fathers, adolescents, and clinical groups: A meta-analytic search for normative data. *Journal of Consulting and Clinical Psychology, 64,* 8–21.

Johnson, J. H. (1986). *Life events as stressors in childhood and adolescence.* Newbury Park, CA: Sage.

Kazdin, A. E., Rodgers, A., & Colbus, D. (1986). The Hopelessness Scale for Children: Psychometric characteristics and concurrent validity. *Journal of Consulting and Clinical Psychology, 54,* 241–245.

Luthar, S. S. (1993). Vulnerability and resilience: A study of high-risk adolescents. *Child Development, 62,* 600–616.

Masten, A. S. (1994). Resilience in individual development: Successful adaptation despite risk and adversity. In M. Wang & E. Gordon (Eds.), *Risk and resilience in inner-city America: Challenges and prospects* (pp. 3–25). Hillsdale, NJ: Erlbaum.

Masten, A. S., Best, K. M., & Garmezy, N. (1990). Resilience and development: Contributions from the study of children who overcome adversity. *Development and Psychopathology, 2,* 425–444.

Masten, A. S., & Coatsworth, J. D. (1998). The development of competence in favorable and unfavorable environments: Lessons from research on successful children. *American Psychologist, 53,* 205–220.

Masten, A. S., Garmezy, N., Tellegen, A., Pellegrini, D. S., Larkin, K., & Larsen, A. (1988). Competence and stress in school children: The moderating effects of individual and family qualities. *Journal of Child Psychology and Psychiatry, 29,* 745–764.

Moskovitz, S. (1983). *Love despite hate.* New York: Schocken Books.

Parker, G. R., Cowen, E. L., Work, W. C., & Wyman, P. A. (1990). Test correlates of stress resilience among urban school children. *Journal of Primary Prevention, 11,* 19–35.

Pavenstedt, E. (1965). A comparison of the childrearing environment of upper-lower and very low-lower class families. *American Journal of Orthopsychiatry, 35,* 89–98.

Pearson, J., Cohn, D. A., Cowan, P. A., & Cowan, C. P. (1994). Earned- and continuous-security in adult attachment: Relation to depressive symptomology and parenting style. *Development and Psychopathology, 6,* 359–373.

Pickles, A., & Rutter, M. (1991). Statistical and conceptual models of 'turning points' in developmental processes. In D. Magnusson, L.

Bergman, G. Rudinger, & B. Torestad (Eds.), *Problems and methods in longitudinal research: Stability and change* (pp. 131-165). Cambridge, MA: Cambridge University Press.

Quinton, D., Pickles, A., Maughan, B., & Rutter, M. (1993). Partners, peers, and pathways: Assortative pairing and continuities in conduct disorder. *Development and Psychopathology, 5,* 763-783.

Rohner, R. J., Saavedra, J. M., & Granum, E. O. (1983). *Parental Acceptance-Rejection Questionnaire: Test Manual.* Washington, DC: American Psychological Association, Journal Supplement Abstract Service.

Rosenberg, M. (1965). *Society and adolescent self-image.* Princeton, NJ: Princeton University Press.

Rutter, M. (1983). Stress, coping, and development: Some issues and some questions. In N. Garmezy & M. Rutter (Eds.), *Stress, coping and development in children* (pp. 1-41). New York: McGraw-Hill.

Rutter, M., Yule, B., Quinton, D., Rowlands, O., Yule, W., & Berger, M. (1975). Attainment and adjustment in two geographical areas: III. Some factors accounting for area differences. *British Journal of Psychiatry, 126,* 520-533.

Sameroff, A. J., Seifer, R., Zax, M., & Barocas, R. (1987). Early indicators of developmental risk: The Rochester Longitudinal Study. *Schizophrenia Bulletin, 13,* 383-394.

Sampson, R. J., Raudenbush, S. W., & Earls, F. (1997). Neighborhoods and violent crime: A multilevel study of collective efficacy. *Science, 277,* 918-924.

Seidman, E., Chesir-Teran, D., Freidman, J. L., Yoshikawa, H., Allen, L., Roberts, A., & Aber, J. L. (1999). The risk and protective functions of perceived family and peer microsystems among urban adolescents in poverty. *American Journal of Community Psychology, 27,* 211-237.

Werner, E. E., & Smith, R. S. (1982). *Vulnerable but invincible: A study of resilient children.* New York: McGraw-Hill.

Werner, E. E., & Smith, R. S. (1992). *Overcoming the odds: High risk children from birth to adulthood.* Ithaca, NY: Cornell University Press.

Wetzel, R. D., Margulies, T., Davis, R., & Karam, E. (1980). Hopelessness, depression, and suicide intent. *Journal of Clinical Psychiatry, 41,* 159-160.

Wills, T. A., Vaccaro, D., & McNamara, G. (1992). The role of life events, family support, and competence in adolescent substance use: A test of vulnerability and protective factors. *American Journal of Community Psychology, 20*, 349–374.

Wyman, P. A., Cowen, E. L., Work, W. C., Hoyt-Meyers, L. A., Magnus, K. B., & Fagen, D. B. (1999). Developmental and caregiving factors differentiating parents of young stress-affected and stress-resilient urban children: A replication and extension. *Child Development, 70*, 645–659.

Wyman, P. A., Cowen, E. L., Work, W. C., & Kerley, J. H. (1993). The role of children's future expectations in self-system functioning and adjustment to life-stress. *Development and Psychopathology, 5*, 649–661.

Wyman, P. A., Cowen, E. L., Work, W. C., & Parker, G. R. (1991). Developmental and family milieu interview correlates of resilience in urban children who have experienced major life-stress. *American Journal of Community Psychology, 19*, 405–426.

Wyman, P. A., Cowen, E. L., Work, W. C., Raoof, A., Gribble, P. A., Parker, G. R., & Wannon, M. (1992). Interviews with children who experienced major life stress: Family and child attributes that predict resilient outcomes. *Journal of the American Academy of Child and Adolescent Psychiatry, 31*, 904–910.

Wyman, P. A., Sandler, I. N., Wolchik, S., & Nelson, K. (2000). Resilience as cumulative competence promotion and stress protection: Theory and intervention. In D. Cicchetti, J. Rappaport, I. N. Sandler, & R. P. Weissberg (Eds.), *The promotion of wellness in children and adolescents* (pp. 133–184). Thousand Oaks, CA: Sage Publications.

Acknowledgments

Our thanks to the children and parents who have generously given their time to the Rochester Child Resilience Project and to the W. T. Grant Foundation, which has supported our research. We also thank our colleague Emory L. Cowen for his important contributions to the RCRP and Dr. Sydney H. Croog, who provided incisive comments on several drafts of this chapter.

Chapter 7

Becoming a Female Artist: Past, Present, and Future

Lita Linzer Schwartz

Twenty years ago, Sang made several points that are found in almost every study of female artists, visual and otherwise. Two decades later, the patterns have not changed too much in most communities.

> The female socialization process does little to prepare women for original work. Whereas creativity involves the ability to go beyond the known—to take risks, to be autonomous and to seek adventure—most women have been trained to value security, conformity, mediocrity and social approval. Such qualities as competence, independence and mastery are threatening. Several studies show that women who are impulsive, rebellious and rejecting of outside influence are likely to show creative achievement. This means that for women to engage in creative endeavors, they must deviate from the social norm. (1981, pp. 43-44)

In addition, they must have time, as well as a certain amount of solitude, to reflect and to produce. However, whether their talents are artistic, literary, scientific, or in another field, women have been socialized to put the needs of others before their own. Francis Bacon (Simonton 1999, p. 219) has been quoted as counseling men not to become entangled with marriage and a family because they are "impediments to a great enterprise." Simonton (1999) then goes on to say, "If Bacon advises ambitious men to shy away from domestic commitments, how much more this advice applies to women who are socialized to view family matters as a far more serious responsibility." (p. 219).

Put another way, "a woman with husband and children suffers a handicap not experienced by an equally capable man with wife and children. Only the woman has so often had to make such a discrete choice between reproductive success and productive success—between contributing to the gene pool or adding something to the gene pool" (Simonton, p. 220).

Women have been taught to put intensity and involvement into their homes and their relationships, but not into the expression of their ideas and concepts, and they rarely create for themselves the necessary environment that allows for contact with their inner being. If they do, and are married, especially with children, they may reap considerable criticism for being so "self-centered." If they do and are living alone, they may be criticized for not living in a way that meets other gender-biased stereotypes for unmarried women, widows, and divorcées. Ochse (1991), in reviewing the obstacles to women as creative artists in the past, asserts that one factor continues to work against women being as creatively productive as men—their sociability! That is an aspect of having interpersonal relationships—such relationships consume time, the very element of opportunity that women have the most difficulty arranging for themselves

To answer the question about whether female artists differ from other women, they do indeed in the sense that they have a talent, a gift that is special. It is also, at least in part, nonconformity that separates artists from other women if they are to succeed in their self-imposed efforts—their commitment—to use that gift to achieve their goal, whether the goal is fame, recognition and acceptance as an artist, or simply a sense of self-fulfillment. A third element in the ways that female artists may differ from other women is that they have had the opportunity to explore, develop, and manifest their gifts. One factor in this third element may be the presence of a mentor, about which more will be said later. Each of these aspects—talent, commitment, and opportunity—is critical to achievement, although we cannot ascribe a weight in the equation for each aspect. We might express this as a formula in the Lewinian mode (Lewin, 1961):

Achievement = f (talent x commitment x opportunity)

Or we might restate it: Achievement is a function of the interaction of talent, commitment, and opportunity. Another way of demonstrating this thesis is seen in Figure 1 below, where achievement is a "whole" greater than a sum of its three parts but obviously incorporates all three.

It might be noted that commitment includes a wide range of behaviors: "sacrifice," persistence (often termed "stubbornness" by those who disagree with the behavior), perseverance, devotion (of time, energy, and such), and self-dedication, among other terms. Opportunity, in the context of this study, can range from an initial exposure that makes the girl or young woman aware that she has a gift, or the potential to develop a talent, to having a mentor or being given the chance and the means to enhance that talent (including time to learn and to practice her art).

In one part of the current study, contemporary women artists were asked about the kinds of encouragement they might have had, and also about their self-perceptions over time, their motivation at different periods, and the major difficulties they experienced as they entered the world of art. Through an examination of their responses as well as biographical data of women artists and photographers over the past 160 years or so, we are guided to suggestions for helping artistically talented girls move toward achievement. Means of aiding them to achieve artistically (and otherwise) is a principal goal of this chapter.

Setting our Search in Context

In the introduction to her book on women visual artists from the Renaissance to the early 20th century, Tufts (1974) wrote that the women who became artists during the Renaissance were allowed to do so because they were the daughters of artists and had the advantage of being trained by and allowed to work in their fathers' studios. By the Age of Enlightenment, however, more women from nonartistic families were permitted to study art because the position of women (upper-class women, that is) had improved, and those who had talent were permitted to follow

FIGURE **7-1** *Outcome of Interaction*

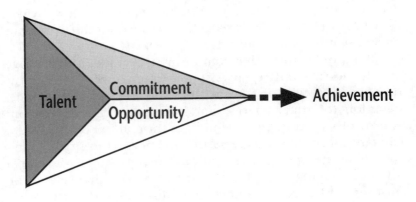

their inclination, but generally as an avocation rather than as a profession. Even during the 19th century, "it remained difficult for a woman to choose and pursue the profession of artist unless she came from a wealthy or artistically involved family" (Tufts, 1974, p. xvi), although this was more acceptable than if her talents were in the scientific realm. This was not uniformly true for artists or photographers as we shall see, although certainly it helped their careers if they were not trying to earn money for personal or family survival.

The artists, most of whom painted portraits or still lifes, had fewer physical risks to take than the photographers, many of whom were on site during civil disorders and wars, or in other geographically hazardous locations. The latter not only took time away from their families but the women were also often absent (and perhaps running risks) physically. As noted earlier, this certainly flew in the face of society's expectations of the past 160 years or so, especially if the women were married, and does so even today to some extent. In studying creativity in women, Tucker (1973), Helson (1990), Stone (1998), and Simonton (1999) have all made the point that the traditional double standard still affects women's attempts to balance family and career. If they try to do both, women are perceived as nonconformists in the eyes of much of society because they have chosen to do both. (Note: The wives of men struggling to make a living have rarely been criticized for working side-by-side with their husbands in the family store while also bringing up children. Successfully performing these multiple roles was a necessity, not a choice, over the centuries for those at or near the bottom of the economic ladder. They were not and are not subject to the same criticism as those who have been provided with options and then made a choice.)

Although some view the young woman's creative aspirations to be the result of incorporating her father's drive or perspective, Kerr (1985) asserted that what distinguishes eminent women from those who accomplish less includes "the determined refusal to acknowledge limitations of gender, an ability to combine roles, a strong sense of one's personal identity, taking responsibility for oneself, and a mission in life" (p. v). The one artist in her study was Georgia O'Keeffe, who certainly exemplified this position. Kerr's "determined refusal" is another way of expressing an element of what here is called "commitment." It is important, even today, for parents and teachers to enable girls to develop these feelings and behaviors. "Support for the lack of conformity that creativity often implies" (Schwartz, 1991, p. 152) is one aspect of opportunity that creativity requires. Punishment for failure to conform may completely douse one girl's creativity, send another off on an asocial or even an antisocial path, prod a third to continue behaviors that are disquieting to some others, and help a fourth learn how to modify her behavior just enough to stay out of trouble while still exploring and expressing her interests.

In what ways do the interaction of life experiences and social context (opportunity), giftedness and creativity (talent), and personality (commitment) combine to produce the work of gifted and creative women in the arts? What factors do these women have in common? How can we use what we learn from the lives of artists past and present to enhance the opportunities of similarly talented girls now and in the future? Answers will be sought through sharing elements of the lives of a number of artists and photographers of the past and through a study of a sample of women in the arts today.

An immediate difficulty in this search has usually been finding information about women artists. If few women are found in standard histories of art or photography, they can scarcely serve as models of creative achievement for the artistically gifted girls who follow (Schwartz, 1994). Indeed, the question has often been asked: "Why have there been no great women artists?" That may be the wrong question. Perhaps we should be asking what impediments were placed in the way of women to keep them from achieving excellence or recognition? (Nochlin, 1994). Darwinians would assert that women's abilities are not equal to men's, or at least do not have the range and variability of men's, not only in the arts but in many fields (Simonton, 1999). Piirto (1991) pointed to the need to encourage commitment and intensity in girls to increase their productivity. Clearly, there is not unanimity of response to the question raised, although we can detect perceptions that relate to the formula stated earlier. There must also be awareness of the orientation or philosophy of the respondent, as obviously these affect perceptions.

Although the work of some female photographers gained positive acknowledgment during their productive years, such as that of Julia Margaret Cameron in England, or Dorothea Lange, Margaret Bourke-White, and Mary Ellen Marks in the United States, the bulk of it was ignored in standard, even significant, histories of the field. The impact of photographs taken by women gained belated recognition in an exhibition at The New York Public Library (1996) and the National Museum for Women in the Arts (1997), the latter site being its own response to the dearth of female representation in larger museums. This exhibition was based on Rosenblum's (1994) book that "corrected" the limitations of Newhall's classic history of photography (1982) which had included only 10 women photographers. Other exhibits have followed, now that recognition of women artists (in all genres) appears to be popular. Indeed, of the 15 stamps offered by the U. S. Postal Service in its group to celebrate the 1930s, two were by women photographers—the first cover of Life magazine by Margaret Bourke-White, and Dorothea Lange's almost legendary portrait of a distraught migrant mother in the Depression. Another facet of the opportunity element has belatedly come to women artists as a group.

The search for characteristics common to these artists, as revealed in their biographies, or in psychological studies, makes this study one of a fairly small collection, for most studies of creativity in women focus on women scientists, writers, or mathematicians rather than their more artistic sisters. The search will be introduced by a review of the findings of historians, biographers, and other psychologists with respect to creativity and giftedness in girls and women. The brief biographical notes for several well-recognized female artists were selected to demonstrate the varied ways in which their lives reflected the three overall aspects of our formula and their interaction.

Women Visual Artists

In examining biographies of female painters, one finds that there may be two, three, or more female artists in the same family, suggesting that there may have been informal mentoring in addition to the more formal instruction received by many of them. Examples can be found in the Bonheur family (two sisters), the Montalba family (four sisters), the Morisot family (two sisters), the Thornycroft family (mother and two daughters), and the four Peale sisters, among others (Dunford, 1990; Elam, 1967; Higgonet, 1990; Rosenblum, 1994). Not all attained the same level of achievement, but certainly the names Rosa Bonheur, Berthe Morisot, and Sarah Peale are familiar to American art lovers even a century after their peak efforts. Let us take as a given that each of these women had talent. Each of them also had opportunity, in that there were teachers—mentors—within the family. Other, possibly less familiar artists and photographers highlighted here represent other backgrounds that demonstrate talent and creativity can arise in and be nourished by a variety of sources.

Sarah Peale (1800-1885), trained in her father's studio along with two of her sisters, was determined to be recognized as an accomplished portrait painter. Although she was attracted to at least two men, she declined marriage because it would deter her from reaching her goal. She moved away from the family enclave in Philadelphia, first to her cousin Rembrandt Peale's studio in Baltimore, then, for 30 years, to St. Louis where she became "the first woman in America to support herself entirely throughout a long life, by the profession of painting" (Tufts, 1974, p. 139). Clearly, she had the opportunity to develop her talent from childhood on; her total commitment, negating marriage because it would distract her from her chosen path, enabled her to achieve her goals—recognition, acceptance, and even financial success as an artist.

Rosa Bonheur (1822-1899) and her siblings were similarly taught to draw and paint by their artist father. As a girl, her nonconformity was seen in her mischievousness, tomboy behavior, and native rebelliousness (Ashton & Hare, 1981). She rejected men and sometimes the whole human race, preferring her pets, but dressed in male attire (with government permission) during her frequent journeys to find suitable subjects for her paintings. Again, opportunity was available in childhood, and again, her commitment to her art was total. Like Sarah Peale, she disdained marriage in favor of her art. Her rejection of men may well have had some other basis in her life, but it certainly seems to have contributed, even reinforced, her commitment to her work.

The women in Berthe Morisot's (1841-1895) family all encouraged her to pursue her interest and talent in painting. She was viewed as highly intelligent and exceptionally willful (i.e., nonconformist?) (Higgonet, 1990). By her early 20s, she had had works accepted by the Salon in Paris, quite an achievement for any artist, and by her early 30s had sold some paintings and perceived herself as a professional. Her mother did begin to nag her about getting married as she approached her 30s, and Morisot married Eugene Manet (brother of Edouard) in 1874, bearing a daughter 4 years later. Her husband was strongly supportive of her painting, however, throughout their marriage, which may have been a prenuptial condition. Unusually productive, Morisot produced more than 850 paintings, and always signed them as Berthe Morisot, as an indication of her independence. (Her sister, also a painter, continued to paint after her marriage, but as an avocation only.) Her commitment to her art is clear, even as she succeeded in having a husband and child. Whether her high level of productivity—her commitment—indicated manic behavior, obsessive behavior, or some other psychopathy is difficult to determine a century and more later. This, however, is not germane to her achievement of being recognized as an artist.

Mary Cassatt (1844-1926) was another nonconformist and, like many other women artists, fortunate enough to come from a financially comfortable family. Her mother encouraged her studies at the Pennsylvania Academy of the Fine Arts and in Paris, although her father would have preferred to see her marry. Like Morisot, she had works accepted by the Salon, and she worked in several media—pastels, oils, etching, drypoint, and color prints (Lindsay, 1985). Higgonet (1990) paired her with Morisot as making new claims for women:

> By the very persistence of their endeavors, as well as by their high pictorial standards, they demonstrated that women could participate fully and continuously in the most rigorous avant-garde art movements...These two women proved that no one model could explain all women's aspirations and achievements any more than one model could explain all men's (pp. 154-155).

Unlike Morisot, however, Cassatt did not marry. She was committed to her art, and to spreading the word of other artists as well, that is, providing opportunity for others.

Another Parisian artist, Suzanne Valadon (1865-1938), came from an extremely poor family setting and was working at menial jobs by age 9. As a child, however, she observed artists on the street, and sketched and drew as she saw them do. Early on it was apparent that she had the curiosity, the visual acuity, and the brain-hand connection—and, as it turned out, the commitment—that only needed opportunity to flower. Toulouse-Lautrec, one of several artists for whom she modeled in her mid-teens, discovered her talent, introduced her to Degas, and the rest is history. Valadon married at age 49 to a man some 20 years her junior, and painted, literally, until the day she died (Dunford, 1990). Valadon was different from the other artists described here in that she needed not only her own inner drive—her commitment—but also the opportunity provided by her mentor. Once the door to opportunity was opened, away she went en route to achievement. Finally, it is significant to note that while we have long been accustomed to the stereotype of the "starving artist" barely surviving in an attic, this has typically referred to males who eschewed other means of making a living. Valadon truly came from a starving family.

Georgia O'Keeffe (1887-1986) had an abundance of talent, and was encouraged by her mother and grandmothers to study art (but also to obtain teacher training so that she could support herself). Definitely a nonconformist in spirit and behavior, O'Keeffe married Alfred Stieglitz, who had first served as her mentor, but they spent most of their married life apart, with her in Taos, New Mexico, and him in New York. She was rarely involved in domestic life, choosing to paint her exuberant, sometimes sexually suggestive works, rather than do anything else (Hogrefe, 1994; Montgomery, 1993). O'Keeffe was enough of an individual to persist in her activities—to be self-driven, but was also fortunate to have not only her family's support but that of the noted photographer and gallery owner who became her husband. As with other artists discussed here, she had an abundance of talent and commitment. Her initial artistic submission to Stieglitz opened a world of opportunity, the necessary third element for recognition and achievement.

Elizabeth Catlett (1915-) knew at age six that she wanted to be an artist, studied art in high school, and by age 16 was enrolled at Howard University studying painting. She later studied watercolors, lithography, sculpture, and other facets of visual arts–all while being married, having children, teaching, meeting other artists, and participating in exhibitions. (Note: It may be that a fourth element should be added to the equation—energy!) Sims (1998) discussed the interplay of the various facets of Catlett's life as well as her prints, paintings, and sculptures in the following statement: "From the mid-1940s, Elizabeth Catlett pursued an approach to art and politics that would continue to characterize her work over the next four decades. Her career is distinctive because she has always embraced the implications of not only her race but also her gender in her work" (pp. 16-17). She had mentors, but principally could be characterized by her tremendous commitment. Like many 20th century artists, she had the advantage of higher education, which gave her exposure to locales where opportunities might be found in a way that was not as readily available to women of the nineteenth century, whether white or not.

Among the women photographers, we might look briefly at a few, again representing a diversity of backgrounds. Julia Margaret Cameron (1815-1879) was English, a mother, and married to a British civil servant. Given a camera by her children in the middle of the nineteenth century, Cameron went on to become the noted portrait photographer of many important British figures, as well as a number of women (Wolf et al., 1998). That she took her talent seriously, indeed sought to ennoble photography (Newhall, 1982), marked her as a nonconformist to both her gender and social class. Once provided with opportunity (the camera), she was able to discover a talent she did not know she had, commit herself to developing it, and then use it effectively.

Gertrude Kasebier (1852–1934) exemplifies both the socially conformist family-oriented woman and the creative woman artist cum businessperson. Some years after the birth of her third child, she began to engage in photography. At age 37, she began to study art at Pratt Institute in Brooklyn, and 10 years later opened her own commercial photography studio in New York. Her work attracted Alfred Stieglitz's attention and he was certainly helpful in gaining exposure for her photographic portraits (Rosenblum, 1994). In the sense that she began her work at this midpoint in her life, somewhat belatedly discovering and developing her gifted "eye," she followed somewhat in the steps of Julia Margaret Cameron. In a sense, she created her own opportunity by enrolling at Pratt, which required commitment as well at a point in her life when she might have been expected to engage in other, more socially-oriented activities.

Among the staunchly unmarried was Frances Benjamin Johnston (1864-1952) who, by her 20s, was actively working with photography in order to illustrate her magazine articles, and subsequently became both a portrait photographer and a photojournalist. One of her outstanding documentaries was a study of the Hampton Institute. The descriptions of Johnston convey her nonconformity so well that a reader today can only smile broadly at them. She "was described as a charming, witty woman, but a bit rebellious because she 'drank beer, smoked and daringly showed her ankles'" (Tucker, 1973, p. 29). Another commentator wrote that she "was an eccentric woman, according to the society she came from—she never married, she smoked, she drank, she hung out with Bohemian friends, and, above all, she was a photographer" (Humphrey, 1975, unpaged). Imagine the shocking quality of that last item! In fact, Johnston herself had such a sense of humor that she took a self-portrait, cigarette and drink in hand, with her hemline high enough to show her ankles. In hindsight a delightful nonconformist, Johnston had an abundance of commitment to interact with her talent and opportunities.

Better known, perhaps, is Dorothea Lange (1895-1965), who studied photography in her early 20s and made her first try then to begin a career. Lange married in 1920, became a mother of two children, embarked a second time on her career as a photographer in 1931, and was divorced in 1935 (very unusual for that time) (Rosenblum, 1994). One of several photographers for the Farm Security Administration during the Depression, Lange married her boss but left her comfortable home and family to travel with migrant agricultural workers from Oklahoma and other migrants to bring their suffering to the attention of others. Her son was quoted as saying that her concern was with the "miserable and the afflicted" (Tucker, 1973, p. 29). A political commitment was thus added to the inner drive that went back to her youth.

All of these women, and many others, shared two traits—artistic talent and commitment to their art which involved persistence in the face of criticism that was social, often familial, and sometimes artistic. They took their art education seriously, as a means to self-fulfillment and a career, rather than as a "ladylike" avocation. They went beyond a polite interest in the visual arts and made it central to their lives. For those who married, there appears to have been an abundance of energy as well as commitment, or they could not have done all that they did. Does this make them different from other women of their time and place? Indeed it does, whether we are considering the 19th or the 20th century.

A Review of the Psychological Literature

A key question in much of the psychological and psychoanalytic literature turns on the relationship between the creative child and each parent (cf. Singer, 1984). To some, like Kavaler-Adler (1993), the young female artist's "internalization" of her father provides the motivation, the drive to create. Certainly, as we have already noted, in the case of many artists of the past the father was the "enabler" if not the motivator for the daughter's accomplishments. On the other hand, it was just as often a mother who had surrendered her aspirations who pushed her daughter(s) forward in their artistic careers, as we have seen in several of the biographical notes (e.g., Hogrefe, 1994; Sweet, 1966). Furthermore, it is not only parents who motivate or enable, although they may literally be the primary influences in the sense of being the first; other relatives from siblings of the child to aunts, uncles, or grandparents may provide the necessary stimulus or recognition.

In examining earlier studies, particularly of adult female artists, it is apparent that each study, no matter how few or how many the subjects, seems to provide much the same portrait. For most of the women, especially those who were married (with or without children), finding time to do one's art was the challenge, since other responsibilities almost invariably had higher priority. For these women, opportunity in the sense of having a few free hours was the critical element in the equation that already included talent and commitment. For younger artists, those still in school, opportunity was more likely to mean the availability of a place to study art, to interact with teachers and possible mentors, or even the encouragement of parents to go forward with their talent. Familial support was also often a key precursor of a woman's success in the field of visual arts (Stariha & Walberg, 1995).

Kirschenbaum and Reis (1997), for example, found that the artistic productivity of their 10 subjects, female artists with children, rested on the interaction of multiple factors whose weight in the equation varied from one time to another: self-discipline, child-rearing responsibilities, spousal encouragement, job demands, financial considerations, and access to materials and equipment as well as work space. Most of these factors come under the heading of "opportunity," but self-discipline clearly represents "commitment." Commitment was certainly necessary, for these women apparently had little encouragement from their husbands, but rather received negative or extremely limited feedback from them (Reis, 1998). Indeed, many of them had low self-esteem with regard to their art because of these weak reactions, and this conflicted with the gratification they felt from creative self-expression.

Bachtold and Werner (1973) and Bachtold (1976) reporting their studies that included 132 female artists, as well as female authors, identified several personality characteristics of their subjects. Using the 16 P-F Questionnaire, they found "women artists, like the authors, were more aloof, intelligent, emotional, aggressive, adventurous, imaginative, radical, and self-sufficient, and less controlled than women in the general population" (Bachtold & Werner, p. 314). Their participants were also found to be more likely to follow their own urges and accustomed to going their own way; the women were found to "tend to be less conventional and less concerned over everyday matters, and more wrapped up in inner urgencies, more self-motivated, and imaginative" (1973, p. 315). In Bachtold's larger study, which included psychologists, scientists, writers, and politicians in addition to the artists, she found that these career women, in contrast to women in general, scored higher on adventurousness (Factor H) (1976, p. 77). Almost all of these descriptors contribute to the sense of commitment in these women. Nonconformists in one or more ways, they had not allowed socialization or demands to be more sociable stand in their way as they moved toward achievement in their fields.

A long-term study from the same period (Brooks, 1973) includes a sample from the Berkeley Guidance Study begun in 1928 to 1929. Of 50 females followed from age 21 months through age 18 years, data was obtained at age 30 for 38 of these women. Notable findings in this study included, for example, the negative correlations found consistently between childhood ratings of "Satisfactions in artistic pursuits" and adult Q sort items (Females) with "Behaves in a feminine style and manner"–significant at the age 8 to 11 years range (-.35), and negative but not statistically significant at later ages (-.25 at age 11 to 14; -.18 at age 14 to 18) (p. 117). (Even where statistically significant, these are not strong correlations, of course.) In addition, there were two other interesting, if somewhat internally conflicting, findings:

- Guidance women with childhood artistic interests were seen as unsociable, unconventional women with unusual thoughts. These women were introspective, insightful about themselves, and seen by others as being interesting, arresting persons (p. 118).

- Girls with artistic interests in childhood experienced a benign early family situation, developed a typical feminine interest, but as adults were unusual in their cathexis of intellectual activity, a trait not associated with the stereotype of the adult female (p. 120).

Nonconformity to the female stereotype, being "unconventional," brought them both criticism and characterization as being "interesting." As always, which view dominated depended on the eye of the beholder.

More recently, Rostan (1998) did a study with 39 youngsters, aged 8 to 11 years, enrolled in an after-school art program, but she did not focus on boy-girl differences, or even specify how many children were included of each age group. What she did find, however, was expression of their pleasure in doing art, of modifying things as a way of being creative, and of decisionmaking. The after-school program was providing an opportunity for these youngsters, in both time and content, that was not typically available to youths of earlier generations. If the teachers of these programs are also instructing the children in how to make decisions and take responsibility for their decisionmaking, even in the limited realm of the arts program, then these children will learn the essence of an internal locus of control that is necessary for commitment.

In other studies, several self-defining adjectives are seen that will be further examined. In one follow-up study, conducted with 10 female artists and writers (5 of each) who had first been nominated by their teachers for participation in the research as "exceptionally creative" teenagers in high school, Schaefer found, 25 years later (1990), that their self-concepts were remarkably stable. They "continued to describe themselves as intelligent, original in thought and expression, open to experience, and indifferent to convention" (p. 685). The key may be that they had already been identified as creative by adults who were in a position to help them move forward. On the other hand, as mature women, Schaefer found that they were able "to reconcile and integrate opposing tendencies such as self versus social interest" (p. 685), and that as a group, they showed a "strong social interest."

The role that the teachers played in Schaefer's study was one that is very important for most youngsters: They were mentors. Kirschenbaum and Reis's (1997) subjects, on the other hand, experienced exposure from some of their high school and college teachers, which is an aspect of mentoring, but more often these individuals were discouraged from pursuing art as a career because of the field's financial instability (Reis, 1998). Torrance (1983) indicated that mentors had three primary roles:

1. encouraging, praising, and prodding;

2. providing role models; and

3. teaching "mentees" how to "play the game" (pp. 12-13).

Although teachers, and in the area of our study art teachers in particular, may serve as mentors more frequently than they sometimes realize, others can also serve as mentors. It was noted earlier that many female visual artists were taught and guided by their fathers, occasionally a mother, sometimes another family member. The mentor may also be a friend who introduces one to the artistic experience with the simple object of sharing something pleasurable, and subsequently acts as guide or mentor.

In attempting to formulate a theory of the creative female's life cycle, Shaughnessy (1987) examined the lives of women "who have succeeded in their chosen field of endeavor against innumerable odds, i.e., in a 'man's world'" (pp. 85-86). In his view of the life cycle, he hypothesized a dozen stages:

Stage 1. Birth...parents may formulate long-range plans for child.

Stage 2. Infancy in the family environment—nurturance and/or adversity.

Stage 3. Early mentor experience—early stimulation.

Stage 4. Early educational experiences and exposures—additional experiences.

Stage 5. Exposure to a "worldview"—further exposures.

Stage 6. Later educational experiences in cultural centers—formal/informal training; experiences through travel or contacts.

Stage 7. Commitment to one's work—vital.

Stage 8. Relocation to chosen cultural center—may be luck or conscious.

Stage 9. Collaboration—work with another talented person.

Stage 10. One's Life Work—makes most valuable contribution—security, recognition, and success follow (age immaterial here).

Stage 11. The retrospective analysis—has she met her goals?

Stage 12. Death—society makes its evaluation.

Although he emphasized commitment in Stage 7, Shaughnessy also wrote that "commitment to oneself is inadequate. A cause must be championed, a new idea, a creative endeavor or a contribution must be given up to humanity and to history...[these] women 'broke the mold' so to speak, and their roles and identities were not based on their relationships to others (daughter, wife, mother) but rather their ties were based on their talents, abilities and creative gifts and their commitment to those gifts and their new roles." (1987, p. 90)

Shaughnessy's women who "broke the mold" were responding in their own way to the ambivalence with which our culture has responded to highly capable women—in any field. Noble's comments in this realm still merit attention: "As a culture, we acknowledge and reward only those talents and abilities that have direct, marketable value, and what has value has largely been determined by and for men" (1987, p. 367). Indeed, Williams (1998), who interviewed several women photographers, reported comments in which some indicated that they believed they had a quality—empathy—that men lacked, which enabled them to be better photographers, although others said that they saw no difference in quality of work by gender. The point was, however, that empathy was not a quality valued by men and therefore was not acknowledged or rewarded.

Tomlinson-Keasey (1998), in her study of contemporary gifted women, which included a review of the long-term study of Terman's gifted women (Terman & Oden, 1959), sought to comprehend the puzzle of women's development. She wrote that "intimacy, relationships, and commitment spill over into the other pieces of the puzzle, modulating the woman's sense of identity and self, increasing the serendipitous aspects of her career, and tempering the goals she sets for herself" (pp. 23-24). Again we see the interactive function of the individual's different roles, self-perceptions, and most notably, recognition that commitment is one of the principal factors affecting the self-set goals. This interaction is also seen in studies of artists in their 40s and older by Brooks and Daniluk (1998) and Stohs (1992).

A brief mention of a pilot study done by the author in the late 1970s...This was an attempt to investigate a possible relationship between gender and sex-role stereotypes of various occupations. Students in six different class sections (N = 144) were asked to rate 20 occupations on their masculinity-femininity on a 10-point scale. Two sections of the six from which these students were selected were taught by one female psychologist, a third section was taught by another female psychologist, two sections were taught by a male history professor, and the sixth section was taught jointly by one of the psychologists and a female history professor. Ratings were compared in terms of sex of the participant and sex of the instructor, and proved to be quite interesting in terms of having live role models. "All students, and female students counted alone, taught by female faculty tended to have higher mean ratings for the occupations of author, professor, psychologist, and social scientist—occupations represented by the three female faculty members—than did students of the male instructor" (Schwartz, 1980, p. 115). Had we sampled art classes, then taught by a male professor, we might have found similar results for that occupation. Having a role model can alter perceptions and, we hope, goals.

The Current Study

Bearing in mind the biographies and research studies already available concerning women visual artists, a sample of women in the Philadelphia (PA) area (N = 60) were asked to respond to a four-page anonymous questionnaire that attempted to have others see them as they saw (and see) themselves at two periods in their lives. Participants were recruited from a camera club and an artists' group that included painters, watercolorists, sculptors, photographers, and craftspeople, as well as a few independent artists. Responses were received from 31 women, just over 50% of the population contacted. Very few, if any, came from families as wealthy as the Cassatts or the Peales, or as social as the Camerons; indeed, for most of the women, the expectation was that they would seek employment until they married and had children. About one-third of the participants responding were old enough to marry in the immediate post-World War II period when middle-class women were expected to be "stay-at-home" wives and mothers except, perhaps, for some volunteer charitable work and an occasional bridge game. These participants were, on the whole, better educated than the 19th and early-20th century women whose brief biographies have been included here, but that is partly a function of higher education opportunities that have become more available since the mid-1800s. Several followed the advice given Georgia O'Keeffe and studied to become art teachers even as they developed their own gifts. Table 1 gives details of their personal backgrounds.

Since having family support for art education, and perhaps art as a career, was characteristic of several of our "historical" subjects, respondents were asked how their families of origin had reacted to their interest in art. Twenty-two of them described family response to be "positive," "supportive," "encouraging," or "enthusiastic." (This is in sharp contrast to comments by Reis' subjects, who were also in mid-life when interviewed [1998].) In addition, 16 of the participants indicated that they had had at least one mentor, of whom eight were male, seven were female, and one participant had had a mentor of each gender. Almost half of the group (15) had majored in some aspect of art, from art education to fashion design, in their higher education, with many of them teaching art at some level of basic or higher education. Fourteen of the participants had had the opportunity, usually as a teacher in basic education or as an art teacher, to work with girls who were interested or talented in some facets of the

TABLE 7-1 *Personal Backgrounds of Questionnaire Respondents.*

	NUMBER
Age Range: 42 to 85 years	
40s	9
50s	6
60s	9
70s	5
80s	2
Highest level of education attained:	
High School graduate	5
Some additional education	4
College graduate	13
Master's degree	10
Doctorate	2
No response	1
Marriage and family:	
Married (at least once)	30
Divorced	9
Widowed	4
Had children (from 1 to 5)	28
Work History:	
While children were young	
F/T	18
P/T	4
Art-related field	14
Currently	
F/T	16*
P/T	10
Art-related field	11
Age of becoming aware of interest in working in the arts:	
Preschool	4
Childhood (age 6 to 12)	11
Teens	2
20s	2
30s+	11
NA	1

*+ 4 retired

arts, with 11 of them indicating that they had indeed served as mentor to one or more girls. Thus, their own commitment helped them to provide opportunities for those younger than themselves.

Thirteen of the participants said that they had experienced barriers in their efforts to combine their artistic activities with other aspects of their life. The most frequently mentioned barriers, hardly surprising, included limitations of time and family responsibilities (mostly child care). Indeed, this group clearly demonstrates the conflict between marriage and family on the one hand and "productive success" on the other quoted earlier from Simonton (1999). Financial restraints were mentioned by a few, in terms of costs of equipment, and lack of self-confidence was mentioned by one respondent. These barriers are those cited earlier by several sources, and also by Rimm's participants (1999) in the visual arts as far as negative impact on relationships and poor financial rewards are concerned. In this respect, these women were consistent with several of their peers from earlier eras.

Respondents were asked two questions about the nature of creativity in terms of its being a fixed ("you have it or you don't") or modifiable ("can be activated through effort") trait. Although seven women initially answered that it was a fixed trait, only one said that it could not be activated. That means, in terms of future artists, that mentoring can activate latent artistic creativity as well as open opportunities for its development.

Although several participants indicated that they knew in childhood that they wanted to be artists, one-third of the group indicated that they did not become involved in art until they were age 30 or older. In a number of cases, they were in their fifties when they became so involved, to their great delight. They parallel a group of women who became eminent after age 50 who were studied by Reis (1998) and who reported that they felt obligated to pursue their abilities actively. As she put it, "They felt obligated because they believed in themselves and wanted to develop their talents in an area of personal importance to them" (p. 271).

The question of how these participants saw themselves both as adolescents, when so many of the female artists of earlier generations had their initial training and exposure, and as mature adults, seemed to suggest some possibilities for consideration. Having provided the participants with a list of 24 adjectives, they were asked to indicate the five that were dominant in their personalities in adolescence and the five that would characterize them now. The results are shown in Table 2 and Figure 2. It was interesting to note, in the highest scoring items, that friendly (n = 15) and intelligent (n = 13) had the same scores for both periods, but that where they were the top two descriptors for adolescence, they were displaced by the then third and fourth choices in adulthood, "creative" and "artistic." Indeed, almost twice as many respondents said they were creative as adults, and exactly twice as many saw themselves as artistic compared to when they were adolescents. At the other extreme, only two described themselves as "conforming" as adolescents, and only one as an adult. These self-perceptions are quite consistent with descriptions noted earlier. Other characteristics that have been found in earlier studies to be associated with female artists were checked off by more participants as adults than for their adolescent periods, as can be seen in the table. Some changes were particularly interesting to note: (1) no one described herself as "Aggressive" at either period, although "Assertive" (more acceptable to most women) was selected by two women as a characteristic in adolescence and four women in adulthood; (2) "anxious" was chosen by five participants to describe themselves in adolescence, but by none as an adult; and (3) "competent" was selected twice as often to describe the participant as an adult as it had been to describe participants as adolescents. (Is active involvement in the visual arts therapeutic?) One respondent added her own terms—"wild" and "out-of-control"—to describe herself as an adolescent. On the whole, though, there is positive correspondence with the self-descriptive adjectives used by Domino and Giuliani's participants (1997), and those in other studies.

In Figure 2, the length of the bar was determined by the highest number choosing that term, with the bar divided by age period (e.g., "artistic" had 8 "votes" in adolescence, shown in white; 16 "votes" in adulthood, with the extended portion shown with diagonal slashes). When a trait had the same number of votes for both periods, both a white bar and a slashed bar are shown.

Asked "Why do you create?," one participant responded: "It quells a thirst...it fills a need." That positive role of artistic activity—that self-fulfilling "achievement"—was expressed also as "for pleasure" (n = 11), "self-satisfying" (n = 11), "a way to express my being and to make my mark in the world" (n = 7), "exposure to new things" (n = 3), "to express creativity" (n = 3), "to contribute something to the world" (n = 2), "for relaxation" (n = 2), "it's exciting" (n = 1). (Obviously, some artists gave more than one reason.) In this, they resembled Cangelosi and Schaefer's "highly creative" participants (1992), the artists and musicians in Rimm's study who would recommend their profession because it is "challenging," "creative," and "fulfilling" (1999, p. 24), and those mentioned earlier in Reis' study (1998). Those participants who then added thoughts for creative girls wrote essentially one message: "Go for it!" One even suggested that a girl delay marriage and having children so that she could experience fulfillment before other commitments claimed her. Apart from this sample, the author has observed that in retirement residences and senior citizen programs, the same kind of pleasure and sense of fulfillment are reported by women engaged in ceramics and other art classes. This creative effort might even contribute to their mental health, as it seems to have done for some of the respondents, as the mind is engaged in the project as well as the eyes and hands.

The most interesting facets of the data from this survey would seem to be the shift in self-perception shown in the changes in descriptors, and the intense feelings of fulfillment and pleasure expressed by the subjects, no matter what their age now or training in the past. In other words, having committed themselves to developing and practicing their talents, and having the opportunity to do so in middle and late adulthood, these participants have a sense of achievement as artists and are

TABLE 7-2 *Self-Perceptions: Adolescence vs. Adulthood (n=31).*

ADOLESCENCE	ADULTHOOD
Personal Qualities Selected with Highest Frequency	
Friendly (15)	Creative (20)
Intelligent (13)	Artistic (16)
Creative (11)	Friendly (15)
Artistic (8)	Intelligent (13)
Independent (8)	Independent (12)
Adventurous (7)	Enthusiastic (11)
Personal Qualities Selected with Medium Frequency	
Enthusiastic (7)	Competent (10)
Inquisitive (7)	Curious (9)
Introverted (7)	Adventurous (7)
Adaptable (6)	Inquisitive (5)
Anxious (5)	Adaptable (5)
Competent (5)	Assertive (4)
Emotional (5)	Inventive (4)
Curious (5)	Persistent (4)
Depentent (4)	Emotional (3)
Sarcastic (4)	Dependent (2)
Assertive (2)	Sarcastic (2)
Conforming (2)	Conforming (1)
Personal Qualities Selected with Lowest Frequency	
Impulsive (2)	Intense (1)
Inventive (2)	Aggressive (0)
Persistent (2)	Anxious (0)
Interesting (1)	Impulsive (0)
Aggressive (0)	Interesting (0)
Intense (0)	Introverted (0)

FIGURE 7-2 *Artists' Self-Perceptions: Adolescence vs. Adulthood (n=31).*

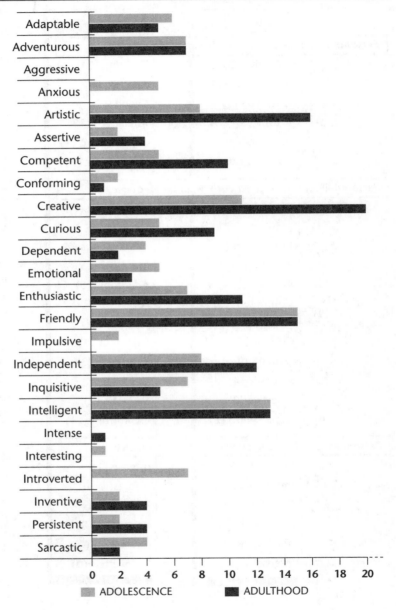

enjoying the experience. Being able to "indulge" in such satisfying behavior is rewarding, and possibly therapeutic—an experience that they seem more than willing to share with younger prospective artists.

Before summing up the conclusions evoked by this project, it seems appropriate to answer here three questions asked of each participant in the 2001 Hartman Conference. Many of the thoughts in the responses have arisen from interacting directly with women artists as well as the research underlying this project. Not being prescient, however, responding to the questions posed becomes a daunting task, but perhaps creativity will arise to meet the challenge.

- *Identify connections between creativity and primary prevention, particularly in the slice of the life course being discussed.*

Looking at children and youth, the opportunity to express oneself creatively and in a socially acceptable way may provide enough self-satisfaction to deter them from less positive activities. After-school art programs, among other extracurricular activities, would provide such an opportunity. Perhaps, by some miracle, legislators will finally get the message that if we do promote the abilities of all children, no matter what their socioeconomic or ethnic background, we will be less likely to have to build more prisons and psychiatric institutions. Self-esteem, praise, and recognition from society in general and family and friends in particular, as well as having tangible creations of one's competence and talent, will reduce some of the reasons for criminal activity.

For the young wife and mother, the opportunity to have something special that is uniquely hers, even for a limited time in any given week, may offset some of the frustrations that occur in those roles even under the best of circumstances. As men assume more responsibility in the home, her time will be more available (as his has been for other nonwork activities) for meeting this need. And once the children are grown and the family demands are somewhat reduced, finding new aspects of creativity and exploring them may well contribute to mental health and the maintenance of mental acuity.

- *In what directions are creativity, research, practice, and policy going in the next decade (in my area of interest)?*

Where are creativity, research, and practice likely to go in the next decade? There will certainly be, indeed we are already seeing, a great impact of computers and digital technology on the visual arts. What already can be done in terms of techniques and products, whether or not we like the results, is awesome. We might wonder whether, a decade from now, images on the computer will be truly three-dimensional and reach out from the monitor, or whether we will be able to feel the texture of something seen on the monitor. (Will there still be a monitor?) In terms of research, as the life span continues to lengthen, there will be more opportunities for longer-term follow-up studies with visual artists as well as others. It will be interesting to see whether women artists will continue to experiment with new techniques when they are in their 80s and 90s (my prediction: Yes, they will). Women of the future may also be fortunate enough to have fewer conflicts as young adults, as compared with the current generation, among the many demands on their time and energy.

- *In what ways can we promote creativity, talents, and giftedness in all citizens?*

Two related factors seem to emerge from generations of research on giftedness, talents, and creativity as keys to promoting these facets of each individual's being: opportunity and mentoring. In some cases, the mentor will create the opportunity as, for example, Toulouse-Lautrec did in Valadon's case; in other cases, having the opportunity to participate in some activity may lead to acquiring a mentor. Going on a field trip to an art exhibit may stimulate a child's (or an adult's) interest in a technique or style, tweak an urge to try it, and then lead the individual to self-fulfilling achievement and possibly external recognition as well.

Friedman and Master (1981) described one such effort involving a collaboration between a school and a museum that yielded positive results for all concerned. More recently, the Guggenheim Museum in New York has published a book for elementary school children that is focused on works in its collection, with sections of the book using art "to engage children in the larger processes of looking, discovering, questioning, and learning" (Goodman, 1999). This delightful introduction to art ties the sculpture or painting to other subject matter, trying to draw the child in by raising questions about the piece, and encouraging the child then to try to create a collage or a sculpture. The book is an excellent prototype for other museums to use as a model for developing their own "eye-openers" for children and adults alike. An alternative approach is to apply the creative problem-solving model to art (Sapp, 1995).

One of the ways in which creative women can aid in this endeavor is to talk with youngsters in school, and to women's groups at varied facilities, about the choices they made at different points in their lives as to which parts of their lives had highest priority. They can go on to explain how these priorities changed over time, resulting in changes in their ability to work with their talents. Sharing the quandaries and difficulties of decisionmaking teaches important life skills as well as being informative about creative development.

It is also true that often we come to forks in the road and serendipitously we choose the path that leads to new opportunities and new challenges, so we need to teach others to be flexible and open enough to some risk-taking to accept such possibilities. We also need to teach, from childhood on, the capacity to make choices and to take responsibility for them—to have an internal locus of control. This is necessary for having the commitment to develop and pursue our creativity and talents. Although equal opportunity to explore and cultivate creativity and gifts of whatever kind may be promoted, that does not mean that everyone will prove to be equally talented. It does, however, offer the possibility that someone will create something—in this case a work of art—that otherwise might never have existed. In other realms, it may mean a solution to a medical or other major problem that might have taken more decades to appear. "Opportunities for creative action abound in all areas of life" (Schwartz, 1977, p. 265).

To summarize, encouraging people of any age to be creative requires several tasks or steps:

- Re-educate society in general, and parents and teachers specifically, about who and what is creative.

- Build self-confidence in the individual by teaching self-acceptance of success.

- Stimulate creativity by interaction with role models.

- Stimulate creativity through productive thinking exercises and brainstorming activities.

- Reduce resistance to creativity and nonconformity.

- With respect to females especially, eliminate stereotypes about their creative potential.

Concluding Comments

It is apparent, even in a relatively brief survey of women visual artists in the past 150 years, that greater recognition is finally being accorded them, perhaps belatedly but in good measure. Some art historians may have acknowledged their abilities, even treasured their works in the past, but the achievement of these women was a well-kept secret from much of society. They were rarely perceived as cultural treasures or given the exposure that would enable others to make that decision for themselves. Today, woman visual artists have a museum of their own and are being given major exhibitions in museums around the country. Opportunity is expanding to meet talent and commitment on the road to recognition and achievement. The individual female artist can take satisfaction in her work and in the appreciation of others for it, but, in a way, she has to allow herself to do that. The present is much richer in this respect than the past for her, and the future for her daughters looks even brighter.

Opportunities may be, and often are, supplied in the family environment, but achieving some degree of eminence in the chosen field, especially one as competitive as art, also requires determination and even sacrifice. Determination may include becoming more vocal, more assertive, more willing to explore areas of interest than was true for girls in previous generations. "Sacrifice" can involve anything from not getting enough sleep to having no leisure time for recreation, lack of participation in children's activities to inability to share a husband's interests. (Note: From a purely psychotherapeutic point of view, the latter two are not recommended for either the health of the marriage or the mental health of the children. One does have to weigh priorities and consequences.) Indeed, one perception of what makes an artist productive and achieving includes strong commitment, which includes sacrifice, interacting with talent and opportunity, the latter frequently being contingent in some way on having a mentor. It seems fair to say that it would be an extremely rare talented individual, with all the commitment to her art that it is possible to have, who could achieve recognition without some external being, some extra-personal figure, providing an ounce, at least, of opportunity. That "ounce" may be any one of a number of possibilities: exposure to an artistic style, an introduction to a master art teacher or to a gallery owner, a scholarship that enables the artist to study and practice her art rather than spend many hours a day washing dishes to pay her tuition. When that helpful "someone" takes the nascent artist under her or his wings, and guides and teaches her, you have a mentor.

The mentor may also wish to impart some realities of life. One is that people, artists included, have to have a priority list when it comes to their commitments and activities. The list is subject to change as circumstances change, but it is the rare individual today who can shut out the world (i.e., family and allied responsibilities, or job and its requirements) totally in favor of doing something she prefers—like her art. Choices have to be made and, as noted above, responsibility for those choices accepted. Sometimes, especially in interpersonal rather than job-related situations, a trade-off can be negotiated so that, for example, a longer block of time for working on art is arranged in exchange for doing something for the other person (spouse, parent). As a person's obligations change, she may be able to devote more time to her art and reap more internal and external rewards with fewer such exchanges. Another reality is that, especially if the artist has more talent than money, she may be able to trade a small piece of her art for professional services as needed, such as accounting, legal, or even psychological. This trade "in kind" has been a practice for centuries. A third thought that the mentor might share is that doing something you enjoy is allowed. Not everything one does has to be duty or drudgery, and the feeling of pleasure that results from artistic activity is healthy.

Almost a quarter-century ago, the comment was made that:

> Because of the traditional barriers in fields as varied as architecture and music, women have to be more assertive in seeking to gain acceptance of their creativity, and *that* may be the crux of the problem. Women have creative potential; they have creative ability. They need stimulation less than they need recognition, acceptance, and opportunity. Perhaps some day, if these needs are met, no man will have to ask how to stimulate women's creativity. He will have been overwhelmed by it. (Schwartz, 1977, p. 267)

In the light of past and current research, there seems to be little reason to change this view today.

Appendix 7A. Questionnaire.

Female Artists: Past, Present, and Future

TODAY'S DATE _____/_____/_____   YOUR BIRTH DATE _____/_____/_____

A little background, please:

1. Your highest level of education completed:
    ☐ High School   ☐ College *Field* _____
                    ☐ Graduate degree *Field* _____
                    ☐ Art School *Field* _____

2. At about what age did your interest in becoming an artist emerge? __
    What was the response of your immediate family? _____
    _____
    Did you have a mentor? ☐ yes ☐ no.
    If yes, ☐ male or ☐ female?
    If yes, in what ways did this mentor help you? _____
    _____
    _____

3. Have you ever been married? ☐ yes ☐ no
    Divorced? ☐ yes ☐ no
    Widowed? ☐ yes ☐ no
    Have you had children? ☐ yes ☐ no
        Ages _____/ _____/ _____/ _____/ _____

4. Have you been employed outside your home? ☐ F/t or ☐ P/t
    Was your job art-related? _____
    Are you employed today outside your home? ☐ yes ☐ no
    Art-related? ☐ yes ☐ no
    Were you employed outside your home when your children were:
        ☐ Pre-school age   ☐ In elementary school   ☐ In High School
    Was this employment art-related? ☐ yes ☐ no *Field* _____

5.   Do you believe that creativity is a fixed trait
     (i.e., you have it or you don't)? ☐ yes ☐ no

6.   Have you experienced barriers in your efforts to combine your art
     with other aspects of your life? ☐ yes ☐ no
     If yes, what were they? _____

     _____

     _____

     In what ways did you overcome them?
     a. _____
     b. _____
     c. _____

7.   Your art specialty? _____
     Neophyte?/ Experienced?/ Professional? _____

8.   Have you had the opportunity to work with school-age girls who
     have been talented or interested in some aspect of the arts?
     ☐ yes ☐ no
     Age range _____
     Have you served as mentor to any of them? _____
     In what ways?
     a. _____
     b. _____
     c. _____
     d. _____
     e. _____

9.   Do you believe that creativity can be activated through effort?
     ☐ yes ☐ no

10. What suggestions do you have to maximize opportunities for girls
     who are gifted and creative in the arts?
     a. _____
     b. _____
     c. _____
     d. _____
     e. _____

11. Do you have suggestions for them relevant to possible conflicts between their art and the other aspects of their lives?

a. _____

b. _____

c. _____

d. _____

e. _____

12. Please check off the 5 qualities below that you believe best describe you as an adolescent:

☐ Adaptable ☐ Adventurous ☐ Aggressive ☐ Anxious

☐ Artistic ☐ Assertive ☐ Competent ☐ Conforming

☐ Creative ☐ Curious ☐ Dependent ☐ Emotional

☐ Enthusiastic ☐ Friendly ☐ Independent ☐ Impulsive

☐ Inquisitive ☐ Intelligent ☐ Intense ☐ Interesting

☐ Introverted ☐ Inventive ☐ Persistent ☐ Sarcastic

Other _____

Please mark the 5 qualities that you believe best describe you today:

☐ Adaptable ☐ Adventurous ☐ Aggressive ☐ Anxious

☐ Artistic ☐ Assertive ☐ Competent ☐ Conforming

☐ Creative ☐ Curious ☐ Dependent ☐ Emotional

☐ Enthusiastic ☐ Friendly ☐ Independent ☐ Impulsive

☐ Inquisitive ☐ Intelligent ☐ Intense ☐ Interesting

☐ Introverted ☐ Inventive ☐ Persistent ☐ Sarcastic

Other _____

One last question: **Why** *do you create?*

_____

_____

_____

_____

Please use this space to express any other thoughts you might have regarding encouraging creative girls to pursue their artistic interests:

_____

_____

_____

_____

Thank you!

Lita Linzer Schwartz, Ph.D.

Distinguished Professor Emerita Pennsylvania State University, Abington College

Fax: 215-884-9693

e-mail: lls2@psu.edu

Please return these pages in the enclosed envelope.

References

Ashton, D., & Hare, D. B. (1981). *Rosa Bonheur: A life and a legend.* New York: Viking Press.

Bachtold, L. M. (1976). Personality characteristics of women of distinction. *Psychology of Women Quarterly, 1*(1), 70–78.

Bachtold, L. M., & Werner, E. E. (1973). Personality characteristics of creative women. *Perceptual and Motor Skills, 36,* 311–319.

Brooks, G. S., & Daniluk, J. C. (1998). Creative labors: The lives and careers of women artists. *Career Development Quarterly, 46,* 246–261.

Brooks, J. B. (1973). Familial antecedents and adult correlates of artistic interests in childhood. *Journal of Personality, 41*(1), 110–120.

Cangelosi, D., & Schaefer, C. E. (1992). Psychological needs underlying the creative process. *Psychological Reports, 71,* 321–322.

Domino, G., & Giuliani, I. (1997). Creativity in three samples of photographers: A validation of the Adjective Check List Creativity Scale. *Creativity Research Journal, 10,* 193–200.

Dunford, P. (1990). *A biographical dictionary of women artists in Europe and America since 1850.* New York: Harvester Wheatsheaf.

Elam, C. H. (Organizer). (1967). *The Peale family: Three generations of American artists.* Detroit, MI: The Detroit Institute of Arts and Wayne State University Press.

Friedman, J. M., & Master, D. (1981). School and museum: A partnership for learning. *Gifted Child Quarterly, 25,* 43–48.

Goodman, M. J. S. (with Lieberman, N. K.) (1999). *Learning through art.* New York: Guggenheim Museum Publications.

Helson, R. (1990). Creativity in women: Outer and inner views over time. In M. A. Runco & R. S. Albert (Eds.), *Theories of creativity* (pp. 46–58). Newbury Park, CA: Sage.

Higgonet, A. (1990). *Berthe Morisot.* New York: Harper & Row.

Hogrefe, J. (1994). *O'Keeffe: The life of an American legend.* New York: Bantam Books.

Humphrey, J. (1975). *Women of photography: An historical survey.* San Francisco: San Francisco Museum of Art.

Kavaler-Adler, S. (1993). *The compulsion to create: A psychoanalytic study of women.* New York & London: Routledge.

Kerr, B. A. (1985). Smart girls, gifted women. Columbus, OH: Ohio Psychology.

Kirschenbaum, R. J., & Reis, S. M. (1997). Conflicts in creativity: Talented female artists. *Creativity Research Journal, 10,* 251–263.

Lewin, K. (D. Cartwright, Ed.) (1961). *Field theory in social science: Selected theoretical papers.* New York: Harper & Brothers.

Lindsay, S. G. (1985). Mary Cassatt and Philadelphia. Philadelphia: Philadelphia Museum of Art.

Montgomery, E. (1993). Georgia O'Keeffe. New York: Barnes & Noble Books.

Newhall, B. (1982). The history of photography (Rev. ed.). New York: The Museum of Modern Art.

Noble, K. D. (1987). The dilemma of gifted women. Psychology of Women Quarterly, 11, 367–378.

Nochlin, L. (1994). Why have there been no great women artists? In A. C. Herrmann & A. J. Stewart (Eds.), *Theorizing feminism: Parallel trends in the humanities and social sciences* (pp. 93–116). Boulder, CO: Westview Press.

Ochse, R. (1991). Why there were relatively few eminent women artists. *Journal of Creative Behavior, 25,* 334–343.

Piirto, J. (1991). Why are there so few? *Roeper Review, 13*(1), 142–147.

Reis, S. (1998). *Work left undone: Choices and compromises of talented women.* Mansfield Center, CT: Creative Learning Press, Inc.

Rimm, S. (1999). *See Jane win: The RIMM report on how 1,000 girls became successful women.* New York: Crown Publishers.

Rosenblum, N. (1994). *A history of women photographers.* New York: Abbeville Press.

Rostan, S. M. (1998). A study of the development of young artists: The emergence of an artistic and creative identity. *Journal of Creative Behavior, 32,* 278–301.

Sang, B. E. (1981). Women and the creative process. *The Arts in Psychotherapy, 8*(1), 43–48.

Sapp, D. D. (1995). Creative problem-solving in art: A model for idea inception and image development. *Journal of Creative Behavior, 29,* 173–185.

Schaefer, C. (1990). Self-concepts of creative girls: A twenty-five year followup. *Psychological Reports, 67,* 683-686.

Schwartz. L. L. (1977). Can we stimulate creativity in women? *Journal of Creative Behavior, 11,* 264-267.

Schwartz, L. L. (1980). Advocating for the neglected gifted: Females. *Gifted Child Quarterly, 24,* 113-117.

Schwartz, L. L. (1991). Guiding gifted girls. In R. M. Milgram (Ed.), *Counseling gifted and talented children: A guide for teachers, counselors, and parents* (pp. 143-160). Norwood, NJ: Ablex.

Schwartz, L. L. (1994). *Why give gifts to the gifted? Investing in a national resource.* Thousand Oaks, CA: Corwin Press.

Shaughnessy, M. F. (1987). Toward a creative female's life cycle. *The Creative Child and Adult Quarterly, 12,* 84-92.

Simonton, D. K. (1999). *Origins of genius: Darwinian perspectives on creativity.* New York: Oxford University Press.

Sims, L. S. (1998). *Elizabeth Catlett sculpture: A fifty-year retrospective.* Purchase, NY: Neuberger Museum of Art.

Singer, E. (1984). Reflections on sexual differences in creative productivity. *Journal of Contemporary Psychotherapy, 14*(2), 158-166.

Stariha, W. E., & Walberg, H. J. (1995). Childhood precursors of women's artistic eminence. *Journal of Creative Behavior, 29,* 269-282.

Stohs, J. H. (1992). Career patterns and family status of women and men artists. *Career Development Quarterly, 40,* 223-233.

Stone, D. (1998, March 11). Should women work? No matter their class, women who work are the targets of a huge guilt industry. *The Philadelphia Inquirer,* p. A21.

Sweet, F. A. (1966). *Miss Mary Cassatt: Impressionist from Philadelphia.* Norman, OK: University of Oklahoma Press.

Terman, L. M., & Oden, M. H. (1959). *Genetic studies of genius, Volume V. The gifted group at mid-life: Thirty-five years' follow-up of the superior child.* Stanford, CA: Stanford University Press.

Tomlinson-Keasey, C. (1998). Tracing the lives of gifted women. In R. C. Friedman & K. B. Rogers (Eds.), *Talent in context: Historical and social perspectives on giftedness* (pp. 17-38). Washington: American Psychological Association.

Torrance, E. P. (1983). Role of mentors in creative achievement. *The Creative Child and Adult Quarterly, 8,* 8-15, 18.

Tucker, A. (Ed.) (1973). *The woman's eye.* New York: Alfred A. Knopf.

Tufts, E. (1974). *Our hidden heritage: Five centuries of women artists.* New York: Paddington Press.

Williams, R. (1998, March). Do women photographers see differently? *American Photo, 9*(2), 26, 89.

Wolf, S., with contributions by S. Lipscomb, D. N. Mancoff, & P. Rose. (1998). Julia Margaret Cameron's women [catalog of the exhibition]. Chicago, IL and New Haven, CT: The Art Institute of Chicago and Yale University Press.

Chapter 8

Toward a Theory of Creativity in Diverse Creative Women

Sally M. Reis

Little research has been completed and little is known about creative women, their creative processes, and the decisions they face about their own creative productivity, and therefore how we can promote creativity in diverse girls and women. The social and political movement focusing on women during the past five decades has provided some understanding of women's creative processes as well as the creative roles that women have played in our society and the forces that shape those roles. In this chapter, current research is analyzed, focusing on the development of women's creativity and the classification of this research into major themes. Internal and external blocks to creativity in women are discussed as is current research on these blocks, and an explanation is suggested for different types of creative productivity exhibited by women. A theory is proposed regarding the diversion of women's creativity into multiple areas in their lives, including relationships, work related to both family and home, personal interests, and aesthetic sensitivities. This diversion of creative efforts may result in different levels of creativity applied to work, as well as different patterns of creative productivity emerging in a diverse group of creative women. The groups of women studied in research cited in this chapter include women of various ages, from adolescence through old age; from various cultural groups, white, African American, Indian, Asian, Australian, South American, and from various Latino groups; and from different domains, including artists, researchers, students, scientists, entrepreneurs, and politicians.

When we reflect on what has been learned about creativity during the last 50 years, we are forced to acknowledge that a gap exists in one major area. Little research has been completed and little is known about diverse, creative women, the choices they make, and the decisions they face about creative productivity in their lives. As Simonton recently indicated, "Psychologists still have a long way to go before they come anywhere close to understanding creativity in women and minorities" (2000, p. 156). This is probably true because the majority of research conducted on creativity and productivity in adult life has concentrated on men (Cattell, 1903; Diamond, 1986; Lindauer, 1992; McLeish, 1976; Schneidman, 1989; Sears, 1977; Simonton, 1978, 1984, 1989). This fact is not often discussed in these data-based studies, and for this reason, Huyck (1990) called for research to investigate how gender and age account for interests, believing that researchers must develop a "sensitivity to issues of gender," through "accepting the possibility that men and women have substantially different basic experiences" (p. 130).

It has been noted that male professors produce more creative work in research publications work than female professors (Ajzenberg-Selove, 1994; Axelrod, 1988; Bateson, 1990), and men earn more degrees, produce more works of art, and make more contributions in professional fields (Callahan, 1979; Ochse, 1991; Piirto, 1991; Reis, 1987, 1998). Even in areas such as literature, in which both younger boys and girls believe that females excel, adult men are more productive in their professional accomplishments. For many years, for example, more men than women have been recipients of grants from the National Endowment Fellowships in Literature. As Callahan (1979) pointed out two decades ago and this still true today, men publish more books than women.

A few recent researchers have questioned why so few eminent female creators exist (Gates, 1994; Ochse, 1991; Piirto, 1991), but Gates (1994) reminds us that the same question was raised by Havelock Ellis in 1894. Gates quoted Ellis as explaining the absence of famous female composers by describing the theory of variability, that is, a greater variation of ability exists in males, as more males than females are geniuses as well as idiots (Gates, p. 27). Although Ellis called this theory the variability hypothesis, some later writers renamed it "the mediocrity of women hypothesis" (Gates, p. 27).

Despite limited research on highly creative women, some explanations have been offered for the small number of women recognized as highly creative in certain domains. Piirto (1991) suggested that one reason for the absence of many famous women artists is how intensely they pursue their passions for art. But how intensely do creative women pursue other fields? Isaac Asimov's *Biographical Encyclopedia of Science and Technology* (1982) is subtitled "The Lives and Achievements of 1,510 Great Scientists from Ancient Times to the Present, Chronologically Arranged." Of the 1,510 scientists included in the book, only 14 are women. When Barbara McClintock won the Nobel Prize for Science in 1983, she was only the fifth woman to receive this award in the eight decades since it was established. Research on the creative processes and personalities of creative girls and women has demonstrated that gender stereotyping throughout their lifetimes, as well as both internal and external barriers in their education, marriage, and family lives, affect their creative productivity (Reis, 1987, 1995a, 1995b, 1996, 1998). The choices that some highly creative women make willingly, or are forced to make, have a profound impact on both the quantity and direction of their creative output. These choices affect the focus of their creativity, either as applied to work or to other essential components of their lives, including: family, relationships, personal interests, and work related to family and home.

The social and political movement focusing on women during the past five decades has provided some understanding of women's creative processes as well as the creative roles that women have played in our society and the forces that shape those roles. Research focusing on the development of women's creativity can be classified into three major themes.

Theme One: Personality Characteristics of Creative Women and the Barriers to and Supports for Their Creative Work

The first theme relates to the personality characteristics of highly creative women, the internal blocks that may prevent them from creating, and the study of these characteristics as a means of helping other women with creative potential to develop their creativity. Research in this area generally falls under the umbrella of either historical views or more modern explanations. To explore historical issues, researchers use retrospective analyses to investigate how creativity evolved in eminent women. Studies have been conducted, for example, on famous writers, scientists, and artists in order to attempt to identify factors characterizing the lives of talented, creative women of the time. These factors have generally included: the ability to overcome challenges or problems, the need for or absence of support, the opportunity to learn independently in the absence of formal education, and the willingness to live a different life from their peers or counterparts. Wallace and Wahlberg (1995), for example, attempted to identify the early conditions of successful adult females by using a historical analysis of psychological traits and childhood environments. Results suggested what is already known, that is, both intelligence and environment are correlates in the success of notable women. As girls, notable women were intelligent, hard working, imaginative, and strong willed. Future writers studied were encouraged by their parents, were culturally and financially advantaged, and learned much outside of school. In addition, girls who became famous writers were more apt to question assumptions and conventions than were those who became notable artists, scientists, lawyers, and politicians.

Subotnik and Arnold (1995) investigated women in science, generally finding what has been noted in previous research, that creative female scientists appear to be motivated largely by deep intellectual engagement and the recognition associated with influential discoveries. The degree to which women scientists resemble or differ from this largely male-derived profile has not been extensively researched. Subotnik and Arnold found, however, that a potential mismatch existed between the single-minded devotion to science, characteristic of eminent research-ers, and the desire to balance family and career that appears so prevalently in reports of professional women. For some groups of culturally diverse creative women, the extended family creates other obligations and blocks to creativity. In a 4-year longitudi-nal study of talented, culturally diverse, highly creative teenage girls conducted using case study analysis, some of the Puerto Rican girls studied indicated that their focus on individual attainment and creativity resulted in negative pressure from their extended family (Reis et al., 1995). In order to support their daughters' creative development, some parents moved to an-other part of the city to enable their daughters to have freedom from extended family criticism regarding the pursuit of the girls' creative talents.

Helson (1996) compared a sample of highly creative women mathematicians with a sample of other female mathematicians. The two groups differed only slightly on measures of intelligence, cognition, and masculine traits, but the creative mathematicians had more research activity, were highly flexible, original, and rejected outside influence. Half of the creative women were foreign-born, and most had professional men as fathers. As compared with creative male mathematicians, the creative women had less assurance, published less, and occupied less prestigious positions. She also found differences between creative and com-parison subjects in background and personality, perhaps indicat-ing that their personality characteristics were powerful determi-nants of creativity in female mathematicians. The traits most characteristic of these creative women were

- rebellious independence, introversion, and a rejec-tion of outside influences;

- strong symbolic interests and a marked ability to find self-expression and self-gratification in directed re-search activity; and

- flexibility, or lack of constriction, both in general attitudes and in mathematical work. Helson attributed differences in creative productivity between men and women after graduate school to social roles and institutional arrangements.

Research with creative women has demonstrated that internal personal barriers often exist in the process of completing creative work (Arnold & Denny, 1985; Callahan, 1979; Hollinger & Fleming, 1988; Kerr, 1985; Ochse, 1991; Piirto, 1991; Reis, 1987, 1998; Subotnik & Arnold, 1995). The way women have been raised and the cultural messages they encounter seem to result in these internal barriers and in failure to develop the belief in self necessary for a commitment to highly creative work (Reis, 1998). Instead, some creative women remain in the background, in a less "center stage" position, as implementers of the ideas of others (Reis, 1998). Creative potential in some women may be directed to lower-profile work. While their male counterparts produce plays, write articles or books, undertake large deals, and are viewed as creative high achievers, many highly creative women make conscious or unconscious decisions to work in a more facilitating role, often implementing the creative ideas of others (Reis, 1998).

Highly creative women who are able to capitalize on this potential in their work often display single-minded purpose, make difficult choices about personal lives, and have support systems to enable their creativity to emerge. These support systems include supportive spouses, or choices made about personal life that have been considered nontraditional in the past, such as remaining unmarried, choosing not to have children, living alone or with a partner, or any combination of these. These decisions are often made to support the adaptation of a lifestyle conducive to the production of highly creative work.

One female composer studied by Reis (1996) lived with a domestic partner who was an older man totally devoted to her talent and her ability to work. She often worked seven days a week on her music and was extremely happy in her choices, feeling, she explained, an obligation to work as hard as she did to make a contribution to a female presence in musical composition. Her first work for orchestra, written in 1981, has become extremely successful, having been played by 30 orchestras including the

New York Philharmonic. Reviews of her work have appeared in major newspapers, journals, magazines, and music periodicals, and she has received numerous awards, commissions, fellowships, and grants from the Guggenheim, Fromm, Naumburg, Koussevitzky, and Jerome foundations. She has been profiled in an award-winning PBS documentary, and major symphonies continue to perform her work. Recently, one of her compositions competed against 140 other new orchestral works to win the Grawemeyer Award, the largest cash prize award in music. She has a long-term relationship with a man with whom she has lived for almost 20 years, and has never had children. She has commissions until 2002 and currently holds a chair at a small college where she teaches for two days each week. She admits that during the other 5 days of every week she often spends 7 or 8 hours a day composing. She does not like to take time off from her work and feels an obligation to be a female composer who continues to contribute. "We still have such a long way to go," she says. "I mean, just look at the statistics. How many pieces by women composers do you know? And how many do you really know? The musicology network is still overwhelmingly a male network. I mean, the standard music history textbook—*the Grout History of Music*—listed two women. That's for the whole history of music" (Reis, 1995b, p. 70).

At the same time, many women with high creative potential are not able to capitalize on their potential in work. A female sculptor who had incredible potential for success in art and won several prizes as a student and young artist explained why her career had been on hold, "I have spent the last 25 years sculpting my three children. They have taken every ounce of my creativity, and there has been little left, either time or creative energy, for my work." (Reis, 1998).

Theme Two: Societal Factors that Facilitate or Impede the Development of Women's Creativity

The second theme in research relates to the societal factors that facilitated or became an impediment to the development of women's creativity. Research in this area is generally divided into either historical or more modern explanations. Ochse (1991) asked why there were so few eminent female creators (scientists, composers, and artists). Researchers who study the history of female achievement have shown that creative works produced by women are often underrated or ignored in history. Historical research indicates that although intellectual stimulation in the home seems to play a major role in the development of creative ability, many girls were typically not encouraged or even allowed to engage in intellectual pursuits by their families or peers. They traditionally received less education than boys, and society often denied women access to certain cultural materials and teachers. In the past, women, and especially culturally diverse women, undoubtedly received little encouragement, stimulation, and access to tools necessary for building intellectual skills and developing the ability to create something of cultural value. Moreover, females were regarded as less able than males to use their intellectual skills creatively. Women who have the need to create may also experience constraints on their personal lives (Kirschenbaum & Reis, 1997).

Some authors have posited "modern" explanations of why there continue to be relatively few eminent women creators, and asked questions similar to those posed by the researchers who have offered "historical" views on why have we not had more female writers, painters, scientists, sculptors, or artists. One explanation offered is that many women do not perceive themselves as creators, follow their interests into career preparation, or place importance on the works they produce (Arnold, 1995; Callahan, 1979; Kerr, 1985; Reis, 1987, 1998). The problem may be further exacerbated when women do produce original, creative works, as some researchers have found that women are more conscious of criticism than men (Baer, 1997; Roberts, 1991; Roberts & Nolen-Hoeksema, 1994) and find it more difficult to deal with negative perceptions of their work.

Other explanations of why there are so few eminent women creators have to do with time commitments. Researchers who have offered "historical" explanations about the limited number of women creators argue that women were burdened with family responsibilities, child bearing, and limited educational opportunities. Contemporary researchers argue that creative women may have too many demands on their time, feel guilty if they attempt to do creative work in time that should be spent with their family, or in some cases, dislike working alone for the periods of time necessary for creative accomplishment (Callahan, 1979; Kerr, 1985; Ochse, 1991; Piirto, 1991; Reis, 1987, 1998). Some researchers have noted that the same years in which Lehman (1953) found the height of male creative productivity to occur characterize the peak period of women's responsibilities to children (Reis, 1998). Some contemporary researchers have noted that in our society, exceptionally able women experience considerable stress related to role conflict and overload, which in many reduces creative urges (Ochse; Piirto; Reis 1987, 1998).

A few studies have examined current highly creative women to investigate the factors enabling them to develop their creativity. For example, List and Renzulli (1991) examined the impact of societal influences on the development of creative artists and studied their formal educational experiences, familial support, the role played by mentors, and the artists' views about the development of their own creative processes. Results indicated that despite negative formal educational experiences, these creative artists generally had supportive families and the benefit of at least one influential mentor in their lives. Each experienced both a strong personal drive to create and a need to share their products with appropriate audiences.

Roscher (1987) studied a group of 12 highly creative successful women scientists who attributed part of their accomplishments to a role model, whether during high school or college, or an individual professor or family member who provided encouragement. The majority of the married women attributed their continued success to the encouragement of their spouse, often a scientist, who recognized the sacrifices necessary for success.

Theme Three: Gender and Cultural Differences in the Creative Process and Product

A third theme relates to the notion that gender differences exist in creativity and the creative process. A growing number of researchers have called for changes in the paradigm of how we view women and creativity, and the need for changes in society that could facilitate the development of creativity in women. Women have made, and continue to make, many creative contributions that are different from the creative accomplishments made by men, yet men's creative accomplishments seem to be valued more by society (Reis, 1987, 1995a, 1995b, 1996, 1998). The creative accomplishments of women are regarded by them as more modest, and do not reflect the types of creative productivity that result in awards, prizes, books, articles, art, patents, professional stature, and financial gain. Rather, their creative efforts are diversified over several initiatives and their creative products are different than those listed above.

A number of researchers have argued that gender differences exist in creativity among men and women. Some researchers perceive that at least some women perceive creative phenomena differently from men. Since women's experiences and situations in society have been vastly different from men's, one would expect differences in perception to emerge, for perception cannot be separated from learning and experience. For example, some female artists believe that their creative growth from both childbirth and parenting can actually contribute to their creative growth in art (Kirschenbaum & Reis, 1997). It is interesting to note that these artists, however, were regional award winners and not artists who have emerged as highly creative in their respective fields, at least at this period in their lives.

Van Tassel-Baska (1995) studied the lives of Bronte and Woolf to investigate whether the path of a talented female writer is different from a male writer, and identified similarities in the lives and work of Bronte and Woolf over the life span. She found three major influences on female writers: adversity (obstacles that the women had to overcome in order to realize their potential), autodidactism (dependence on self-learning due to limited or absent formal educational opportunities), and emotional support (need to have mentors to help these gifted women attain their potential). These areas also surface in other research related to women and the creative process across domains.

Explanations for gender differences in creative productivity vary. Some researchers point to studies from the 1950s indicating that women are more conservative, conventional, and unlikely to posses the traits most associated with creativity. However, in later replication studies, Eisenman & Johnson (1969) found that creative females preferred more complexity than males and that women were more open than males in terms of emotional expression.

Perhaps the most controversial issue related to women and the creative process is the claim that there may be a potential mismatch between the single-minded devotion necessary for creative accomplishment and the desire to balance family and career that appears so frequently in research about creative women. In fact, many women have the potential to display single-minded devotion to their work, but they also choose to diversify their creative efforts. One highly productive female scientist who had several patents and had published over a hundred scientific papers admitted she did her scientific research in addition to being dean of a large science college in a very competitive university. She had the responsibility for almost a hundred faculty members, over $20 million in budget and grants, and she ran a large laboratory on her own research initiatives. She was committed to having more economically disadvantaged and culturally diverse students become scientists, so part of her work continued to be the mentoring of young talented African American students from urban high schools. She explained that she was very efficient and could do multiple tasks. She also explained that on many weekends, she did not do science, but rather pursued another love, gardening. She had three children who had all graduated from college and a loving relationship with her husband, an architect. He indicated that his work had always been secondary to that of his wife. "She is," he explained, "brilliant," and he had always been committed to encouraging her career. They have a close marriage and by all accounts she had been an involved and loving mother. Their marriage appeared close and happy and had survived over 30 years (Reis, in press).

This female scientist may never win a Nobel prize or become a household name and she clearly has that potential and a single-minded devotion to work. But she has chosen, like many creative women, to diversify her creativity potential; it was applied to her laboratory, to her work as an administrator, to mentoring poor African American high school students, to her spouse and children, and to her gardening. More work remains to learn more about diversion of creative potential in women.

The creative process in women may emerge differently than in males, and in some women, it may have difficulty in emerging. Women's perceptions of the creative process in art as well as other areas have been filtered through male perspectives and the cultural roles developed for women but not by women. Therefore, female writers, artists, scientists, and creators in all domains deal with male conceptions of creativity and a creative process that has been accepted as the standard within that domain, but may only be the standard for male creators (Reis, 1998). Again, more research is needed in this area.

New Initiatives or Research on Women and Creativity

New research about women and creativity is sorely needed. Intriguing issues have not been widely researched, such as one study that indicates that some women's timelines for creative work may occur at a later time than men's. In research with older women who achieved eminence in their respective fields after age 50, later years were found to be very productive for the development of women's creativity (Reis, 1996). Drawing on research conducted with creative women during the last twenty years, a model of talent realization in women depicted in Figure 1 was provided by Reis (1996; 1998). The model includes: abilities (intelligence and special talents), personality traits, environmental factors, and perceptions about the social importance of the realization of talents. Each of these separate factors contribute to the development of belief in self and the desire to develop one's talents, depicted in the middle block that then leads to the development and the realization of talent in women.

A Model of Talent Realization in Women

Five factors emerged from the data that suggested the model of talent realization in women depicted in Figure 1. This model evolved from separate research studies conducted over a decade (Kirchenbaum & Reis, 1997; Reis, 1987, 1991, 1995a, 1995b, 1996, 1998; Reis & Callahan, 1989; Reis, et al. 1995; Walker, Reis, & Leonard, 1992). The samples for this work were extremely diverse. The groups of women participating in the research included women of various ages, adolescence through old age; from various cultural groups, white, African American, Indian, Asian, Australian, South American, and from various Hispanic groups; and from different domains, including artists, researchers, students, scientists, entrepreneurs, and politicians.

The factors in the model include

- above average intelligence, contextual intelligence, and/or special talents,
- personality traits,
- environmental contributions, and
- the perceived social importance of the use or manifestation of the talent.

This combination of factors results in a belief in self and a desire to actively develop one's talents.

Above Average Ability and Special Talents

Women who realized their talent indicated that they were good but not superior students during the time they were in school, reflecting the distinction made by Renzulli (1986) between schoolhouse giftedness and creative-productive giftedness. The women

FIGURE 8-1 *A Model of Talent Realization in Women.*

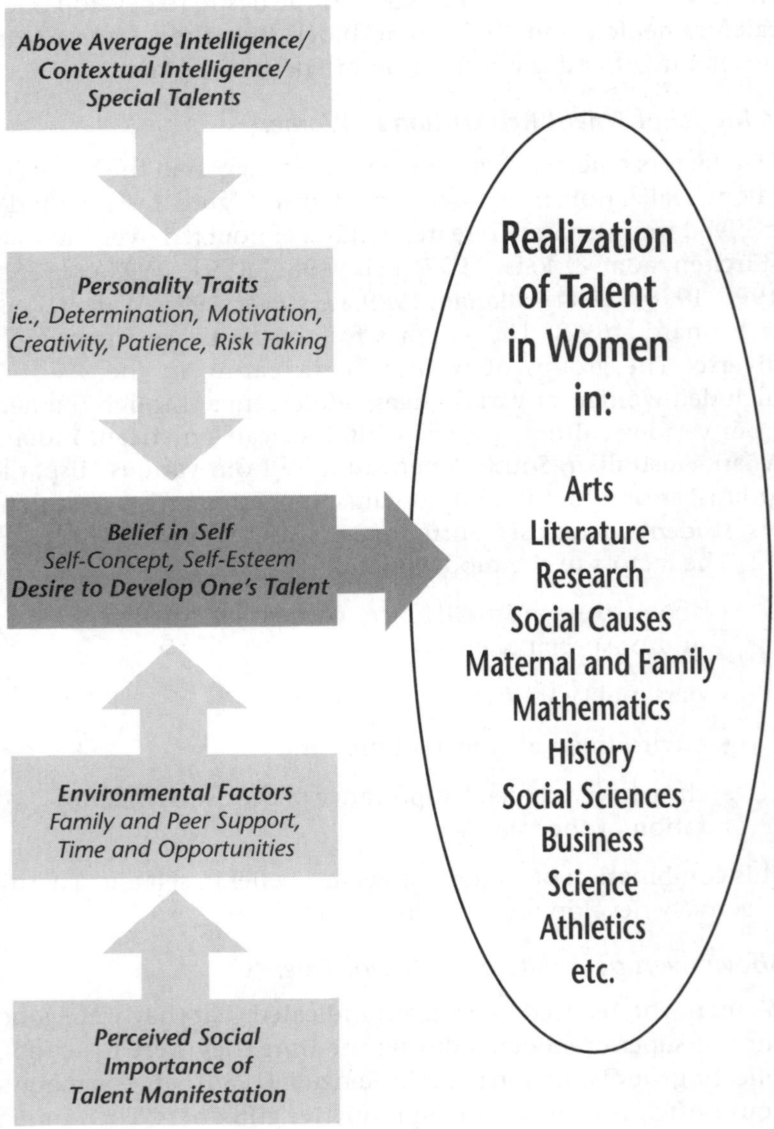

Above Average Intelligence/
Contextual Intelligence/
Special Talents

Personality Traits
*ie., Determination, Motivation,
Creativity, Patience, Risk Taking*

Belief in Self
Self-Concept, Self-Esteem
Desire to Develop One's Talent

Environmental Factors
*Family and Peer Support,
Time and Opportunities*

Perceived Social
Importance of
Talent Manifestation

**Realization
of Talent
in Women
in:**

Arts
Literature
Research
Social Causes
Maternal and Family
Mathematics
History
Social Sciences
Business
Science
Athletics
etc.

who displayed creative productive giftedness chose creative options as opposed to another route that would have resulted in high grades or superior performance in school. In almost every case, the creativity, interests, and talents of the subjects merged to enable the development of their talent. Contextual or practical intelligence (Sternberg, 1985) was also manifested by all of the participants as each was able to creatively cope with the problems encountered. They displayed skills such as adapting to existing environments; shaping existing environments in ways that rendered them a better fit to their unique abilities, values, and interests; and selecting new environments when existing environments were not and could not be made suitable.

Personality Traits

Personality traits emerging from interviews or other primary source data included determination, motivation, various ways of manifesting creativity, patience, and the ability to take—and in some cases thrive on—risks. Determination was clearly exhibited throughout the life of every study participant. The ability to strive for success and to continue to work hard, sometimes under adverse odds, with or without the support of family, was evident in most cases. The participants explained their motivation and creative processes differently. Some were certain it had developed from the positive role modeling of their parents. Others believed they developed their motivation because of their strong need for a purpose in life, such as preserving the environment, being a successful female composer, or bringing theater to disadvantaged urban youth. Still others believed that their motivation came from a desire to produce, leave a mark upon the world, or from the sheer joy of the creative act. Their creativity was also evident in their love for their work, the sheer volume of their work, and their persistent evolution into higher and more challenging talent forms.

Patience was also a characteristic of all of subjects in this study. Some had to wait years for the opportunity to invest considerable blocks of time in the development of their own talent. Some worked steadily over the years only to be acknowledged for their specific talents later in life. One woman (Reis, 1995b) postponed her congressional career until her youngest daughter was ready for college. A composer worked consistently to improve her art form. This "wait time" differs markedly from research conducted on achievement in males. Lehman (1953), for example, concluded that achievement tended to be a curvilinear function of age: From the onset of a creator's career, productivity increases rapidly, levels off at a productive peak age, and thereafter, declines with increasing age. While some have questioned Lehman's belief in a creative decline in later years, Simonton (1989, 1990a, 1990b) has indicated that recent research employing multivariate techniques has demonstrated the general truth of Lehman's basic conclusions, even though specific details often need to be qualified. For example, Simonton (1990a) cites specific domains such as pure mathematics and theoretical physics in which early peaks of productivity exist (late 20s or early 30s). Later peaks (late 40s or even 50s with a minimal, if not largely absent, drop-off afterward) exist, according to Simonton, in domains such as history, philosophy, and general scholarship. What is not always discussed in these data-based studies is that the research leading to these findings was conducted with populations primarily or exclusively consisting of males. It is for this reason that research is needed to investigate how gender and age interact with high levels of creative productivity.

Another trait clearly displayed by these creative, talented women was their willingness to take risks and engage in tasks that others might not have the courage to attempt. One woman who achieved eminence was almost 50 years old and financially insecure when she chose to return to graduate school to work on a Ph.D. in Renaissance literature. Another was elected to the national House of Representatives after her children had graduated from high school. How many women who are over 50 will run for Congress in the future, exposing themselves to the rigors of public life and a forced separation from home and family? Another was a forester who became a conservation activist and continued to move across the country from job to job, sleeping in tents and living under adverse conditions, simply to do the work she loved, until she was almost 80 years old.

Finally, the participants in this research displayed a trait that was difficult to define but can be described as high creative energy or vitality, and a contentment about life. Some were enthusiastic while others were quiet; some laughed frequently and moved constantly, others were very calm and almost reserved. However, each exuded a creative energy and intensity about her life and work, and a spirit of satisfaction about the direction her life had taken.

Environmental Factors

The participants in some of the studies, such as the study of older eminent women (Reis, 1995b, 1996) were more educated than the participants in other studies (Kirschenbaum & Reis, 1997; Reis, et al., 1995). Some participants came from upper middle class families, others from relatively poor families. Some attended prestigious women's colleges, some went to large state universities, and some flunked out of high school. Some received advanced degrees but most did not. Some had nurturing families but some had families who were abusive or distant. Almost all had siblings. Almost all were members of families in which sufficient income was present to provide them with food, a materially good home, and a commitment to future education. Some were born to parents with college degrees, who were of middle- to upper-middle class socio-economic status, and encouraged their daughters to attend college and graduate. Some were born to parents who had not attended high school. Some were white and others reflected culturally, ethnically, and linguistically diverse populations. Many were single; most who married or had long-term relationships had children. The women who did not have children believed that they labored more steadily on their journey to accomplishment. All participants who had children, however, delayed placing primary emphasis on their career because of their children's needs, and worked in different ways to prepare themselves for their future work. The congresswoman, for example, waited until her daughters entered college to run for office, while maintaining a steady record of community, civic, and other responsibilities that contributed to her eventual election to the House of Representatives. She did not initially realize how qualified she had become to run for public office until she sought help from her college career office. That help was vital to her and integral to her success:

> I don't know how I got the idea that I should go back to the career office at my college. Somebody suggested it to me when I applied to law school and didn't get in because I applied late. You see, I didn't know what to do with my life so I applied to law school and the School of Social Work. My career office helped me to arrange all of the volunteer stuff I had done and to put it into professional terms. Then I began to see that all of the programs that I'd developed and marketed, all of the leadership that I'd provided in the PTA to get parents more involved and all of the other stuff that I'd done could be marketed in professional terms. And I can remember saying: 'Look at all the things I've done'. The career office counselor helped me realize that all of the things I've done fit into the real world of business and after that, I said I'm not going to do volunteer work any more, I'm not going to repeat this phase of my life. I'm going to move forward. (Reis, 1995b, p. 71)

Perceived Social Importance of Talent Manifestation

All participants had a strong desire to use their talents in ways that were personally satisfying and would benefit society. They did not simply have a drive to succeed; rather, they defined success in their own unique ways that involved ways their talents could benefit society. Before she became a congresswoman, one participant was asked to be the first woman in her area to chair the United Way Fund Drive and to be the first president of The League of Women Voters. Later she consciously decided that volunteer work would no longer help her to achieve her goals. The composer started her own instrumental group but also sought to become a successful and famous composer. A poet worked to produce poetry that was personally joyful and which would also help teachers make poetry enjoyable for their students. An African American researcher discussed her research efforts in the context of her status as a woman and someone who was black, calling herself "twice exceptional." She also spoke of her need to be a role model to other young African American women considering doctoral work and a career in research.

Belief in Self and Desire to Develop and Contribute their Creative Productivity

Each of these women developed a belief in her self and a desire to make a creative contribution and each had a personal desire to develop her talents and creative productivity. Each had reasonably high levels of self-esteem, found to characterize other successful women (Northcutt, 1991; Steinem, 1992), although many had problems dealing with criticism of their work. Most believed their self-concept and self-esteem came from their own successes, as well as from the love and support they received from family and friends.

Each participant also wanted to contribute. None were satisfied with their lives unless they could actively develop their talent. Most, when asked, discussed friends and siblings who were just as smart or even smarter (if one uses school performance as the basis for assessment) but who were content to lead lives that did not involve the constant work and energy needed to develop one's talent. Why did these women continue to strive? Why did they work so hard when their friends and colleagues were content to live such different lives? My research has indicated that these women had no choice; they wanted to contribute in some way, they believed in themselves and their creative potential. Several of them explained this simply and eloquently: "Something inside of me had to come out." Gruber (1985) has referred to this as moral giftedness which requires a commitment to prolonged, steady work. Some of these women had to delay the time in which they could make a prolonged, steady commitment because of family responsibilities but once they began, they continued. Many were not able to focus their creative potential simply on their work, but rather they diversified their creative efforts to multiple venues. Some mentioned their cultural diversity as a stimulus to creative effort, indicating that they made greater creative efforts due to their understanding of the necessity for creative contributions from minority women.

The Diversification Theory of Female Creativity

Research (Reis, 1987, 1995a, 1995b, 1996, 1998) has demonstrated that women's creativity is diverted to multiple areas in their lives, including relationships, work related to family and home, personal interests, aesthetic sensitivities, and appearance. This diverse creativity emerges in their work but also in other areas including their relationships with family and friends, the ways they decorate their homes, prepare meals, plan complicated schedules for their families, balance time between work and personal life, and stretch the family budget. This diversification of creativity (see Figure 2) emerged across several studies and was eloquently explained by one participant in a study of older creative women (Reis, 1996; 1998). When asked about various periods of creative productivity in her life, one of the first female producers on Broadway discussed her beliefs about the ways in which women's creativity evolves in a different pattern than men's:

> Women spend their lives moving from one creative act to another and they find satisfaction from their creative expression in many different outlets. I have found that men, on the other hand, see an end goal and move directly toward the pursuit of that creative goal. That is why men are able to achieve goals and fame more quickly than women, but I think that women have a richer creative journey, find joy in the diversity of their creative acts, and in the end, enjoy the creative process so much more. (Reis, 1998)

Women have different ways of demonstrating their creativity. As suggested by other researchers, it may be that they are so frequently involved in multiple tasks, they are less capable of focusing only on one aspect of creativity, such as their work. This research indicates that the diversity in their creativity occurs because

FIGURE 8-2 *Diversification of Creativity in Women.*

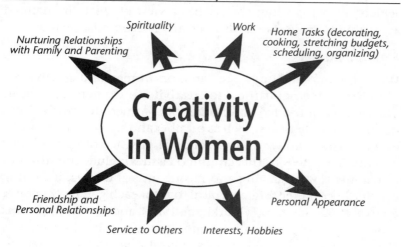

they enjoy and derive pleasure from diverse creative acts and that the diversification of their creative potential is natural for these women. Because women have had to struggle to find a place for themselves in many work situations, they have not yet had the time or experience to be able to engage in the single-minded devotion to work that many of their male peers have had. Perhaps the barriers that they have experienced over time have led to the need to diversify their creative talents, as several external and internal barriers to creativity have been identified in recent work conducted about creative women (Kirschenbaum & Reis, 1997; List and Renzulli, 1991; Ochse, 1991; Piirto, 1991 Reis, 1987; Reis, 1995a, 1995b, 1996, 1998; Roscher; 1987). Or it may be that they enjoy many diverse expressions of creativity, as indicated by many participants in the research studies leading to this theory.

External and Internal Barriers to Creative Accomplishment in Women

What types of barriers cause women with high levels of creative potential to fail to realize their potential, at least according to traditionally male standards of realizing potential? It may be that their creativity is manifested in ways not generally recognized by society, or perhaps our society has a view of creativity defined according to male standards of creative accomplishment.

External Barriers

When the limited body of research on women and creativity is examined, external barriers to creativity in women seem clear. The first set of barriers to creativity in women deal with childhood and family issues, such as number and sex of siblings, birth order of the siblings, and presence or absence of one or both parents (Reis, 1998). Other childhood issues include the attitudes of parents toward having and raising girls and boys, including purchasing different stereotypical toys for each gender (Kuebli & Fivush, 1992; Schwartz & Markham, 1985), and decorating rooms differently. Girls' rooms have more dolls and dollhouses, and boys' rooms have more vehicles, educational and art materials, and machines (Rheingold & Cook, 1975; Pomerleau et al., 1990). Some parents hinder the creative process in their daughters. In a study of young gifted female sculptors, Sloane and Sosniak (1985) found that it was most important to parents that their daughters be happily married. Parents also hoped that their daughters would be able to do something in which they were interested, finish their education, and become financially secure. If parents are primarily encouraging their talented daughters in these areas, little encouragement may have been given to their creative potential. Socialization also involves breaking cultural stereotypes and assumptions. Many of the talented Latino young women we studied discussed issues relating to their movement away from their families as they received higher levels of education and the negative cultural stereotypes they encountered.

Jeanne H. Block (1982), a pioneer in gender research, believed that a fundamental task of the developing individual is the mediation between internal biological impulses and external cultural forces as they coexist in a person's life space and life span (p. 2). She further believed that the socialization process, defined as internalization of values, appears to have differential effects on the personality development of males and females. Socialization, Block asserted, narrows women's options while broadening men's options (p. 220). Unfortunately, as girls get older, many of them learn that their perception of reality differs from the life experiences they encounter.

Because many women still assume the primary responsibility of family nurturer and caretaker, their creative energies are diverted into several different areas including work, relationships, family, and home, while many men's creative energy is more available to be directly applied to work. While female nurturing has in the past been directed primarily to child care, people are living longer and the need for care has been shifted to elderly parents. In the early 1970s, for example, only 25% of people in their late 50s had a surviving parent, but by 1980, 40% did, as did 20% of those in their early 60s, and 3% of those in their 70s. The need for care has become most necessary for the oldest people in our society, those over the age of 85, a group that has grown from fewer than 300,000 in 1930 to over 3 million today (Beck et al., 1990). The majority of those who care for elderly parents are women, and thus, the responsibilities for care increase.

Completing creative work requires long periods of concentrated effort which are not available to many women in their peak work and childbearing years, and perhaps not even in their older years. Many women of all ages who have families simply do not have that kind of time available for their professional work. A study of gifted females who selected a traditionally female career was conducted to identify the social forces, if any, that caused these women to select a career in teaching or business and to learn whether they regretted their decisions (Reis, 1995a). A questionnaire was administered to 67 gifted women aged between 25 and 62, and follow-up interviews were conducted with 25 women. When asked how much free time each respondent had each day, the mean amount of time listed by respondents was slightly more than one hour each day (X = 1.20 hrs.). The most frequent response about the amount of free time these gifted women had daily was 1/2 hour. When asked what percentage of household work and chores respondents did as compared to spouse/partner and/or children, a larger percentage than might be expected was indicated. Deleting the responses of unmarried participants, who did 100% of their housework, the mean percentage of household work and chores undertaken by these gifted females was 70.8%. Only 31% of the sample did less than 75% of the work, and 90% of this group attributed the lower percentage to their children's contributions rather than their spouse's.

Those talented females who selected a traditional career (Reis, 1995a) present a contradictory picture of parental influence on the development of creativity and emerged talent. Parents usually encouraged these gifted females to do well in school but provided little encouragement beyond the college years. Approximately 20% of the participants believed that their parents had reserved this encouragement solely for their sons. When encouragement was given to daughters, it was not applied to a specific career goal. Accordingly, these talented females learned to do well in school but had no idea how to focus their good grades and achievement scores into career aspirations. Another theme that emerged from the questionnaires and interviews involved parental expectations that these women would marry and have a family. Some respondents said their parents encouraged their education and career only when combined with family. Many of these talented females were discouraged by their parents (especially their mothers) from pursuing their careers after they had children. They were often encouraged to pursue a career only if it allowed them to "put their family first," so teaching and nursing were considered appropriate career choices and excellent outlets for creative energy by many parents of the women who participated in this study.

Runco (1991) suggested that two broad personality and cognitive "transformations" occur in the development of high levels of creativity in persons of high potential. The first is the development of outstanding creative ability during the first two decades of life. The second begins in adolescence and entails the transformation of creative abilities into an integrated set of cognitive skills, career-focused interests and values, specific creative personality dispositions, and moderately high ambitions. Accordingly, if parental encouragement of any creative work is regarded as less important than encouragement to marry and have children, a different set of priorities may be embedded in creative females than in males.

Some creative young girls are willful and determined, and their parents strive to "correct" creative aspects of their daughters' personalities. Too many parents squelch their daughters' enthusiasm and spirit under the guise of manners and behavior codes, and sometimes squelch some of the passion in their creative, spirited daughters (Reis, 1998). Recent research (Reis, 1998) indicates that the mixed messages creative girls receive emanate from the interaction of family variables, their parents' relationship, and their expectations that their daughters will have certain types of manners and behaviors. Many highly creative young girls have problems reconciling messages that have emerged from home and school with their creative potential, which causes external barriers to create internal barriers. Parents' strict guidelines about manners for their daughters create confusion about roles and expectations. Being praised for appearance, encouraged to consistently mind their manners, and told to be polite and ladylike may conflict with the characteristics that are necessary for girls with high creative potential to evolve into women whose creative potential is manifested in adult productivity. These characteristics include the ability to challenge convention, to question authority, and speak out for change (Reis, 1998). The very characteristics found to be associated with older creative women (Reis, 1996) including determination, commitment, assertiveness, risk taking, and the ability to control one's life, directly conflict with good and appropriate manners parents demand from daughters.

Internal, Personal Barriers to Creative Expression in Women

Another reason why fewer creative women fulfill their potential to complete professional and creative endeavors is their different priorities. Miller (1976) wrote in *Toward a New Psychology of Women* that women she saw in her practice were preoccupied with how their actions affected others, with questions about connecting and giving, and whether they were perceived as being selfish or measuring up. Highly creative women often value relationships as much or more than creative work (Reis, 1998). A sick child or elderly parents who need care, a friend who is in trouble, and many other personal issues cause talented women to make choices about what is more important to them, and since creative energy may be finite, force them to make difficult decisions. For many creative women, having to split time between the people that they love and creative work they want to do is a difficult and often wrenching choice (Reis, 1995a; 1996; 1998). The *greatest* conflicts found in talented, creative women in their 20s, 30s, and 40s concern the interaction between their career and personal life (Reis, 1998).

This intensely personal struggle to try to develop their personal talents while they also try to meet the needs of those they love causes creative women the most conflict, guilt, and pain. Maric Mileva Einstein, Albert's first wife, was a gifted mathematician with extremely high potential who was a fellow classmate at the prestigious Swiss Federal Polytechnic. In a biographical study of her life, Andrea Gabor found that "the more insecure Maric became in her relationship with Einstein, the more she came to identify her interests with his, ultimately putting Einstein's welfare ahead of her own" (1995, p. 12). After she married and had children, however, her life changed drastically, and friends recalled that she often spent all day cleaning, cooking, and caring for the children and then would busy herself in the evening, proofreading her husband's work and doing mathematical calculations to help him in his writings.

Lee Krasner, a talented artist, married Jackson Pollock, following a similar path to Maric Mileva Einstein, defined by Gabor as the Invisible Wife Syndrome. "In her marriage to Jackson Pollock, she succumbed to a potent brew of upbringing, social expectations and precedent by deliberately choosing to exercise much of her artistic devotion through the work of her husband" (1995, p. 58). It was only after his death that Krasner created art that seemed to be a reaffirmation of life but this creative energy in art stemmed from her loss of this complicated man she so deeply loved. Sculpting a personal and professional life for highly creative women is an intensely difficult challenge, and putting the needs of their husbands ahead of their own needs is an ongoing personal decision, one which does not seem to have been reconciled effectively in many women's lives. Consider the reflections of Mary Catherine Bateson: "As a young woman, I never questioned the assumption that when I married what I could do would take second place to what my husband could do" (1990, p. 40).

Another reason that women with high levels of creative potential may not pursue creative productive work is that they may possess certain personality traits often conflicting with high-profile creative endeavors (Reis, 1998). These traits occur in many women, whether they work within or outside of the home, are married or single, and whether or not they have children. One of the most common traits is perfectionism, which causes some girls and women to expend maximum energy at all times, attempting to do everything and do it well. Often, it is not enough to try to be outstanding in work; perfectionistic women also feel they have to strive for a flawless body, a beautiful house, and perfect children. Creative women often wear themselves out trying to do everything well, often with minimal help from their spouses. Despite these accomplishments, they still feel plagued by guilt that they may not have given enough to their husbands, children, home, and career.

A tendency exists for many females, regardless of their age, to try to minimize their differences. Both young girls and older women have been found to have a greater need to be accepted and to have others like them. Defying the Crowd, the title of a recent book on creativity by Sternberg and Lubart (1995), illustrates a fundamental difference in creative endeavors for women. Defying the crowd is the last thing that many women with high creative potential seek to accomplish, as many creative women want to minimize differences through quiet work completed without calling attention to themselves (Reis, 1998). Many creative women want to create quietly, in an environment in which their differences do not appear so obvious (Kirschenbaum & Reis, 1997; Reis, 1987, 1995a, 1995b, 1996).

Many creative women with firm religious backgrounds and beliefs have grappled with the religious training that conflicts with what is required if they are to develop their own talents (Reis, 1998). Selflessness, modesty, turning the other cheek, and the subjugation of individual pursuits for the good of others are learned from earliest interaction with religious training, and these lessons may conflict with experiences that occur later in life. Concerns that pursuing one's creative talents will be misconstrued as selfish consideration has been mentioned repeatedly by creative women (Reis, 1998) who have been raised with religious beliefs. Many struggle with learned beliefs and perceptions that to pursue their own talents is selfish. Guilt seems intertwined with many creative women's struggles to understand the relationship between their own talent development and what they learned in their previous experiences, including their religious training, about their responsibilities to those they love. As a result, little time is left for individual creative work. As one extremely creative artist explained, she can work only:

> When my life is in order, the kids are happy, dinner is cooking, the house is clean, the laundry is caught up, and there's a semblance of calm in the household. It just seems like ideas flow. I can sit down and write poetry just like that. I can sit at the computer and turn out two or three pages of a screenplay. (Kirschenbaum & Reis, 1997, p. 261)

The guilt experienced by creative women from putting work ahead of other responsibilities, perhaps, explains why selecting work that results in social change or the improvement of the human condition is so important to some talented women with strong religious backgrounds.

Females across the life span hide or mask their abilities so as not to appear too different, or to appear as if they are immodest (Callahan, 1979; Kerr, 1985; Noble, 1989; Reis, 1987). Parental influences, such as teaching daughters to be modest or polite, seem to confound this issue. In many interviews with young and adolescent gifted girls, they explained that they did not like to share the news of a high grade or a special accomplishment because it would seem as if they were bragging (Reis, 1998).

Many talented, creative females often compare themselves more, express more doubt about their abilities, and criticize themselves and others more (Arnold, 1995; Bell, 1989; Callahan et al., 1994; Cramer, 1989; Hany, 1994; Kramer, 1991; Leroux, 1988; Perleth & Heller, 1994; Reis, 1987; Reis & Callahan, 1989; Subotnik, 1988). Creative women artists (Kirschenbaum & Reis, 1997) were hesitant to show their art to others because they believed it wasn't good enough or feared rejection in some form. This low self-esteem might have affected their creative process and productivity. One stated, "I make things and hide them because I don't think they're good enough. I'll bring them out and somebody will say they're pretty good and it surprises me. If I get enough positive feedback on a piece, I'll show it somewhere. Several of the women avoided the prospect of having their efforts (and, consequently, their self-confidence and self-esteem) diminished by either having their art rejected in art competitions or ignored by the buying public.

Another internal barrier concerns strong feelings of loneliness and isolation on the parts of highly creative women. In research with both older and younger creative females, feelings of loneliness were often discussed (Reis, 1998). A successful college president, widely acclaimed for her novel ideas and creative contributions, when asked about friendships replied simply, "I have none." Some of the reasons that many talented women had few friends and were often lonely revolved around the extremely limited time they have for friendships. The ambivalence of other women to highly creative women who achieve has also been identified in successful women who recounted situations in which their success was viewed negatively by both other women and men. Creative women who had successful careers often reported that they were pitted against women who stayed at home and worked to raise their children (Reis, 1998).

Simonton (1978) suggested several external factors that affect creative development, including a set of philosophical beliefs essential to the development of creative potential. In a society in which the majority of our leaders, politicians, artists, musicians, and inventors are male, how does a woman *develop* a philosophical belief about her own creative potential? How might she overcome her upbringing, her parent's and teachers' advice and imprinting on manners and personal characteristics, and the knowledge that creative contributions take great amounts of time? When Maria Goeppart-Mayer made the discovery that later resulted in a Nobel Prize, she delayed publishing her results for months. Her biographer concluded that modesty caused this delay (Dash, 1988, p. 322). However, her hesitation may also reflect the intrinsic belief imposed upon highly able women by our society—that discoveries, inventions, and creations are usually the work of men. Until many more women are visible as discoverers, inventors, or creators, they may be relegated to the traditional roles they have generally held in the past—implementers of others' ideas, organizers, service providers, and the painters of the backdrop of creation.

Perceptions about Personal Creativity

Levels and types of creativity must also be investigated in creative women. It is clear that many women with creative potential do not believe they have been as creative in life as they might have been, given their early promise. In a study of 67 talented women who pursued a more traditional career, participants were asked to compare life today with the dreams they had for their future when they graduated from college (Reis, 1995a). Sixty percent indicated they experienced a conflict between the "real world" and the cultivation and realization of their own creative talents. Societal expectations often led them not to plan a career that was personally satisfying, to put their talents and aspirations on hold while raising their families, and eventually to stop regarding themselves as capable of more creative lives than they were currently living. Many indicated that they had not been able to pursue their own creative talents because of the pressures of marriage and family. Their creative achievements, "a grant from my district," "a curriculum unit I developed," "developing an innovative program," "a workshop I gave," might be considered modest when compared to those that are often considered important by either societal or male achievement standards (books written, national awards won, and such). Half of the women studied were apologetic when discussing their creative accomplishments, indicating that they knew their achievements in this particular area might seem "modest," but they were also often defensive, acknowledging how hard it was to accomplish anything given their work and family commitments.

Many creative women do not have role models who exemplify how creativity can be applied to work, and even if they do, their availability may not be enough to overcome the social forces they overcame in their life. Consider the explanation of this phenomenon by Mary Catherine Bateson, whose mother was Margaret Mead, on the negative influences of social factors she experienced in her life:

> I believe the issue of female inferiority still arises for virtually every woman growing up in this society. I grew up in an environment where no one told me females were inferior or that significant achievement would necessarily be beyond my reach, but the belief was all around me (p. 40).

This sentiment was also expressed by the culturally diverse creative women studied (Reis, 1998). Highly creative African American and Hispanic women consistently mentioned expressions of feeling different, negative societal pressure, negative feelings from family and peers. One African American woman explained she was a double exceptionality. "I am an accomplished, highly educated, creative woman and I am black. Imagine how hard that was for the men I encountered in my life," she explained, while discussing why she had not married.

The Importance of Creative Expression

Current research (Reis, 1998) indicates the need creative women have for creative expression in their work. In research conducted on creative female artists, participants also commented about the value of the process of creating art. For those involved in some aspect of sculpting, the feeling of doing physical work as they created was very gratifying (Kirschenbaum & Reis, 1997, p. 262). One woman explained:

> The process of doing art is often more important [than the product] to me because of my feeling that I have to get something out. The act of welding, of fusing metal together, is very important to me. The passion I feel, the violence of creating something with an arc-welder as the sparks fly everywhere, watching the metal heat up, then manipulating it by bending, hammering, and cutting it, gives me feelings that are hard to describe. It's a rich feeling, one of power, I guess (p. 262).

Another creative artist explained, "I may not be in the mood to paint, but if I don't do something [artistic], it's like I'm suffering from drug withdrawal. If I don't take care of this creative urge, I feel like I'm going to blow up. I need that high of being creative." (Kirschenbaum & Reis, 1997, p. 262) When asked about their futures, the goals mentioned by these female artists included being able to keep learning and doing their art, obtaining necessary equipment and materials when the money was available, and completing specific projects in the near future. In other areas of creative expression, similar views were consistently expressed by women about their need for creative expression in work (Reis, 1998).

Conclusion

The accomplishments of some highly creative females and the failure of others to realize their creative potential is a complex issue dependent upon many factors, including personal choices and social-cultural forces. "It is obvious that the values of women differ very often from the values which have been made by the other sex. Yet, it is the masculine values that prevail," wrote Virginia Woolf in *A Room of One's Own*. Our current societal structure eliminates the possibility that many highly creative females, especially those who are married and have children, can produce at a similar level as their male counterparts. While the importance of women's traditional contributions cannot be underestimated, these contributions are often not enough for highly creative women (Reis, 1998). These women may want a different life, or have a sense of destiny about applying their creativity to areas of choice, especially after they have been exposed to a range of options available to them.

The exploration and discussion of the personality issues and personal choices facing girls and women with high levels of creative potential should be encouraged. The development of a creative life is intricate and complex. What one young girl regards as an impossible obstacle, another may see as an intriguing challenge. Some creative women were negatively influenced by their parents' lack of support for their career preferences, and they changed their career plans, regretting it later. A much smaller group of women were so angry that their parents tried to steer them away from their dreams that they rebelled and became eminent in their selected areas of endeavor (Reis, 1995a, 1995b, 1996, 1998). The ways in which the same obstacles differentially affect girls and women provides the fascination of researching their creative accomplishments. Resilience, rebellion, multipotentiality, different cycles of creativity, and high creative accomplishment in the face of obstacles such as poverty and a complete absence of support characterize many highly creative women (Reis, 1998). Yet, they persist. Is this type of persistence, determination, and inner will learned, or is it the result of innate personality traits?

.   Many creative women develop these characteristics throughout their lives, and it is precisely this development that creates their success—which is actively learned throughout their lifespan. Exploring how and when creative women develop these characteristics may help other creative young females in their journeys. Continuing to have limited research on this topic will result in what Gerda Lerner described. Noting the long history of extraordinary women, she raised a similar concern about women with special talents:

> Their individual achievements are awesome and inspire respect, yet it must be noted that their individual effort

could not lead to a collective advancement in consciousness. The women of talent existed, they struggled val-
iantly, they achieved and they were forgotten. The women
coming after them had to start all over again, repeating
the process (Lerner, 1993, p. 274).

The unique pattern of the lives of creative women seems
almost to defy general theories of human development, yet some
recent trends have emerged (Reis, 1998). There is no clear path for
creative women, whose lives are intimately connected with
relationships with family and friends in addition to work. Creative productivity in women is more diffused than that of their
male counterparts. Because relationships are central to women's
lives, they often have an impact on their work and individual
creative attainment. Yet, without meaningful work, creative
women are not satisfied.

The realization of the creative potential in women requires effort, conscious decisionmaking, and an understanding that the full range of creative talents in many women may
be unrealized in our world today. Virginia Woolf, in *A Room of
One's Own*, wrote that the creative powers of men and women
were different, "that the creative power of women, though
highly developed differs from the creative power of men"
(1957, p. 91). However, many people do not fully understand
the creative potential of women as opportunities for creative
work and productivity are less often encountered by girls and
women. We live in a world in which our realities and daily
experiences reinforce certain roles, expectations, and obligations that limit creative opportunities for girls and women.
And the creative opportunities that women continue to have
are often diversified over many different outlets. More research needs to examine this complex phenomenon in diverse
creative women before we can understand the reasons for this
diversification and whether it will change as work for women
becomes more of a predominant theme in life. In the meantime, some of the suggestions included in the Appendix may
be helpful as we consider encouraging creativity in ourselves,
our colleagues, children, and friends.

Appendix 8A. General Recommendations for Promoting Creativity in Girls and Women

These ideas emerged from several years of research with creative girls and women. They can be implemented by parents, teachers, and administrators as strategies in the classroom or at home. They were developed from research-based studies as well as from practical applications of creativity training programs and enrichment opportunities. It is, of course, unrealistic to expect that all of these suggestions can be implemented, but implementing several should be a goal for each group.

Creative girls should:

1. be exposed through personal contact and the media to female role models and mentors who have successfully balanced career and family;

2. develop independence and intellectual risk-taking, as well as an understanding of sex-role stereotyping/cultural biases/gender prejudices and high social-self perceptions;

3. be involved in career counseling at an early age and be exposed to a wide variety of career options;

4. become involved in leadership roles and extracurricular activities;

5. participate in sports, athletics, and multiple extracurricular activities;

6. learn to question, speak out, and take action;

7. learn from mistakes and try again;

8. discuss issues related to gender and success in supportive settings with other girls;

9. learn various communication styles and the value of planning for the future;

10. delay becoming involved in romantic relationships until formal education is completed;

11. find peers and friends who support their academic goals and help them identify interests; and

12. identify a dream for important work and develop a plan to make that dream come true.

Parents, teachers, and counselors should:

1. form task forces to advocate for programming and equal opportunities and to investigate opportunities for talented, creative girls;

2. spotlight achievements of creative females in a variety of different areas, encourage girls and young women to become involved in as many different types of activities, travel opportunities, and clubs as possible;

3. show sensitivity to the different nonverbal ways girls express themselves;

4. encourage girls to take advanced math/science courses as well as courses in the arts and reinforce successes in these and all areas of endeavor;

5. understand some of the personal characteristics of highly creative females that may impede their success;

6. encourage relationships with other creative girls who want to achieve;

7. maintain options for talented, creative girls in specific groups such as self-contained classes, groups of girls within heterogeneous classes, science and math clubs, or support groups;

8. ensure equal representation of girls in advanced classes;

9. constantly point out options for careers and encourage future choices but help girls focus on specific careers;

10. stress self-reliance, independence, creative training and creative problem solving and decisionmaking;

11. educate and raise males to assume equal partnership in relationships and support the talent development of those they love;

12. express a positive attitude about creativity and talents in girls in all areas and be a constant source of support, avoiding criticism as much as possible;

13. not attempt to remediate all behaviors which show spirit, passion, resiliency, or anger since some of these characteristics are essential to adult creative productivity;

14. consciously discuss and actively challenge obstacles and barriers to success by pointing out negative stereotypes in all environments; and

15. foster a secure sense of self by helping talented girls understand and develop a belief in self and their talents and abilities.

Parents should:

1. become assertive advocates for the development of their daughter's interests and creative talents;

2. maintain a proactive, supportive role to support their daughter's interests;

3. provide career encouragement and planning;

4. provide extensive experiences in museums, travel, and interaction with adults;

5. develop independence and an inclination for creative action;

6. encourage interests but not insist that their daughter achieve the honor roll;

7. not criticize too much and never make fun of appearance or weight—do not focus on their daughter's appearance as it sends negative messages about what is most important;

8. encourage humor and positive risk taking;

9. encourage their daughters' decision making and allow their daughters to make her own decisions;

10. encourage participation in sports, competition, and extracurricular activities—teach their daughters that everybody loses sometime; and

11. monitor television viewing and media exposure—watch out for   magazines such as *YM, Cosmopolitan,* and many other teen magazines which primarily stress appearance.

12. encourage creative action across domains: art, dance, cooking, and science, and help daughters narrow interests as they mature.

Teachers should:

1. provide equal treatment in a non-stereotyped environment and in particular, provide encouragement in math/science classes;

2. reduce sexism in classrooms and create an avenue for girls to report and discuss examples of stereotyping in schools;

3. help creative, talented females appreciate and understand healthy competition;

4. group gifted females homogeneously in math/science or within cluster groups of high ability students in heterogeneous groups;

5. encourage creativity in girls;

6. use problem solving in assignments and reduce the use of timed tests and timed assignments within

class periods; rather, provide options for untimed work within a reasonable time frame;

7. expose girls to other creative females through direct and curricular experiences—field trips, guest speakers, seminars, role models, books, videotapes, articles, movies, etc.;

8. provide educational interventions compatible with cognitive development and styles of learning (independent study projects, small group learning opportunities, and so forth.) and use a variety of authentic assessment tools such as projects and learning centers instead of just using tests;

9. establish equity in classroom interactions; and

10. provide multiple opportunities for creative expression in multiple modalities.

Counselors should:

1. provide individualized, goal-oriented career counseling and maintain an interest in talented girls with high potential who need help to develop their creative talents;

2. provide group counseling sessions for gifted and talented girls who share issues such as multipotentiality, underachievement, or absence of belief in ability;

3. encourage participation in honors and advanced placement courses, and in extracurricular activities and summer and out-of school programs such as college science and math classes;

4. sponsor conferences, workshops, and symposia for and about gifted, creative women for talented girls and their parents;

5. provide bibliotherapy and videotherapy in small group sessions; provide readings in a wide variety of

excellent resources and view films (such as *The Joy Luck Club* based on the novel by Amy Tan) about the struggle of talented, creative women;

6. establish support groups with a network of same-sex peers;

7. contact parents when highly creative girls begin to underachieve or seem confused about abilities, aspirations, or careers;

8. provide a variety of career counseling and exposure opportunities;

9. provide information about societies, web pages, and resources that encourage and support gifted girls and women; and

10. discourage the encouragement of well-roundedness and encourage selection of specific areas of creative pursuit.

(Adapted from Reis, 1998, pp. 326-330)

References

Ajzenberg-Selove, F. (1994). *A matter of choices: Memoirs of a female physicist*. Brunswick, NJ: Rutgers University Press.

Arnold, K. D. (1995). *Lives of promise*. San Francisco: Jossey-Bass Publishers.

Arnold, K. D., & Denny, T. (1985). *The lives of academic achievers: The career aspiration of male and female high school valedictorians and salutatorians*. Paper presented at the annual meeting of the American Educational Research Association, Chicago, IL.

Asimov, I. (1982). Biographical Encyclopedia of Science and Technology. Garden City, NY: Doubleday.

Axelrod, T. (1988). Patently successful. *Ms., 16*(10),44–45.

Baer, J. (1997). Gender differences in the effects of anticipated evaluation of creativity. *Creativity Research Journal, 10*, 25–31.

Bateson, M. C. (1990). *Composing a life* (p. 40). New York: Plume.

Beck, M., Kantrowski, B., & Beachy, L. (1990, July 16). Trading Places. *Newsweek*, 48–54.

Bell, L. A. (1989). Something's wrong here and it's not me: Challenging the dilemmas that block girls' success. *Journal for the Education of the Gifted, 12,* 118–130.

Block, J. H. (1982). *Sex role identity and ego development.* San Francisco: Jossey-Bass.

Callahan, C. M. (1979). The gifted and talented woman. In A. H. Passow (Ed.), *The gifted and talented* (pp. 401–423). Chicago: National Society for the Study of Education.

Callahan, C. M., Cunningham, C. M., & Plucker, J. A. (1994). Foundations for the future: The socio-emotional development of gifted, adolescent women. *Roeper Review, 17,* 99–105.

Cattell J. M. (1903). A statistical study of eminent men. *Popular Science Monthly, 62,* 359–377.

Cramer, R. H. (1989). Attitudes of gifted boys and girls toward math: A qualitative study. *Roeper Review, 11,* 128–133.

Dash, J. (1988). *A life of one's own* (p. 322). New York: Paragon House.

Diamond, A. M. (1986). The life-cycle research productivity of mathematicians and Scientists. *Journal of Gerontology, 41,* 520–525.

Eisenman , R., & Johnson, P. (1969). Birth order, sex, perception, and production of complexity. *The Journal of Social Psychology, 79,* 116.

Gabor, A. (1995). *Einstein's wife: Work and marriage in the lives of five great twenty-first century women* (pp. 12, 58). New York: Viking/Penguin.

Gates, E. (1994). Why have there been no great women composers? Psychological theories, past and present. *Journal of Aesthetic Education, 2,* 27–34.

Gruber, H. E. (1985.) Giftedness and moral responsibility: Creative thinking and human survival. In F. D. Horowitz & M. O'Brien (Eds.), *The gifted and talented: Developmental perspectives* (pp. 301–330). Washington, DC: American Psychological Association.

Hany, E. A. (1994). The development of basic cognitive components of technical creativity: A longitudinal comparison of children and youth with high and average intelligence. In R. F. Subotnik & K. D. Arnold (Eds.), *Beyond Terman: Contemporary longitudinal studies of giftedness and talent* (pp. 115–154). Norwood, NJ: Ablex.

Helson, R. (1996). In search of the creative personality. *Creativity Research Journal, 9*, 295–306.

Hollinger, C. L., & Fleming, E. S. (1988). Gifted and talented young women: Antecedents and correlates of life satisfaction. *Gifted Child Quarterly, 32*, 254–260.

Huyck, M. H. (1990). Gender differences in aging. In J. Biren & W. W. Schaie (Eds.), *Handbook of the Psychology of Aging* (3rd ed., pp. 120–134). New York: Academic Press.

Kerr, B. A. (1985). *Smart girls, gifted women*. Columbus, OH: Ohio Psychology Publishing Company.

Keubli, J., & Fivush, R. (1992). Gender differences in parent-child conversations about past emotions. *Sex Roles, 27*, 683–698.

Kirschenbaum, R. J., & Reis, S. M. (1997). Conflicts in creativity: Talented female artists. *Creativity Research Journal, 10*, 251–263.

Kramer, L. R. (1991). The social construction of ability perceptions: An ethnographic study of gifted adolescent girls. *Journal of Early Women in Culture and Society, 16*, 158–172.

Lehman, H. C. (1953). *Age and achievement*. Princeton, NJ: Princeton University Press.

Lerner, G. (1993). *The creation of feminist consciousness* (p. 274). New York: Oxford University Press.

Leroux, J. A. (1988). Voices from the classroom: Academic and social self-concepts of gifted adolescents. *Journal for the Education of the Gifted, 11*, 3–18.

Lindauer, M. S. (1992). Creativity in aging artists: Contributions from the humanities to the psychology of old age. *Creativity Research Journal, 5*, 211-231.

List, K., & Renzulli, J. (1991). Creative women's developmental patterns through age thirty-five. *Gifted Education International, 7*, 114–122.

McLeish , J. A. B. (1976). *The Ulyssean adult: Creativity in the middle and later years*. New York: McGraw-Hill/Ryerson.

Miller, J. B. (1976). *Toward a new psychology of women*. Boston: Beacon Press.

Noble, K. D. (1989). Counseling gifted women: Becoming the heroes of our own stories. *Journal for the Education of the Gifted, 12*, 131–141.

Northcutt, C. (1991). *Successful career women: Their professional and personal characteristics*. Westport, CT: Greenwood.

Ochse, R. (1991). Why there were relatively few eminent women creators. *Journal of Creative Behavior, 25,* 334–343.

Perleth, C., & Heller, K. A.(1994). The Munich longitudinal study of giftedness. In R. F. Subotnik & K. K. Arnold (Eds.), *Beyond Terman: Contemporary longitudinal studies of giftedness and talent* (pp. 77–114). Norwood, NJ: Ablex.

Piirto, J. (1991). Why are there so few? (Creative women: Visual artists, mathematicians, musicians). *Roeper Review, 13,* 142–147.

Pomerleau, A., Bolduc, D., & Malcuit, C. (1990). Pink or blue: Environmental gender stereotypes in the first two years of life. *Sex Roles: A Journal of Research, 22,* 359–367.

Reis, S. M. (1987). We can't change what we don't recognize: Understanding the special needs of gifted females. *Gifted Child Quarterly, 31,* 83–88.

Reis, S. M. (1995a). Talent ignored, talent diverted: The cultural context underlying giftedness in females. *Gifted Child Quarterly, 39,* 162–170.

Reis, S. M. (1995b). Older women's reflections on eminence: Obstacles and opportunities. *Roeper Review, 18*(1), 66–72.

Reis, S. M. (1996). Older women's reflections on eminence: Obstacles and opportunities. In K. D. Arnold, K. D. Noble, & R. F. Subotnik (Eds.), *Remarkable women: Perspectives on female talent development* (pp. 149–168). Cresskill, NJ: Hampton Press Inc.

Reis, S. M. (1998). *Work left undone.* Mansfield Center, CT: Creative Learning Press.

Reis, S. M. (in press). Toward a theory of creativity in diverse creative women. *Creativity Research Journal.*

Reis, S. M., & Callahan, C. M. (1989). Gifted females: They've come a long way—or have they? *Journal for the Education of the Gifted, 12,* 99–117.

Reis, S. M., Hebert, T. P., Diaz, E. I., Maxfield, L. R., & Ratley, M. E. (1995). *Case studies of talented students who achieve and underachieve in an urban high school* (Research Monograph 95114). Storrs, CT: University of Connecticut, The National Research Center for the Gifted and Talented.

Rheingold, H. L., & Cook, K. V. (1975). The content of boy's and girl's rooms as an index of parent behavior. *Child Development, 46,* 459–463.

Roberts, T. (1991). Gender and the influence of evaluations on self-assessments in achievement settings. *Psychological Bulletin, 109,* 297–308.

Roberts, T., & Nelson-Hoeksema, S. (1994). Gender comparisons in responsiveness to others' evaluations in achievement settings. *Psychology of Women Quarterly, 18*, 221–240.

Roscher, N. (1987). Chemistry's creative women. *Journal of Chemical Education, 56*, 748–752.

Runco, M. A. (1991). *Divergent thinking*. Norwood, NJ: Ablex.

Schneidman, E. (1989). The Indian summer of life: A preliminary study of septuagenarians. *American Psychologist, 44*, 684–694.

Schwartz, L. A., & Markham, W. T. (1985). Sex stereotyping in children's achievements. *Sex Roles, 12*, 157–170.

Sears, R. (1977). Sources of satisfactions of Terman's gift ed men. *American Psychologist, 32*, 119–128.

Simonton, D. K. (1978). Creative productivity, age, and stress: A biographical time-series analysis of 10 classical composers. *Journal of Personality and Social Psychology, 35*, 791–804.

Simonton, D. K. (1984). Artistic creativity and interpersonal relations across and within generations. *Journal of Personality and Social Psychology, 46*, 1273–1286.

Simonton, D. K. (1989). The swan-song phenomenon: Last-work effects for 172 classical composers. *Psychology and Aging, 4*, 42–47.

Simonton, D. K. (1991a). Career landmarks in science: Individual differences and interdisciplinary contrasts. *Developmental Psychology, 27*, 119–130.

Simonton, D. K. (1991b). Emergence and realization of genius: The lives and works of 120 classical composers. *Journal of Personality and Social Psychology, 61*, 829–840.

Simonton, D. K. (1991c). Latent-variable models of posthumous reputation: A quest for Galton's G. *Journal of Personality and Social Psychology, 60*, 607–619.

Simonton, D. K. (2000). Creativity: Cognitive, Personal, Developmental, and Social Aspects. *American Psychologist, 55*, 151–158.

Sloane, K. D., & Sosniak, L. A. (1985). The development of accomplished sculptures. In B. Bloom (Ed.), *The development of talent in young people* (pp. 90-138). New York: Ballantine.

Steinem, G. (1992). *The revolution from within*. Boston, MA: Little, Brown.

Sternberg, R. J. (1986). A triarchic theory of intellectual giftedness. In R. J. Sternberg & J. E. Davidson (Eds.), Conceptions of giftedness (pp. 53–92). Cambridge, MA: Cambridge University Press.

Sternberg, R. J. & Lubart, T. I. (1995). Defying the crowd. New York: The Free Press.

Subotonik, R. (1988). The motivation to experiment: A case study of gifted adolescents' attitudes toward scientific research. Journal for the Education of the Gifted, 11, 19–35.

Subotnik, R., & Arnold, K. (1995). Passing through the gates: Career establishment of talented women scientists. Roeper Review, 13, 55–61.

Van Tassel-Baska, J. (1995). A study of life themes in Charlotte Bronte and Virginia Woolf. Roeper Review, 13, 14–19.

Walker, B., Reis, S., & Leonard, J. (1992, Fall). A developmental investigation of the lives of gifted women. Gifted Child Quarterly, 36(4), 201–206.

Wallace, T., & Walberg, H. (1995). Girls who became famous literalists of the imagination. Roeper Review, 13, 24–27.

Woolf, V. (1957). A room of one's own (p. 91). New York: Harcourt, Brace & Jovanovitch.

Chapter 9

Riding the Tiger: The Challenge of Creative Renewal in the Later Adult Years

Robert Kastenbaum

Are you enthusiastic today? Are you inspired? When we are radiant with enthusiasm it is because a whiff of the divine has wafted into our mortal being. The word entered language as *en-theo-siasm*: god within us. In all probability, God entered us as a subtle spirit through our breath. We were *in-spired* by God. This tells us something about creativity, perhaps more than we really want to know. The study of lives also tells us something about creativity, again, perhaps not always what we would like to hear. I will be asking you to open your thoughts both to the dangers and the facts of creativity before we surrender ourselves completely to enthusiasm and inspiration.

Miss Eggerton's Last Task

But first let's knock on a door and see if Miss Eggerton will let us in. I worked for years in a geriatric hospital, first as a psychologist, later as director. Today one would never speak of an unmarried elderly woman as a "spinster," but Miss Eggerton—not her real name—described herself as "a tough old spinster." At age 94 she was among the oldest of our 600 residents, and one of the few to have a room of her own. Miss Eggerton was a dignified, imperial, and rather crusty person who took no prisoners. She was respected by all that knew her.

And she was dying. Miss Eggerton insisted on completing her life's journey in the small room that had been her home for the past several years. She summoned visitors from throughout the hospital—just the people she wanted to see one more time. It would have been a terrible slight to be snubbed by Miss Eggerton in her version of a farewell tour. But she did invite me, and I stood before her door.

"Miss Eggerton? Miss Eggerton?"

I entered. She spoke first.

"I am dying. You probably want to ask me some questions for your study!"

"Tell me your answers," I proposed, "and I'll make up the questions later."

Miss Eggerton explained that death should be taken seriously.

"It affects your plans!"

When she felt the first slight touch of death's hand upon her, Miss Eggerton discontinued her practice of spending much of the day in what was called the "Times Square" area of the hospital, the public space where much of the socializing transpired.

"They will just have to get along without me!"

Now she keeps to this room, which, as she said, "is all that death and myself need."

By this time, I did have a question for her.

"Miss Eggerton—what are you embroidering on those panties, and why?"

Miss Eggerton is not discomforted by the question. She raised her handiwork for my inspection. The backside of the pink underpants was scripted in valentine-red letters: "Egger..."

She informed me, "It will be Eggerton before I am finished. You know the hospital laundry. Clothes wind up anywhere, on anybody's body. When I am gone, this will be covering somebody else's rear end. I want them to know whose they were."

"Your parting gift," I replied, "Your mortal end." Miss Eggerton quickly triumphed with the last word. "My mortal *ass*, young man, and my immortal panties!"

Expressions of Creativity in the Later Adult Years

That is precisely what happened when I saw Miss Eggerton for the last time. It would not be until years later that I could recognize seven features of Miss Eggerton's example that also can be found in many other examples of creativity in the later adult years.

- The creative expression was unexpected and essentially unpredictable. One does not usually find a dignified elderly woman or a dying person engaged in embroidering her name on the backside of a pair of panties. *Creative expressions often are unexpected and unpredictable in some way.*

- The creative expression made do with available materials. Miss Eggerton did not require special equipment or resources to spark her imagination. *Creativity often excels in the utilization of limited materials.* To put it another way: an abundance of lavish supplies, high tech equipment, and other amenities do not guarantee creativity: It is the mind and spirit of the individual that counts.

- The creative act expressed a significant truth in the situation. In this instance, two aspects of her reality were expressed: (a) the prospect of her death, and (b) the nature of life in a geriatric institution where the vagaries of the laundry were part of a general loss of privacy and assault on individuality. *Creative acts often symbolize significant aspects of reality and integrate these aspects in an effective and original way.*

- The creative act transformed passivity and helplessness into action and mastery. Here was an aged and dying woman, to all appearances a recipient, a target, a victim of forces beyond resistance. Nevertheless, Miss Eggerton stirred herself, organized herself, directed herself to do something in her situation. She gave herself a task with a purpose, and thereby kept herself going as an integrated person. *The creative act can be an affirmation of purpose and meaning in the face of risk, loss, and disaster.*

- The creative act could be accomplished with limited physical strength and energy. Some creative activities do make substantial demands on strength and energy; the person may even become exhausted. Nevertheless, there are other creative acts that accomplish their purposes with a minimum of physical exertion, although still requiring attention and concentration. *The creative act depends more on impulse and purpose than on stamina and dexterity.*

- The creative act was a gift to other people. I am not speaking of the embroidered panties, but of the real gift that Miss Eggerton fashioned as she and Death moved toward their rendezvous. Miss Eggerton offered herself as a model, a heartening example to all who would one day be in her condition. How should we face aging? How should we face institutionalization? How should we face loss? How should we face death? Perhaps none of us would choose to do so with a sewing needle, red thread, and a pair of pink panties. But all of us who had our final meetings with Miss Eggerton were awarded the gift of her poise, her resolve, her ironic wit, her ability to transform and express her thoughts and feelings under distinctly unfavorable conditions. *The creative act is a gift for those who are capable of recognizing and receiving it.*

- Finally, the creative act serves as a bridge across time and space. This is one of the most fundamental characteristics of any symbolic expression. The human animal has its flaws and vices, but also the ability to encompass the past, the future, and distant places within our imagination and with various forms of language as our primary tools. Miss Eggerton has given us an example that involves two types of expression: the visual and the narrative. The embroidered panties are a visual and tactile product that presumably led a useful life for some time after Miss Eggerton's death. More significant is the fact that her creation of this item provided the basis for her self-narrative, the expression of her attitude toward the situation in which she had been living and from which she now was dying. With the panties in hand as a visible artifact, Miss Eggerton could direct and embroider the conversation. The fact that this incident has stayed with me for 30 years is a testimony to the ability of her creative act to bridge time and space. And if you happen to remember this incident and perhaps share it with others—why, then, Miss Eggerton's panties and their meanings will take on an even more encompassing life. *The creative act enables us to transcend particular times and places even when it serves to symbolize a particular time and place.*

There is another characteristic of the creative act that can be illustrated more clearly with a different example. Some years ago I met a distant branch of my wife's family for the first time. This clan had lived in a small town in Vermont for as long as anybody could remember. I perceived the central person as being as much of a traditional patriarch as Miss Eggerton had seemed like a traditional spinster. John Curtis—and that was his actual name— was in his 89th year. He was a taciturn and solemn man with a lean and weathered appearance. He looked as though he were a part of the natural environment that had learned to withstand centuries of bitter-cold winters.

The family was very much concerned about him. He was a fiercely independent person who was not willing to concede anything to the aging process. Their anxiety was focused on his stubborn insistence that he would walk alone wherever and whenever he felt like it. And, no, he would not consider using an assistive device. I saw right away that the family had ample reason for this concern. The family home was set in a rocky and hilly area that held many a risk for the unwary or unsteady foot.

Somehow John Curtis and I seemed to connect with each other despite the fact that we had almost nothing in common. I was a kid from a dead-end street in the Bronx, New York, and more or less accustomed to the noise, pace, and conflicts of city life, while he was, as described, a rural Vermonter down to his stubborn toes. When I returned home I searched the shops until I found a truly wonderful walking stick. It was a powerful, gnarled, no-nonsense specimen: You would display it in a museum. I secretly wished that I had some excuse to have such a walking stick myself! I sent it to the patriarch with a note explaining that this item had caught my eye and seemed to be made for him. I also wrote a little poem in honor of his 90th birthday.

> To be ninety! To be ninety!
> To feel the apple wind fresh, yes,
> And mellow, now, as then, new,
> Renewing this, each, every day
> Deep, deep this day renewing
> In his deep roots,
> God's word
> Why, then—here's to John Curtis!

Word came back quickly from his family that their beloved patriarch was very much taken with the walking stick and now used it all the time, to their immense relief. I have told you all this just to set up what happened next. I received a letter from John Curtis, actually, a poem. It was written in a firm and strong hand with just the slightest of tremble:

> Three months ago that good cane came,
> And life has not been quite the same.
> I've learned on that where e'er I went,
> Life's been a little more content.

One trip downtown 'twas left behind.
The slush and ice were most unkind.
Next time that cane supported me.
In debt to it I'm glad to be.
A stronger Stay my steps sustain.
I never seek His help in vain.
Him to my friends I recommend.
He'll be your Stay until the end.
March 22nd, 1962, J. A. C.

The old man had shaped a letter into a poem and the poem into a sort of prayer. He had made a connection in his mind between a walking stick and the support he found in his religious faith. By praising God he was affirming and strengthening his relationship to God. And by having composed a poem of praise, he was also emulating God—God, the Creator.

Playing with Fire: The Temptation and the Risk

We have arrived at the following proposition: *The creative act is an expression of the spirit of divine creativity within the individual.* This proposition is a part of the core belief system in several of the world's great religions. Among God's creations is a creature who is also capable of creation, of transforming reality and engendering new meanings. The sense of divinity in the creative act has long been appreciated in such works as the great cathedrals of Europe, the ancient carvings, murals and mosaics of India, and such musical masterpieces as the requiems by Mozart, Brahms, and Verdi. People differ greatly in their ability to create in the spirit of a universal creative force, but the impulse may well be within every person, and even a small and fleeting expression may be accompanied by a sense of joy, renewal, or participation in a transcendent mystery. The creative act may bring us as close to the generative spirit of the universe as we can come within our limited frame of being.

There is a risky side to all of this. Prometheus was cruelly punished for daring to steal the divine fire. In the golden age of mythmaking, there was more attention to rejuvenation than to creativity in our sense of the term. People who tried to re-create themselves through rejuvenation had to pass through ordeals of pain and fire, ordeals they might not survive. This, by the way, was almost exclusively a male occupation or preoccupation. An ancient Egyptian treatise, for example, explained how a man of 80 can become once again a man of 20.

For millennia, rites of passage have required the initiates to pass difficult and dangerous tests before they could enter the inner circle of the wise and powerful. Unlike the mysteries of rejuvenation where they were usually excluded, females often did participate in these rituals as they moved from girl to woman and, in some circles, from woman to crone (a mature and wise woman). The dangers increased for those who presumed to serve as intermediaries between gods and mortals. Priests, magicians, sorcerers, and necromancers who communicated with the spirit world were risking their lives: Often they were literally playing with fire. Alchemists incinerated themselves from time to time and people considered to be witches were burned by a frightened public.

Science inherited society's ambivalence toward those who would attempt to cross the uncertain border between the human and the forbidden divine. The character of Dr. Victor Frankenstein soon became the prime example of a human who dared too much. To make sure nobody missed the point, Mary Wollstonecraft Shelley subtitled her classic novel, *The New Prometheus*. At the time of her writing there were indeed bodysnatchers who came around to the back doors of the most avant-garde physicians to peddle their merchandise. Perhaps needless to say, both the grave robbers and the elite medical researchers were usually men. Meanwhile, women continued to suffer in the throes of childbirth as they had for centuries and often died because of medical ignorance and incompetence. Mary Shelley's own mother had been one of these casualties. Scientific creativity and daring was largely a male enterprise; females were expected to bear and raise children as their contribution. In our own time the controversy about how far is too far continues to rage. Cloning is a particularly interesting example because here science is making a move to alter the female monopoly on bringing life into the world. Whatever our personal feelings on the matter, creativity has a significant historical link with the gods, rejuvenation, and status passage, all of which have traditionally operated along culturally-prescribed gender tracks.

The living heritage of this tradition is the risk involved in unbridled creative activity. Humankind has long believed that the gods create and the gods destroy. We have something of that divinity in or available to us. It is dangerous, however, to emulate or challenge the gods beyond a certain—actually, an uncertain—point. Creation and destruction are intimately related. One swiftly can turn into the other. The people of the village have their reasons for lighting torches and grabbing pitchforks when strange things are happening in the old castle on the hill.

We don't encourage children to play with matches. Should we encourage children, youth, adults, and aged adults to play with divine fire?

I remind us of this "divine spark" tradition because I find that our society today has a tendency to tame and downsize creativity. If we are to consider creative renewal in the later adult years we might do well to shake off the shackles of triviality as well as those of gender restrictions.

Tyger, Tyger!

There is an assumption in our society that creativity is a pleasant and comfortable activity that we can toy with in our leisure time. A little dabbling here and there. A little producing of "nice" and unobjectionable objects. A casual activity that will not interfere with meals, watching television, or nap time. Something we can pick up or put down. Something that others can look at and say, "Oh, isn't that adorable." Something that will not lead us to sweat, curse, destroy, offend, or confuse. And, of course, creative activity surely will not produce unsettling changes within ourselves and our relationships with others. Creativity is "nice."

No, I don't think so! Creativity is not nice, nor is it safe. It is not a trivial pursuit that can fill little spaces of time that become available in our schedules. What *is* this creativity we seek to promote across the life course?

Tyger Tyger, burning bright
In the forests of the night.
What immortal hand or eye,
Could frame thy fearful symmetry?
In what distant deeps or skies
Burnt the fire of thine eyes?
On what wings dare he aspire?
What the hand, dare seize the fire?
And what shoulder, and what art,
Could twist the sinews of thy heart?
And when thy heart began to beat,
What dread hand? And what dread feet?
What the hammer? What the chain,
In what furnace was thy brain?
What the anvil? What dread trasp,
Dare its deadly terrors clasp?
When the stars threw down their spears
And water'd heaven with their tears:
Did he smile his work to see?
Did he who made the Lamb make thee?
Tyger Tyger burning bright,
In the forests of the night:
What immortal hand or eye,
Dare frame thy fearful symmetry?

William Blake brings us face to face with a heart-stopping image. The tyger is awesome not only for the power of its physical frame, but also for the burning fire of its eyes, and for the brain that was forged in a diabolical furnace. The tyger is the very embodiment of "deadly terrors" and moves majestically through "the forests of the night"—not a place where we would feel safe and secure.

The tyger is also the embodiment of the untamed creative spirit—be it divine or human. The creative spirit is not sentimental; it is not respectful; it is not interested in being popular. When the creative spirit is aroused, it cares nothing for the niceties of everyday life. At any given moment, the creative spirit is likely to be disruptive and demanding. It can be oblivious to the give-and-take and the little compromises that help us to hold our lives in balance. The creative spirit may also strike alarms for the haunts it prefers and the company it keeps. It may disappear into "the forest of the night" into which we, with our cultivated judgment, hesitate to venture. It may take up with feelings, ideas, relationships, materials, and situations that make us distinctly uncomfortable.

The creative spirit likes to play and it likes to destroy, as did many gods who did not make it into the Judeo-Christian pantheon. The tyger in us just will not let things be. When others are behaving themselves and the status is comfortably quo, the tyger may leap and pounce—not necessarily to kill but for the pure joy of delighting in its strength and making things happen.

The tyger at play is a beautiful or an alarming sight—depending on whose eyes are viewing the antics. It is beautiful and exciting if we ourselves can participate in the spirit of unbridled creative play; it is alarming if we tremble in fear at the power expressed by the tyger outside or the tyger starved and trapped inside.

Creative people in many fields of endeavor describe this activity as a kind of liberating play that requires all the energy, concentration, and skill that one can summon. It is passionately serious and capriciously playful at the same time. The person who has either lost or failed to develop the spirit of play is likely to find creative pursuits laborious and burdensome. This person might come up with inventions, designs, books, and other products, but the process is not likely to be joyful nor the results original and transforming.

But the aroused tyger is not always content to be playful. It is also in the nature of the beast to destroy. For some people, it is incomprehensible that destruction has a major role in the creative enterprise. How can this be? It is wrong, it is not proper for destruction to be an intrinsic part of creativity! Perhaps it is wrong; perhaps it is improper. Nevertheless, destruction is an intrinsic part of the creative process. We will never appreciate the creative process if we know it only by those selected products that have met with general approval. We will have little idea of what the creative person had to go through in shaping this product, and even less idea of the frustrations, failures, and conflicts that were encountered along the way.

Creative people destroy in order to give themselves the space, the momentum, the energy to generate something new. The familiar saying, "You have to break the eggs to make an omelet" applies especially to some of the crucial early phases in the creative process. This is one of the reasons why "good little boys and girls" may have difficulty in turning loose their creative potential in the adult years. "Being good" has often meant not being adventure-some and unpredictable. Even so, creativity often will find some way to express itself, running just enough risk to make it exciting without courting major punishment.

Once I led a discussion of the worst thing each individual in the group had ever done in high school. A senior business executive who looked the very model of prosperous respectabil-ity struggled with himself for a moment. Finally:

"I need to tell somebody," he said.

All ears tuned to him.

"The night before junior prom, we filled the swimming pool with Jello. Yes, it was my idea, I guess."

"What flavor Jello?"

"Lime. We figured it would look most slimy."

"You got away with it?"

"Until now."

His revelation encouraged others to divulge some of their youthful pranks. The common theme was their having felt stifled through their years of schooling as they tried to meet parental and their own expectations. They were good kids who just had to do something bad, but not too bad. As the discussion deepened, several reflected that they had learned to keep that prankish, boundary–breaking, creative–destructive side of their personali-ties under wraps in the service of a career and a persona.

Creative Destruction

Destruction takes various forms in association with the creative process. Intellectual destruction is common. This type of destruction occurs every time a scholar or scientist demolishes a respected theory in order to replace it with a radically different version. Brahms destroyed his compositions and Monet his paintings when they did not measure up to their exacting standards. Dedicated artists sometimes destroy what is merely "good" in order to challenge themselves to create something better.

The dynamics of destruction and creativity can be experienced in our closest interpersonal relationships as well. For example, when a person disrupts a stale and limiting relationship, it might be on the impulse that the relationship has to be broken before it can be fixed. This destructive act might end the relationship, but it might also stimulate a much-needed reconstruction. "I'm tired of being treated like a child!", for example, is a disturbing line that either an adult child or that child's parent might use on each other. Often it is not easy to distinguish between the energies of anger and love, creation and destruction. Perhaps we should think of passionate outbursts as a force that can be turned to either destructive or creative use—and that the way to creativity can pass through anger and rejection.

Otto Rank, one of Freud's most gifted disciples, suggested that there were three basic personality structures, the normal, the neurotic, and the creative artist-type. The normal was on the lowest rung of the developmental ladder. This is the person who follows the dotted line, who lives the expected life and is not interested in the great questions of existence or in his or her own potentials. The neurotic person is in some kind of tizzy most of the time. To put it another way, the motor is running, but the person doesn't seem to get anywhere. The neurotic is caught between conflicting impulses to advance and retreat. In Rank's idiom, this would be the will to live versus the will to die. Although the neurotic suffers and stumbles and can be an ordeal to others, there is hope for this person. From our standpoint, the creative and destructive impulses of the neurotic person are often out of balance, the shining and the daring brought to ruin by self-destructive habits and unchecked fears. The creative artist-type person lives in a more spontaneous and holistic manner. This person moves ahead through life, exploring possibilities and taking risks. There can be many failures along the way, such as projects that are flawed or rejected, but there is also continued personal growth. According to Rank, then, the people society considers "normal" have given little play to either their creative or their destructive potentials. The neurotic is often self-lacerating and self-defeating, but is also sometimes graced with moments of creative insight and action. There are not many creative artist-type people, but these are the ones who are also prized for their wisdom and sometimes known as sages.

Can We Tolerate Creative Tension?

Some creative acts do have the intention of unsettling or even destroying our expectations. We are confronted with different versions of reality or possibility. So-called modern art, music, and drama quickly faced condemnation. "You call *that* art? You call *that* music?" Dali, Picasso, and Mondrian perpetuated outrages on traditional ideas about what and how we see; Stravinsky, Schoenberg, and Webern did the same for our perceptions of organized sound. Ionesco, Pirandello and Beckett pulled the rug from under our expectations of drama. How do we respond when somebody dares to challenge our opinions, our assumptions, our approach to life? Perhaps we say, "Thank you very much! You've certainly opened my eyes and ears and given me something new to think about!" Most people, however, are not receptive to being confronted by challenges to their expectations, assumptions, and beliefs.

The creative person frequently encounters resistance, anger, and rejection for having disturbed our comfortable mindset. This means that creative people are often at risk in their relationships. Furthermore, passionate engrossment in one's creative activity can have the effect of shutting other people out even when this is not intended. Some creative activities bring people together. In theater, music, and dance, for example, the participants may become a temporary family for each other, while at the same time having little to do with their own families. Other creative activities are inherently solitary, such as writing. A person caught up in sustained creative activity can therefore either drift away from others or suffer rejection.

In our society, there is a tendency to look at creative people as being "weird" and incomprehensible. We edge away from them. The stereotypes of the mad scientist and the bizarre artist help us to keep our distance and not have to pay any real attention to what they are doing. Artists with disturbing visions and scientists or scholars with challenging ideas are likely to find many minds and doors closed to them. And woe be the person whose creativity involves social, political, or religious change! Over and over again, society has demonstrated that while it might have problems with the old ways, it stands ready to ridicule and attack those who offer alternatives.

There are also acts of destruction that grow out of intergenerational tensions. We can usually count on some members of the younger generation to attack the art, the music, the politics, and even the hairstyles of the senior generation. Symbols of the establishment are useful to joust with when practicing developing skills. Years later, many of these confrontational individuals will have become the establishment whose achievements will then be challenged by the next generation. In the meantime, the senior generation may be attempting to restrict or limit the creative expression of the younger generation. This process occurs in both small traditional societies and high-tech mass societies, although it may be played out differently from one culture to another.

The young generation's challenge to the older generation has the potential to stimulate both generations to original, significant, and valuable creative activities. This positive function of intergenerational rivalry is obstructed when both sides lock themselves into fixed positions. What should be a healthy spirit of challenge becomes instead a kind of trench warfare in which both sides dig in too deeply to appreciate what each has to offer the other. In such situations the most truly creative person may be the one who is able to overcome intergenerational fear and hostility whether from the side of youth or age.

"Senseless Violence": A Creativity Substitute?

There are even more dangerous types of destruction that can occur as part of the creative purpose. The shift from the destructive to the creative mode can be difficult, especially for people with relatively little experience and little guidance. At a particular point, the creative person might insult, offend, and reject not merely other people's creative products but the people themselves. Careers and even lives can be ruined in this way. Destruction can become scattershot. Instead of destroying what seems to be in the way or taking it apart to see what it is made of, one might revel in the power to do harm. Destruction then transgresses beyond its useful function in the creative process. The joy and zest of creative activity transfers to the exercise of power, violence, and destruction for their own sake.

Consider for a moment a term that has recently established itself as an American idiom: "senseless violence." There is no doubt that this expression encodes part of our reality today. Most of the criminal violence is done by young people; the evidence is conclusive on this point. Let us add another fact that is perhaps not as well known. It is in youth that the first stirrings of creativity emerge. Many of the great contributions to mathematics, music, poetry, and other human endeavors have been made by people who were of the same age as those who are stealing, vandalizing, and making vicious assaults on other people. It is a significant but almost entirely overlooked fact that these cruel and terrible acts of destruction are being carried out by people who should be entering a bright, creative, and productive phase of their lives. (Kastenbaum, 2001; Dennis, 1966; Lehman, 1953). What's going on?

I offer another proposition for your consideration: *Much of this "senseless violence" is the result of aborted and misguided creativity.* It may sound "weird" as well as unappealing to propose a link between youth violence and the creative process. Nevertheless, I ask you not to reject this proposition on first hearing. Think about it from time to time as you observe the world around you and the world within you. The approach I am suggesting here could yield surprising benefits. We might devote more attention to helping troubled young people experience and emphasize the productive rather than the destructive components of the creative process. The satisfactions and sense of self experienced in creative activity make it perhaps the most potent alternative to senseless violence—but, first, the individual must somehow enjoy the personal experience of creative activity.

If the creative process goes seriously wrong in youth, it may have the unfortunate consequences that have just been mentioned. But what if the creative process goes seriously wrong in the later adult years, or just seems to go away? What are the consequences? My experience suggests that the loss or distortion of creative potential in the later adult years does contribute to significant problems, including depression, social withdrawal, and suicidality. We will be in a better position to examine this issue after considering a few other aspects of the creative process in general.

The Receptive Side of the Creative Process

The first of these considerations requires us to look at the other side of the coin. I am speaking of the coin that has as one of its faces the image of the tyger with its untamed and dangerous creative spirit. What is on the other side? Again, the answer is provided by William Blake, this time in his collection of poetry and drawings called *Songs of Innocence* (Blake 1970). This poem takes its impetus from a persistent question:

Little Lamb, who made thee?
Dost thou know who made thee?

Gave thee life and bid thee feed,
By the stream and o'er the mead;
Gave thee clothing of delight,
Softest clothing, woolly bright;
Gave thee such a tender voice,
Making all the vales rejoice?
Little Lamb, who made thee?
Dost thou know who made thee?

The final verse answers the question and gives us access to the other side of the mystery of creativity:

Little Lamb, I'll tell thee,
Little Lamb, I'll tell thee.
He is called by thy name,
For he calls himself a Lamb.
He is meek and he is mild;
He became a little child.
I a child and thou a lamb.
We are called by his name.
Little Lamb, God bless thee!
Lamb Lamb, God bless thee!

You will recall Blake's question of the tyger: "Did he who made the lamb make thee?" Now we have the answer. The majestic and dangerous power of the tyger and the tender innocence of the lamb do indeed come from the same source. The generative spirit of the universe conceived two beings with radically different modes of relating to the world. Somehow, we must have needed both.

Within each of us the tyger and the lamb coexist. Friedrich Nietsche, Sigmund Freud, Carl Jung, Karl Menninger, Viktor Frankl, the Dalai Lama, and other students of the human condition have expressed this truth in various ways. A common point is that each of us must make some kind of arrangement between an active, aggressive, and risk-taking impulse, and a receptive and appreciative orientation. Unlike the tyger and the lamb, we have a choice. Theoretically, we can deal with the world either with tooth and claw, or with a naive and trusting belief in the goodness of the world and the intentions of others. In actuality, few of us give full rein to either of these impulses. We learn to protect ourselves against the consequences of acting in an aggressive, destructive, and high risk-taking modality. And we learn to protect ourselves against deceit and danger by building fortifications around the childlike innocence that would have us believe the world to be a loving and secure place.

Is it necessary to protect ourselves from both the tyger and the lamb within? Probably so. But probably not to the extent that the development of creative propensities has been discouraged through formal and informal education. Curiosity, experimentation, and playful exploration of possibilities occur in our schools when teachers burning with their own sparks of creativity find a way to protect this impulse from the standardized grinding of the educational system. The heightened emphasis on standardized testing at present is threatening to roll back what progress has been made in liberating and guiding the natural curiosity of the young. If teacher and student are required to focus on material likely to be on the test, there is much less opportunity to explore the world in their own ways. Furthermore, gender studies have made it abundantly clear that there is intense social pressure on females to inhibit their exploratory, aggressive, and risk-taking impulses. It is one of the great struggles and therefore one of the great triumphs when a woman reclaims the tyger powers in the middle or later adult years.

Society's attitude toward the lamb is more complex. The major social institutions in most societies encourage obedience, conformity, and predictable behavior. Going into the twentieth century, "patriotism" and "faith" were among the most common terms used to praise attitudes of uncritical acceptance. Social institutions with their keen interest in self-preservation seldom encourage questioning attitudes and critical thinking that might be turned against them.

As we move deeper into the new millennium, we can see the dominance of another social institution whose power has been much enhanced in recent years: the network of mega-corporations. It is to their advantage to shape consumers' buying habits—indeed our total lifestyles—for their convenience in production, distribution, and marketing. To take one brief set of examples: your local book or audio-video store is most likely to be part of a large franchised operation which, in turn, is probably a subsidiary of a huge media corporate network. It is in their commercial interests to stock a relatively few titles that are in great demand. It is more cumbersome and less profitable if we, as consumers, have a diverse range of interests in books, compact disks, and videos. The lamb is therefore of some commercial value, especially the modern lamb with its several credit and debit cards. Persistent advertising campaigns are intended to herd consumers together into flocks with the same preferences. In a somewhat parallel manner, the educational system tends to encourage a simplistic approach to understanding the complexities of life. The controversial changes in curriculum can be viewed as a shift from one oversimplification to another. With respect to both business and public education, the lamb is indulged because it is perceived as a docile and controllable component of our personality.

These considerations suggest that the lamb is favored by society. The tyger is in chains; the lamb is free. Unfortunately, this is not quite the case. The lamb is free only to become a sheep who will use the pathways established by society, paths that lead from one approved destination to another. This is a convenience for social stability, but a serious impediment to the development of creativity. Recognizing that both potentials are within each of us, we also should be able to recognize what the lamb must learn before the tyger can leap. It is the lamb's enthusiastic curiosity that absorbs what the world has to offer and brings in the raw materials for creativity and keeps the mind fresh through the years. When we read the biographies of celebrated artists, scientists, and inventors, we learn again and again of their fascination with a broad spectrum of sensory images and ideas. These people often observe the odd little details and irrelevant little patterns that others ignore. They may become fascinated with seemingly trivial phenomena and questions. They may nose around in places that right-thinking people have learned to avoid. While a hundred others hustle about their structured routines and narrow purposes, the creative person pauses to squint at something that seems delightfully strange, or to mull over a conversational phrase that everybody else has forgotten. The lamb continually refreshes the mind with sights, sounds, interactions, and ideas that engage its "idle curiosity"—a misnomer if ever there was one: hardly anything compares to the vigor of the human mind enlivened by a question.

The typical socialization process comes down pretty hard on the lamb side of the creativity coin. As a child moves into formal education and then ever closer to adult responsibilities there is increasing restriction on what realms of experience and activity are considered to be appropriate. Children are differentially reinforced to lead them away from whatever society frowns upon, fears, or considers a waste of time and effort. What splendid preparation for becoming an elder who obediently accepts a diminished role in society! What practice in blunting one's curiosity!

Here are two related examples that are of particular consequence for the developing child's inclination to experience the world in a fresh and individual manner. The first example:

"Jason! Are you daydreaming? You're not daydreaming? Well, why don't you just put that work down and let your mind wander around wherever it wants to go. You spend so much of your time doing and thinking useful things, Jason. I wish you'd lie around more, looking up at the sky, or imagining stuff that's fun to imagine."

The second example:

"Jennifer, what do you have for our family poetry reading tonight? Is there a problem? You look a little uncomfortable...Oh, you wrote something yourself but you don't know if it's any good. I definitely want to hear it. We all do. If that poem wanted to be written, there has to be something to it! You've heard my poems, even the awful ones! We sometimes have even more fun with the bad ones, and they seem to prepare the way for the good ones."

How often have you heard comments of this kind directed to schoolchildren? The practice of allowing one's thoughts to drift and spin as they choose is often criticized in our society. Children who do not stay on the straight-and-narrow, goal-directed path in their thoughts might grow up to be idlers and underachievers. Years of criticism from multiple sources discourages children from engaging in the free play of their own minds. Similarly, children's exploration of their inner experience is systematically neglected.

The fragile and peripheral place of poetry in American life is one manifestation of this attitude. There will come many times in a person's life, many crucial times, when there is a desperate need to understand one's own thoughts and feelings and convey them to another person. Unfortunately, the person may flounder and fail in this effort. Our society is weak in its appreciation, weak in its education, and weak in its communication of the most intimate thoughts and feelings. Addictive, depressive, and hostile behaviors are among the alternatives when people cannot consult their own inner depths and share with others. Communication of intimate and complex inner states of being requires and deserves attention from parents and educators. When this perceptive and expressive ability is cultivated, the person has a lifelong resource for dealing creatively with both the festive and the catastrophic aspects of life. When this ability is blunted and mocked, people face a lifetime of groping inarticulately toward self-understanding. Communication within core interpersonal relationships may also falter at crucial times because people cannot find the words. I spoke once with a young man who had nearly incinerated himself. He suffered painful burns and came close to death when he poured gasoline on his clothes and set himself on fire. This was in the presence of the young woman who had told him a few hours previously that their relationship was over. "I was so—like you know—I was so—I don't know what. I don't—you know—I don't have the words." I think some relationships die and some people die because they lack poetry. I admit immediately that some very good poets have taken their lives, but I believe that usually it was the poetry that had kept them going up to that point.

Stagnation or Renewal in the Later Adult Years?

There are some fantastic people among us who bring the resources of both the tyger and the lamb with them into their later adult years. They have the daring and the power to take risks and to reject what has become useless or restrictive. The past informs but does not constrain them. They may catch us by surprise when they share their latest creative work. For example, a composer in his late 60s smiled when I reacted with surprise to his most recent piece. "Sure, it's different! Why not? I'm different, the world is different: shouldn't the music be different, too?" He is among the many creative artists who choose not to rely upon their established reputations but to explore new possibilities and to accept the risks of misunderstanding, risk, and failure. The same elderly creative person who retains the tyger's zest is also likely to retain the lamb's receptivity to experience. This is the kind of person whose ability to appreciate the variety of life on its own terms has escaped the numbing socialization process, the kind of person who in advanced age is still quite capable of noticing something new that he or she can turn to creative use.

It is obvious that some people continue to be highly creative in their later adult years. This creativity may show itself in one particular kind of activity, or it might show up in everything they do, including their relationships with others. They have been fresh, productive, and stimulating since childhood, and a long life's experience has added depth and nuance. It has become obvious through research that some people renew their creative selves in the later adult years. This renewal may be assisted by a reduction in chores and responsibilities that had previously claimed much of their time. There may be more opportunity to rediscover interests one had many years ago but which had to be set aside in the service of family and career. Travel may stimulate new thoughts and feelings. Elderly couples may start to know each other in new ways as they can turn from being "Mom" and "Dad" to exploring further potentials in their relationship.

Unfortunately, it is also true that some people seem to be without the creative spark in their later adult years. They are repetitive in their thoughts, communications, actions, and inter-actions. Today is pretty much a replica of yesterday—or as near so as they can make it—and tomorrow will be more of the same, if things go as they should. Until recently, it was rare for anybody to question this state of affairs. Health professionals, life scien-tists, and social and behavioral scientists often accepted the general stereotype that our creative juices dry up with age. We become inflexible in our routines, past-oriented in our conversa-tions, and increasingly less capable of giving or receiving pleasure in an adult manner. We spend our time worrying about our bowels and the cost of funerals. Zestful and passionate creative activity has seemed far out of character for people who have reached their later adult years, and even our human service professionals have acquiesced to this assumption.

Even today, after some years of public education, most people still do not expect elderly men and women to be creative in any meaningful sense of the term. This negative expectation smacks us in the face like a boomerang when we get up in years ourselves. Nevertheless, the urge for creative expression is strong and persistent and may be felt even under these unfavorable circumstances. Unfortunately, the urge may be felt—and seri-ously misinterpreted. Here is an excerpt from one of a series of conversations I had with a woman in her late 80s:

> I started being cross. Restless. I did not feel at peace with myself. Nothing was right. Nothing could be made right. I could not let myself be satisfied, that was the problem because actually everything was as it should have been, but that was no longer good enough for me. The chil-dren figured I was either upset at them or getting mental. The doctors wanted to load me up on pills so I would sleep all night and zombie around all day. That was not

for me. A vexation, that is what I called it! I tried to talk myself out of this vexation, but that was not working either, and I definitely did not enjoy having to live with myself at this time. I feel sorry for those who did. I must have been a real pill or perhaps I should say prune!

Mrs. H. did not long remain a prisoner of her strange vexation. She decided to work some of this apparently useless and directionless energy out of her system by walking over to our campus every day and popping in here and there to see what was happening. This involved a walk of about two miles to the campus, and quite a bit of perambulating while there. She soon fell into conversations with students, staff, and faculty members. One day everything fell into place. "I want to be a student," Mrs. H. told several of us, "and learn how to teach other old people to be students!" And so she did. Mrs. H. took courses in several departments over a period of about three years, sometimes for credit, sometimes as an auditor. She made a profound impression on the other students and on me in the two courses she took with me. Generally, Mrs. H. would speak only once or twice during a class session, but her penetrating observations were often the highlights of the day. Furthermore, she recruited several other people of advanced age for meetings in her home where they would discuss their educational interests and how to pursue them. I know of at least one of these elders who followed Mrs. H's initiative and also became a student at Arizona State University.

During all this time, Mrs. H. seemed to be in robust health. She never complained of health problems, and somehow found the energies she needed to walk to the campus, participate in a class, hang with students and faculty, and then walk home again. Mrs. H. had rediscovered her love of learning that early in her life had to take second place to family responsibilities. She had developed a creative vision in which highly motivated elders could help each other to renew and extend their education and enjoy the give-and-take of intellectual dialogue.

At first both Mrs. H. and the people in her life had assumed that something was "wrong" with her or with them because she had become jittery, short-tempered, and dissatisfied. This sense of frustration, however, this unsettled mood, proved to be a necessary precondition to the rediscovery and recovery of her creative potential. A creative adventure is often preceded by a phase of unrest, of searching, of strong but unfocused impulses. Mrs. H. did activate her creative spirit and did find a guiding purpose to which she could devote her considerable powers of intellect and persuasion. But who knows how many elderly men and women today are having their suppressed creativity misdiagnosed as illness, personality disorder, or senseless agitation? And who knows what medications and interpersonal responses are being applied to a "problem" that is, in fact, the awakening sign of opportunity? The burgeoning signs of creative activity are all too easy to misinterpret in our society as agitation and deviancy. This misinterpretation is especially common when the individual is elderly and therefore expected to be thoroughly routinized and predictable, if not inert.

There are some cultures in which creativity is expected of elders. Creativity is expected especially of those people who had pursued artistic excellence throughout their earlier adult years. Furthermore, not only the art but the person is expected to reach a higher level of creative distinction with age. An excellent example has been documented in Nathdwara, a small pilgrimage center in Western India. This town is the headquarters of a Hindu sect that places high value on artistic creativity. An in-depth study was conducted a few years ago by the late Renaldo Maduro, a psychiatrist and anthropologist who knew the Hindu culture as both an insider and a trained researcher. Maduro reminds us that the Hindu concept of the life course includes a positive role for the elderly person. Age is not a failure; it is a very significant stage or ashrama in the human journey.

Not everybody has the ability, character, and discipline to become both a more spiritual artist and a more spiritual person with age, to achieve in all its meaning the final ashrama of Sanyasa. It is an ideal of the religion and the culture as well as the individual. Here is an excerpt from one of Maduro's interviews with an elderly man who was regarded as a highly creative painter. This is how the elderly artist explained himself and others at his level of age and creative activity:

> Now the truly creative painter—as a man in the elder's stage—he is unconventional, original, and somewhat less sociable. He is really different from others because of his age and because of his mind, which remains very sharp-witted and especially sensitive to messages from within for his artistic work. He listens more carefully for messages from inside, from the gods...and he is less outgoing.

> *But he is able to be more original and creative now—also more individualistic. He paints whatever he likes. He doesn't give a hoot sometimes about other people...He happily does his own thing, just like the water buffalo. This means he is more imaginative, mature/ripe, and religious—not religious with mantras and tantras and temple service...but with self-development and independence. He is closer to the power of the gods within him now, and closer to root emotion* (Maduro 1981).

This description is both illuminating and challenging. It is illuminating because it reveals the possibility that a person may be more rather than less imaginative and creative in the later adult years, as well as more unconventional, more liberated from the opinions and demands of others, and more in contact with the root sources of human emotion and religious experience. It is challenging because it deprives us of the stereotypical image of a passive, routined, and predictable elder. Like Blake's tyger, Maduro's elderly painter is not inclined to waste time in trivial pursuits and does not care much about public opinion. Creative elders go their own way. They are faithful to their inner voices and emotions. They will not be trapped in the nets of either negative or positive social stereotypes; for example, they are not "dear, sweet, adorable old things." They have minds and purposes of their own, and teeth and claws to achieve and protect these purposes.

Can our society accommodate itself to an increase in the number of elderly people who are vital and creative and, therefore, difficult to predict and control? Or do we actually prefer that elders twiddle their time away in routine and inconsequential activities? These are questions to keep in mind during the years ahead.

There is one question that can be answered with some assurance right now, however. *Does it make a difference whether an elderly person's creative potential is expressed or suppressed?* It does make a difference, a tremendous difference. People who have been unable to maintain or reclaim their creative spirit are much more likely to suffer from depression and anxiety, much more likely to seek desperately after satisfaction and meaning, much more likely to criticize the people in their lives and even the food on their plates (Csikszenmihalyi 1996). They may turn in many directions to identify and overcome the source of their discontent—but this question is not likely to be successful unless they turn inward to renew their own creative spirit.

People who do nourish their own creative spirit are likely to have more energy at their disposal and less time to cultivate the attitude of victim or patient. They are also more likely to recognize and encourage the creative spirit in others, regardless of age.

Creative activity requires the integration of thought and emotion. It is at the same time a physical and a spiritual venture. Furthermore, the most creative elders are able to take the greatest risks, to confront the greatest doubts and the horrors of existence. And, not least, the most creative elders have the power to *heal*— to heal not only themselves, but the ravaged soul of the world.

Research Support for Creativity in the Later Adult Years

There is solid research to support the proposition that people can remain creative throughout a long life. What do the studies tell us?

- People who were creative when young are those most likely to be creative in their later adult years. The mental skills that contribute to creativity continue to develop if they are exercised throughout the life span. These abilities include tolerance for ambiguity, preference for complexity, flexibility and fluidity of thought, and the knack for recognizing problems as opportunities and the willingness to experiment with possibilities (Guilford, 1959; Adams-Price, 1998).

- The quality of creative activity remains intact throughout the life span. In general, people produce fewer creative works in their later years, but the ratio of "hits" and "misses" in their output is about the same as it was in earlier years (Simonton, 1996).

- There is often a renaissance of creativity deep into the later adult years. Interests and talents that had to be put aside earlier in life may now be given a new opportunity. Furthermore, both the perspective and the challenges of advanced age can stimulate creative activities (Einstein, 1937).

- Women often have more opportunity for creative expression in the later adult years because of reduced family obligations. Furthermore, women often provide emotional support for other people's creative activities and express their own creativity in ways that are subtle and indirect (Helson, 1990; Kallir 1982).

- Elderly people with a history of creative activity often learn how to accomplish and communicate more with less effort. They get to the heart of the matter. The spare but affecting brush strokes of the artists studied by Maduro provide excellent examples (Kastenbaum, 2000; O'Connor, 1979).

A history of alcohol or drug abuse, inadequately managed health problems (especially with overmedications), and lack of opportunity and support can stand in the way of creative expression in the later adult years. Sometimes the most formidable obstacle is the attitude of society. I well remember an example that occurred in a geriatric facility when I was new to this field.

A professor of art at a local college volunteered to help us work toward a more stimulating and normal social climate within the institution. He noticed several residents painting under the supervision of the occupational therapy department. They were restricted to copying picture postcards. The professor earned their confidence and encouraged them to paint not so much what they saw, but what they felt. He sat back and observed with wonder and pleasure as two of the residents started on new paintings that were as different from the postcard as from each other's drawings. Both brushed color over color to create vibrant and expressive paintings. Even more impressively, they were completely engrossed in their projects, eyes glowing with purpose. The professor himself was so excited that he returned the next day to see the finished products and visit with the elder artists. To his puzzlement, the paintings had been scraped down to approximate a representation of the postcard picture. An occupational therapist proudly admitted that she had improved their paintings. The residents were supposed to paint pictures of pictures and do them the right way! She could not begin to imagine that there was more than one way to paint, let alone that there could be profound emotional release in expressing oneself through the creative process. The professor and I realized that we had a lot of work to do in understanding institutional dynamics if we were to offer opportunities to the residents.

Promoting Creative Expression in the Later Adult Years

If we agree that Rome was not built in a day, then we might also be ready to admit that the same is true of creative older people. To promote creative expression in the later adult years it would be useful to attend both to the whole life course, as well as to the situations that are encountered as a long life continues to lengthen. I would make the following suggestions:

- In childhood, allow for "idle times" in which the meter is not running and nobody is keeping score.

This will help to cultivate curiosity, and a sense of self that may be otherwise submerged under parental or media influence. Useless free time without expectations or pressure—there's nothing like it!

- Encourage experimentation; don't have a cow about "failure." The creative process is inherently risky at all levels of endeavor. Many children start to put away their creative impulses early because it only seems to get them into trouble.

- Provide positive models. "Look how different that one flower is from all the others. I wonder why?" "That sure didn't work, did it? Let's try it another way."

- Welcome dreams, daydreams, and fantasies into everyday conversation. Accept indecision, hesitation, and ambiguity as part of life. This will safeguard against the tendency to button up one's inner life in favor of a brittle and restrictive facade.

- Help the young to develop positive but realistic attitudes toward aging and the aged. Frequent contact with a variety of elderly adults is often the most effective way of doing this.

- Cultivate the ability to recognize the signs of "settling in" as we move into the middle adult years. A comfortable and predictable lifestyle can sedate the creative impulse. See the same people, discuss the same topics, hold the same opinions, make the same rounds—this is pleasant enough, but it also gradually softens the edges of life, drawing back from the boundaries where the most vital creative encounters take place. Many of those who appeared routinized and hyperhabituated in their later adult years had already lapsed into a noncreative lifestyle in their 30s or 40s.

- Recognize that depression is not a natural or intrinsic part of aging. Many elders suffer with depression that is associated with bereavement, unmodulated transitions and discontinuities, and concern about their future. Alcoholism, overmedication, and suicidality are sometimes part of this picture. But many also respond well to sympathetic and knowledgeable attention. Creativity can be unleashed when the heavy burden of depression is lifted. Conversely, encouragement to creative endeavors can also help to lift a depression.

- Remember that long-term care facilities are still part of the community. Staff are more likely to take that extra step themselves when they see family and community demonstrating a keen interest. Proprietors and directors of long-term care facilities can also encourage community participation themselves by selecting from effective programs that have fostered creativity in institutionalized elders or innovating their own.

Years ago we established a pub (The Captain's Chair) inside a state geriatric facility that generated creative activity throughout the hospital. Effective programs throughout the nation range from creative cooking to the production of original theater pieces. With a little creativity on the part of the staff—and receptivity to the ideas of the residents—it is possible to establish a milieu in which personhood is respected and individual expression welcomed.

The daunting tyger and the receptive lamb make uneasy but stimulating companions if we have the nerve to take both of them along with us on a long life's journey.

Further Readings

Adams-Price C. E. (Ed.) (1998). *Creativity and aging: Theoretical and empirical approaches*. New York: Springer Publishing Co.

Blake, W. (1970). Songs of innocence and experience (original work, 1789). In D. V. Gurdurn (Ed.), *The poetry and prose of William Blake* (pp. 7–32). New York: Doubleday.

Csikszenmihalyi, M. (1996). *Creativity.* New York: HarperCollins.

Dennis, W. (1966). Creative productivity between the ages of 20 and 80 years. *Journal of Gerontology, 21,* 1-8.

Einstein, A. (1937). Opus ultimum. *Musical Quarterly, 22,* 269-286.

Guilford, J. P. (1959). Traits of creativity. In H. H. Anderson (Ed.), *Creativity and its cultivation* (pp. 142-161). New York: Harper.

Helson, R. (1990). Creativity in women: Outer and inner views over time. In M. A. Runco & R. S. Albert (Eds.), *Theories of creativity* (pp. 46-58). Newbury Park, CA: Sage.

Kallir, J. (1982). *Grandma Moses: The artist behind the myth.* Secaucus, NJ: Wellfleet.

Kastenbaum, R. (1989). Old men created by young artists: Time-transcendence in Tennyson and Picasso. *International Journal of Aging & Human Development, 28,* 81-104.

Kastenbaum, R. (1995). *Dorian, graying: Is youth the only thing worth having?* New York: Baywood.

Kastenbaum, R. (2000). Creativity and the arts. In T. R. Cole, R. Kastenbaum, & R. E. Roy (Eds.), *Handbook of the humanities and aging* (2nd ed., pp. 381-401.) New York: Springer Publishing Co.

Kastenbaum, R. (2001). *Death, society and human experience* (7th ed.). Boston: Allyn & Bacon.

Lehman, H. C. (1953). *Age and achievement.* Princeton, NJ: Princeton University Press.

Madruro, R. (1981). The old man as creative artist in India. In R. Kastenbaum (Ed.), *Old age on the new scene* (pp. 71-101). New York: Springer Publishing Company.

McCrae, R. (1987). Creativity, divergent thinking and openness to experience. *Journal of Personality and Social Psychology, 52,* 1258-1265.

O'Connor, F. V. (1979). Albert Berne and the completion of being: Images of vitality and extinction in the last paintings of a ninety-six-year-old man. In D. D. Van Tassel (Ed.), *Aging, death, and the completion of being* (pp. 255-289). Philadelphia: University of Pennsylvania Press.

Simonton, D. K. (1996). Creativity. In J. E. Birren (Ed.), *Encyclopedia of gerontology* (pp. 341-351). New York: Academic Press.

Chapter 10

Creativity, Primary Prevention, and the Paradoxical Extension of the Conventional: The Final Chapter as Prelude

Martin Bloom and Thomas P. Gullotta

We have met some interesting people in the course of this volume, from the feisty, creative 94-year-old Miss Eggerton who had some sewing to do before she died (Kastenbaum), to the new and super shy kindergartner Tiffany who unexpectedly became "too busy" to go home because she was wondrously engaged in "writing" a story (Doyle). They have taught us a great deal about their own creativity, and we hope we can capture something of this ecstatic resolution of a challenge involving unknowns, whose solution has social value—that is, our primary prevention-oriented definition of creativity offered in the introduction to this volume.

Let us return to our working definitions. In characterizing primary prevention, we introduced an equation involving ten elements, which we mercifully shortened to six. This was the primary prevention cube involving six general facets: To obtain a primary prevention outcome, we seek to increase the strengths of individuals, the supports of social groupings, and the resources of the physical environment; and we seek to reduce the limitations of individuals, the stresses of groupings, and the pressures from physical environments, viewed as an interrelated system.

311

Not every facet is necessarily involved in every situation, but as a checklist, we postulate that we must consider each of these facets in our multidimensional approach to primary prevention.

Likewise, with creativity, we summarized the conceptual aspects of what is involved in any form of innovative and socially useful entities (products, processes, ideas, and such). We employed the same metaphor: The cube of creativity, briefly summarized, refers to that system of individual, sociocultural, and physical environmental factors whose interactions lead to the production of a novel and socially useful outcome. Some of these individual, sociocultural, and physical environmental factors are strengths and may contribute positively to creativity in the given individual; others are limitations and may be inhibiting.

Now we have to come to terms with the chapters in this anthology in order to understand the promotion of creativity across the life course. We note that for the most part, the authors emphasized the strengths of individuals and, to a slightly lesser extent, the support offered by the sociocultural environments in which young talented people are raised. Yet, there was recognition of a dark side of life, where individual talents and group supports are inhibited, sometimes as part of the broad cultural norm that operates against women, minorities, and the aged as creative people. The physical environment was seen to play little role, except for some accessible resources and available support groups.

Readers of these chapters can point to even more specific factors, such as adequate (but not necessarily extraordinary) intelligence; self-motivation for a future that is fulfilling—of some dream, or minimally, of a full stomach; a strong sense of self as a person with talents to be expressed, even in the face of social or personal obstruction but often with at least one supportive mentor; a capacity for risk taking, for divergent thinking, when others around them are conventional and play it safe.

Likewise, certain specific sociocultural themes reemerge: that social support from significant others to do innovative work is very important; that some degree of resources is necessary—the tools, time, and themes of which creativity or creative adaptations are made; and especially the importance of an appreciative audience. Likewise, some dark sociocultural themes emerge as barriers to women's progress in conventional creativity, as well as the barriers that poverty, ethnicity, and other status characteristics may impose.

Given these, and other themes discussed in the preceding chapters, how are we to combine individual and sociocultural factors, strengths and limitations, into our assignment: promoting creativity across the life course? Let us enter, so to speak, the inside of the cube of creativity, which is the life space of pushes and pulls with regard to some outcome. Everyone every day is involved in these pushes (toward) and pulls (away from) some desired goals. Probably, the creative person is more involved as contributor to his or her creative fate than the average person—this is where the independent, risk-taking aspects of the creative person come into play—but nonetheless, even the most creative individual is still subject to the pressures (stresses) and resources (supports) of the sociocultural and physical environments. Our question thus reduces to activating the positives and minimizing the negatives in persons' environments toward the end of producing some novel and socially useful creation.

However, the paradox of promoting creativity is in its very unconventionality. We want to encourage risk taking but not behavior so far out as to be unacceptable to the relevant audiences. We want to support young and old talent but not so much as to infringe on the originality of the creative person, which includes the freedom to fail as well as to succeed. We want to educate for best conventional techniques to express ideas and feelings but not so much as to emphasize coloring within the lines as the ultimate act of artistry. As Pelz and Andrews (1966) wrote long ago in their analysis of creativity within scientific organizations, the evidence suggests that it is only with high levels of challenge (risk taking) along with supportive resources (security) that creativity can thrive.

The primary prevention cube involves an analysis of the ways of moving people and groups toward desired ends (and away from undesired ones) (Bloom, 1996). One of the insights we obtained from reading these chapters is that primary prevention largely addresses conventional challenges—how children can get along with each other in school; how parents can best raise their children to maturity; how to prevent school dropout, unwise sexual activity, drug use, and so forth. However, creativity involves the unconventional, how to break rules (to achieve better solutions), how to take risks (in order to move beyond yesterday's solutions to tomorrow's challenges), how to put ordinary ingredients together in novel and socially useful ways that do not currently exist.

This unconventionality being the case, we had to rethink our primary prevention practices as being the vehicle of making constructive changes in human affairs. This perspective led us to a concept we named the *paradoxical extension* for promoting creative outcomes. Let us take an example of a well-established primary prevention practice and see how it has to be transformed by paradoxical extension.

Shure & Spivack (1988) summarize a quarter century of research in helping young children (and others) to problem solve. Their underlying cognitive theory suggests that having some sense of the rules of problem solving enables possessors to make their way through socially conflictful situations with a minimal of problems. Those who lack these cognitive skills have more problems with others, and consequently, get into various kinds of trouble. The solution is to teach young children the critical steps of problem solving: identifying alternatives to any problem situation, and recognizing probable consequences of each alternative, so that the individual can make a decision as to the best course of action. This would be a conventional primary prevention practice; it has been used with many young children in different contexts with very encouraging results.

Now, the paradox: How shall we promote the kind of divergent and innovative thinking for creative solutions that still involves getting along with others in age-appropriate ways? On the one hand, we are most likely to encourage the line of thinking that involves the most sharing and the least fighting over the toy one kindergartner has and the other kindergartner wants. (This is the way we oversocialized adults think.) But Shure and Spivack (1988) are very clear in saying that they do not impose solutions onto children, only a broadening of methods for them to find their own best solution. However, what if one child's method for finding the best solution involves telling the other child that she has germs on her hands and should wash them with soap and water immediately, so as to stay healthy. He volunteers to watch over the coveted toy in the meantime. It is a novel suggestion, and socially useful up to a point. (What 4-year-old wouldn't reap benefit from a good hand washing?) But it is ... well, far out. And maybe a bit too original for the observing teacher to accept, even though it might be a "creative solution." However, let us suppose the teacher does accept it, since no real harm has been done. She may not positively reward our pint-sized hero directly (since she suspects a Machiavellian subtext), but he has won a unique victory—he has come up with a novel solution that has value in the preschool setting. He has learned one step toward becoming a creative problem solver.

What we see in this hypothetical example is a ratcheting up of a conventional solution that goes beyond the conventional response to one that is original and intentional, while producing some positive social results for himself and his playmate. The less likely alternative appears to have been chosen rather than the more likely one—"I'll give you my garbage truck if you'll give me your steam shovel truck." Now our little Machiavelli can play (for a while) with both trucks, and his playmate will indeed benefit from cleaner hands that reduce the spread of germs (for a while).

How did he know that this proposal was novel and socially useful? We doubt that he did, in so many words, but he did know the territory—about what conventional ploys are encouraged and that they are as likely to be refused as not. So he tried something else, something original, something that was a "better solution" to a common challenge. It was risky in the sense that he did not know how his "audience" was going to respond, either the other child or the observing teacher. But the lesson he learned was to have trust in himself and in his innovative solution.

How are we to set up rules for rule breaking? We want and need extensions of conventional rules that no longer satisfy the new demands placed on them. And we need people to break old rules so as to establish new ones. We are in the paradoxical situation of needing to promote both conventionality and nonconventionality, rule following and rule breaking, innovative outcomes using conventional methods, innovative methods leading more effectively to conventional outcomes. We—who are the social context for creativity—have to help young people, the middle aged, older people, all people to expect and ecstatically enjoy their own creativity; we have to provide opportunities for this creativity; and we have to reward creative outcomes. Not just for their sake, but for the sake of everyone.

Here, then, is our proposal for rules for rule breaking: Select the least likely (least conventional) alternative for action, which promises the most likely degree of positive consequence—with some minimal degree of acceptable outcome. This rule prescribes two contradictory tendencies—the search for the nonconventional solution and the provision of a degree of social responsibility. It provides for both risk and security, in Pelz' and Andrews' terms, for the creator and the audience, which makes it an optimal solution.

Let us try it out with a second example, on the use of social support groups in primary prevention. There are two major functions of such groups: (1) to buffer members of the group from the oppressive forces of the larger society, and (2) to encourage and support members' self-expression within the boundaries of conformity to group norms (Bloom, 1996). However, consider the creative extension of a group of artists or scientists or practical problem solvers: Here the norms are nonconventional ones, and the paradoxical function of such support groups would be to encourage more divergence from conventional thinking, by a kind of leapfrogging on each other's creative ideas. A support group for the creative produces divergent synergy, not convergence. The expectation is for the unexpectable. However, there is the expectation also for some audience approval (and sales) to make the productions viable. Even starving artists have to eat sometimes.

Again, we believe that our rule for rule breaking applies: The least likely alternative will involve nonconventional actions as sanctioned within the artistic support group, while the reasonable degree of positive social consequence will involve some positive viable social product.

In general, we believe that this rule for rule breaking allows us to "eat our cake and have it too." We invite readers to experiment with it in different contexts—to be creative while recognizing their own social responsibilities, and to therefore be socially constructive.

References

Bloom, M. (1996). *Primary prevention practices.* Thousand Oaks, CA: Sage.

Pelz, D., & Andrews, F. (1966). *Scientists in organizations: Productive climates for research and development.* New York: Wiley.

Shure, M. B., & Spivak, G. (1988). Interpersonal cognitive problem-solving. In R. Price, Cowen, E. L., Lorion, R. P., & Ramos-McKay, J. (Eds.), *14 ounces of prevention* (69–82). Washington, DC: American Psychological Association.

About the Contributors

Martin Bloom, PhD, received his doctorate from the University of Michigan, and has pursued a career in teaching and research. He has written a number of books and papers, concentrating on primary prevention, the evaluation of practice, and on human behavior and development. He currently teaches social work at the University of Connecticut.

Charlotte Doyle, PhD, conducts research on creativity ranging from story-telling by preschool children to the process by which fiction writers create their works to a woman mayor's remarkable leadership. A generalist, Doyle is author of *Explorations in Psychology*, and she just defined "psychology" for the American Psychological Association's *Encyclopedia of Psychology*. She writes books for young children, too. Her most recently published title is *You Can't Catch Me* and her other new title, *One Baby, Two Babies*, is in press. Doyle is professor of psychology at Sarah Lawrence College.

Emma Forbes-Jones, MA, is a doctoral candidate in clinical psychology at the University of Rochester. She is presently conducting research on risk and protective processes in the development of aggression. Forbes-Jones is the cofounder and developer of a classroom-based program to reduce violence and promote conflict resolution in young children.

Thomas P. Gullotta, MA, MSW, is CEO of Child and Family Agency and is a member of the psychology and education departments at Eastern Connecticut State University. He is the senior author of the fourth edition of The Adolescent Experience and is the founding editor of *Journal of Primary Prevention*. He is the senior book series editor for *Issues in Children's and Families' Lives*. In addition, he serves as the monograph series editor for *Prevention in Practice*. Tom holds editorial appointments on the *Journal of Early Adolescence, Journal of Adolescent Research, Adolescence,* and the *Journal of Educational and Psychological Consultation.* He serves as vice-chairman for Children and

319

Prevention on the Board of National Mental Health Association and works frequently as a consultant for several branches of the U.S. government. He has published extensively on adolescents and primary prevention.

Alice Sterling Honig, PhD, is a Professor Emerita in the Department of Child and Family Studies at Syracuse University and a licensed psychologist specializing in parenting problems and custody cases. She received her undergraduate education at Barnard College, Columbia University, and her doctorate in developmental psychology from Syracuse University. Dr. Honig is a fellow of the Society for Research in Child Development and of the American Psychological Association and a member of the International Society for Infant Studies. For 12 years, Dr. Honig was the program director for the Family Development Research Program. For more than 25 years, she has conducted the National Quality Infant/Toddler Workshop held annually at Syracuse University. Dr. Honig is the author/editor of numerous books and articles on infant and toddler development.

Robert Kastenbaum, PhD, is Professor Emeritus, Hugh Downs School of Human Communication, Arizona State University. He has served as clinical psychologist and geriatric hospital director in addition to his teaching and research. His books include *Dorian, Graying: Is Youth the Only Thing Worth Having?* and *The Psychology of Death.* His works for the theater include *Tell Me About Tigers*, and the operas, *Dorian*, and *Closing Time.*

Sally M. Reis, PhD, is a professor of educational psychology at the University of Connecticut where she also serves as Principal Investigator of the National Research Center on the Gifted and Talented. She was a teacher for 15 years, 11 of which were spent working with gifted students on the elementary, junior high, and high school levels. She has authored more than 130 articles, 8 books, 40 book chapters, and numerous monographs and technical reports. Dr. Reis has traveled extensively conducting workshops and providing professional development for school districts on gifted education, enrichment programs, and talent development programs. Sally serves on several editorial boards, including the *Gifted Child Quarterly*, and is the current President of the National Association for Gifted Children.

Joseph Renzulli, PhD, is the Neag Professor of Gifted Education and Talent Development at the University of Connecticut, where he also serves as the director of The National Research Center on the Gifted and Talented. He has served on numerous editorial boards and as a senior research associate for the White House Task Force on Education for the Gifted and Talented. Renzulli's major research interests are in identification and programming models for both gifted education and general school improvement, including his widely-used Enrichment Triad Model the Three Ring Conception of Giftedness. Dr. Renzulli has contributed numerous books and articles to the professional literature and has been a series author with the Houghton Mifflin Reading Series. Although Dr. Renzulli has generated millions of dollars in research and training grants, his proudest professional accomplishment is the annual summer Confratute program at the University of Connecticut, which originated in 1978 and has served more than 14,000 persons from around the world.

Mark A. Runco, PhD, is professor of child and adolescent studies at California State University, Fullerton. He is also editor of the *Creativity Research Journal* and past president of Division 10 (Arts and Psychology) of the American Psychological Association. His recent works include the *Encyclopedia of Creativity* (co-edited with Steven Priztker) and *Creativity: Theories, Themes, and Issues.* He earned his PhD in Cognitive Psychology from the Claremont Graduate School in 1984 and lives in La Habra, California.

Lita Linzer Schwartz, PhD, Distinguished Professor Emerita at Pennsylvania State University, combines her interests in creativity, gifted and creative personalities, and photography in this chapter. She relishes the opportunity to do such interdisciplinary research. Her other research and professional efforts focus on children and their welfare in adoption, surrogacy, and divorce situations. She is a Fellow of the APA, holds a Diplomate in Forensic Psychology, and is an active photographer.

Peter Wyman, PhD, is associate professor psychiatry and psychology at the University of Rochester and Director of the Rochester Child Resilience Project, based within the Children's Institute, Inc. Wyman has written numerous articles and chapters on the development of competence and adaptation to adverse environments. A second interest area is the development and evaluation of preventively-oriented interventions for at-risk children. Wyman is presently directing a coalition of New York State agencies to plan and coordinate school-based prevention for young children.